An introduction to intercultural communication

THE BOBBS-MERRILL SERIES IN *Speech Communication*

RUSSEL R. WINDES, *Editor*
Queens College of the City University of New York

JOHN C. CONDON
International Christian University, Tokyo

FATHI S. YOUSEF
California State University, Long Beach

An introduction to intercultural communication

Bobbs-Merrill Educational Publishing
INDIANAPOLIS

The Bobbs-Merrill Company, Inc.
4300 West 62nd Street
Indianapolis, Indiana 46268
First Edition
Ninth Printing-1984

ISBN 0-672-61328-X

Library of Congress Cataloging in Publication Data

Condon, John C
  An introduction to intercultural communication.

  (The Bobbs-Merrill series in speech communication)
    1. Intercultural communication. I. Yousef,
Fathi S., joint author. II. Title.
HM258.C59   301.14   74–14633

Editor's Foreword

Professors Condon and Yousef have written a very special book, which we believe to be the first comprehensive introduction to the vital subject of interpersonal communication across cultures. There have been a number of books which have touched on selected aspects of intercultural communication: the mass media and international communication; nonverbal behavior; communication in or with specific cultures; cultures and subcultures. Recently we have begun to see frequent articles on intercultural communication, some of which have been collected into books of readings. But thus far no book has attempted to provide the student of culture and the student of communication with a thorough background of the many issues which underpin the study of intercultural communication. As instructors well know, one simply cannot take relevant but scattered articles from different disciplines, written from different perspectives for different purposes, and put them together to make a unified course of study. There must be a basis for selection, a sense of emphasis and balance, and, above all, some unifying themes and assumptions which not only **bring** necessary issues together, but **hold** them together. **An Introduction to Intercultural Communication** is the first book in its field to make this attempt. So successful is the result that, we believe, this book is likely to define the field of intercultural communication for years to come.

The significance of this study can hardly be overestimated. Any work in contemporary history and politics; any survey of educational exchange programs, technical assistance, tourism and multinational conferences; any study of world economics and multinational corporate growth and activity are evidence that communicating with persons of other cultures has become a daily necessity. If we do not yet live in Marshall McLuhan's "global village," we at least inhabit its suburbs, within easy commuting distance. Moreover, in the United States today we need not travel at all in order to encounter significant differences in attitudes, values, language, nonverbal behaviors, and ways of thinking. The communication problems we often label as "race relations," "interethnic relations," or even "the generation gap," are really not so very different from those we experience in communicating across more clearly defined cultural and national lines.

This much-talked-of "shrinking world" has produced some standardizations of behavior. At the same time, however, it has made us more aware of differences in ways of speaking, reasoning, gesturing, and acting—differences which no longer are viewed at a distance. Technological and political realities have conspired, not just to permit, but to require a secretary of state to race from one part of the globe to another, a process which has underscored the necessity of **personal** communication among men of varied and varying cultures. Of lesser consequence, no doubt, but of far greater frequency, each of us may decide whether we wish to stay at home this year (in our own country) or to see the gardens in Edinborough, to watch the sunsets in Vienna, or to go trucking the back roads of Yucatan. The study of intercultural communication is a subject of concern not only to communicologists and anthropologists, but to diplomats, missionaries, businessmen, Peace Corps volunteers and exchange students; it is, in fact, a reality which embraces us all.

It is not surprising that more colleges and universities are offering additional courses in this field, or even that Bobbs-Merrill is adding this volume to our Series in Speech Communication. What is surprising is that our discipline, dating back two thousand years, has failed to produce such a book until now. One possible reason may be simply that, until recently, the conduct of international relations was essentially a matter of secrecy and subterfuge, and that the humanistic concerns of communication were most often reserved for the citizenry at home. In ancient Greece a barbarian was any foreigner; in the world of today we seem at least a bit more sophisticated. A second reason for the late appearance of such a book probably lies in the great disparity between the vastness of the potential subject matter and the obvious limitations felt by any scholar. As the authors of this book make clear, however, this problem can be somewhat diminished if the focus of study is not "all about other cultures," but rather "something about our own cultural behavior as sensed through interaction with some other cultures." Thus, the book invites self-awareness and introspection as much as it informs about the behavior of others. For this reason alone, the book ought to be highly relevant to many courses not primarily concerned with international or cross-cultural communication. **An Introduction to Intercultural Communication** is one book from speech communication which is likely to find its way into courses in other allied disciplines—sociology and anthropology, political science and international relations, urban studies, linguistics, and in certain interdisciplinary studies. At the same time, within the speech-communication discipline, the book should be highly relevant to many aspects of interpersonal communication, nonverbal communication, semantics, rhetorical criticism, political communication, and courses which relate to conflict and decision-making (argumentation, persuasion, for example).

Professors Condon and Yousef are highly qualified by education and experience to write an introductory book in intercultural communication. Professor Condon, who prepared a major share of the book, has spent ten years studying and teaching abroad—in Mexico, Brazil, Tanzania, and Japan. He taught for five years at Northwestern University. His first book, **Semantics and Communication** (Macmillan, 1966), continues to be an important book in the discipline and he has published more than thirty articles in several nations. Professor Yousef also brings impressive credentials. Born and raised in Egypt, he spent many years working with Americans in the Middle East (chiefly with Aramco in Saudi Arabia) and in Europe. His studies at the University of Minnesota centered around intercultural communication, and he has published several important articles in the field. Between the two of them, the authors speak and understand eight languages and have spent over twenty years outside their own cultures.

By choice of topics, organization, and balance of theory and example, this introduction to intercultural communication is an innovative, practical, and fascinating book. Because its emphasis is on communication, and not on all facets of culture, the introduction, Chapter One, surveys selected principles of interpersonal communication. It not only provides common ground for a potentially diverse readership, but it makes even familiar concepts seem fresh as they are viewed in their application across cultures. Chapter Two, in which the authors present a series of cases drawn from actual intercultural encounters, sets the tone for the remaining chapters of the book. Its overall purpose is to make the reader aware of some of his own culture-bound assumptions and some of his own difficulties in knowing what other people might be thinking, as well as what he might or might not do in simple but unfamiliar situations.

Chapters Three, Four, and Five form the core of the book: an introduction to the concepts of values and value orientations, followed by a study on value orientation and cultural beliefs. Often the relationship to communication is left implicit, but never far from the surface. The reader should emerge from these chapters with a far clearer sensitivity to the cultural roots of his own behavior, as well as a sensitivity to the richness and variety of alternative values and assumptions of persons in other societies. These chapters are impressive not only for the wealth of insights drawn together, but because they leave the reader with a means of interpreting other cultures not specifically referred to in the chapters. Thus, most valuable here is the perspective and framework for further analysis.

Because of the structuring of the book, the reader finds himself well into the theory before he begins to consider in some detail those specific topics that often, individually, masquerade for the whole of "intercultural communication." Chapter Six, on nonverbal behavior and communication across cultures, is selective enough to complement other more exhaustive studies of nonverbal communication. Following this, Chapter Seven describes home styles and communication patterns, reminding us that culture, if not always charity, begins at home.

Chapter Eight, on language in culture, is no less original in its content and design. The much discussed "Whorfian hypothesis" is included, but it is included in the perspective of more recent linguistic theories. Here, as elsewhere throughout the book, the writing is neither technical nor popularized. Information and examples provide insights and at the same time raise significant questions. Another original contribution, a consideration of the importance of translation and interpretation, follows in Chapter Nine. Up to now, almost no information has been available on the many roles and influence of those anonymous people providing the link between speakers of different languages.

The next to final chapter, Ten, discusses the issues which once comprised almost the entirety of the speech discipline: rhetoric. Viewing rhetoric, language, and cultural values as essentially interdependent, we believe that this chapter alone is sufficient to revise many traditional and culture-bound treatments of reasoning and persuasion.

The final chapter, Eleven, written in question-answer format, gives a partial review of some of the most important considerations raised by the previous chapters. It also underscores two important themes in the book: first, the knowledge that both the study and facility in interpersonal communication across cultures begin with the awareness of our own culturally influenced patterns of communication; second, the importance of realizing that each intercultural encounter is unique and complex. Thus, the advice of "do this," or "don't do this," must be regarded with suspicion. Therefore, the perspective from any one area—theory of speech communication, rhetorical theory, language, nonverbal behavior—is of necessity incomplete.

An Introduction to Intercultural Communication is a richly human, often fascinating experience which embraces insights and conclusions from many disciplines and from many cultural experiences. For all that, there is a modesty about the book which helps to make it an excellent introduction for readers who wish to enhance their knowledge about and proficiency in that which is the most human of all human experiences: communication.

Russel R. Windes

Preface

This book is an **introduction** to intercultural communication. And while the handling of such a complex subject requires a measure of immodesty, even to attempt an introduction, it seems surprising that this attempt is one of the first, so far as we know, to provide such a study. The area of intercultural communication remains largely uncharted. The speech communication field has explored very little, claimed little, and contributed little thus far. But the potential is great. While we stake no claims, either, we hope this book will stimulate greater interest in the subject.

Looking back, we can see that more than a little progress has been made. When I was at Northwestern twelve years ago, completing doctoral research on intercultural communication and values, there were no courses, no books, and few articles in the field. Attitudes were reflected in the graduate school directives. Although my research was conducted in Mexico, the graduate school refused to allow Spanish as the foreign-language requirement. I was told to take the French examination instead, because, they said, too little serious scholarly research was published in Spanish! Since then, however, the Department of Communication Studies has supported a number of excellent dissertations in this field, including two excellent ones prepared in East Africa. Now Swahili is regarded as highly as French. Now there are courses in intercultural communication and cultural patterns of communication; there is an excellent newsletter, **Communique,** with a circulation in the thousands; there are international conferences—even three or four per year. At least two state legislatures have passed a law requiring a course in intercultural communication as part of teacher certification requirements.

Five years ago, at the University of Minnesota, Professor William Howell—a pioneer in intercultural communication—introduced me to Fathi Yousef. One summer we worked together in a seminar and, finding that our interests coincided and our backgrounds were complementary formed the idea for writing a book together. He had worked with Americans in the Middle East and later came to the United States as a foreign student (and has since become a citizen). My perspective, on the other hand, was directed **out** of the U.S., and my experiences were in other parts of the world. Hence, this book evolved more out of personal experiences and questions than a survey of literature in the library. While there are certain obvious limitations inherent in this kind of approach, and we cannot begin to cover **all** aspects of intercultural communication, we believe there are advantages, too. For one thing, through working together we hoped to minimize biases that result from personal or cultural peculiarities. The examples we used come mainly from the United States, Brazil, Mexico, the Middle East, Japan, and East Africa, with linguistic examples from the corresponding languages.

A study of this kind depends heavily on the insights of many colleagues and friends who have unknowingly assisted over the years. We acknowledge gratefully the contributions of my colleagues at International Christian University in Tokyo, including Professor Mitsuko Saito (Japan's "First Lady" of communication studies), Noah Brannen, Holloway Brown, Anatol Gorshkoff, and—most of all—our magnificent students who live intercultural lives at ICU. Also we are indebted to friends and associates in Japan: Masao Kunihiro, Sen Nishiyama, and to the gentle Kobayashi family, with whom my barbaric family has lived for five years. We are grateful, also, to Caroline Yousef, for observations on homes in Germany, where she grew up, and to my wife, Camy, who worked for three years in northeast Brazil. Also in Brazil we wish to acknowledge the wise counsel of Frei Joao Vogel, former Director of the Centro de Formacao Intercultural in Petropolis. In Tanzania, others are to be thanked: the dedicated students at Kivukoni College in Dar es Salaam, Griff Cunningham, former Director, George Shilaka, Lionel Cliffe, and Ezekiel Ngonyani. At Northwestern University the Council on Intersocietal Studies was of great assistance, and the Ford Foundation made possible the year of teaching and research in East Africa. In Mexico we were helped by Ivan Illich and his associates at CIDOC in Cuernavaca, and by the good people at the **casa** Solis—including the sixteen children. In the United States many colleagues and friends have helped, only a few of whom I can mention here: Ethel Albert, Mary Badami, Dean Barnlund, Karen Carlson, William Howell, Bill Neher, Lee Roloff, and Edward Stewart. We have been aided also by Helmut Morsbach, now at Glasgow, and Heinz Gohring at Heidelberg. Several typists in different locations worked on the manuscript, including Yoko Yamada Kubota, Anita Mermel, and Ann Pyshos. Finally, we wish to express special appreciation to Russ Windes and Ralph Smith, who made many helpful editorial suggestions, most of which have been incorporated into the manuscript.

The book is dedicated to: Kaemi, Mama Bahati, kanai, Carmelita, and Camy—for reasons best known to her.

John Condon

Cuernavaca, Mexico
January, 1974

Contents

xv

ONE

Communication perspectives

The ambassador's dandruff

We were talking with some Japanese students in Tokyo about a former U.S. ambassador to Japan, whose knowledge of the Japanese language and culture was widely praised. One girl remarked, "Yes, he was excellent, but . . . I think his wife was not such a good wife, if you know what I mean." We didn't know. Was this some gossip from one of the notorious Japanese weekly magazines? No, the girl said, it was nothing like that. She simply had seen the ambassador interviewed on television a few times and "noticed he had dandruff on his shoulders." That was the end of the explanation. But it was sufficient for the other students, who agreed that, yes, perhaps his wife was not such a good wife. To this writer, an outsider at that time, these were **non sequiturs;** the "explanation" made no sense. So they all patiently explained that in Japan a good wife is responsible for her husband's personal appearance. If he is not well groomed, obviously it is his wife's fault. But what did the girl remember hearing the ambassador **say** when he was interviewed? She said she couldn't remember anything he said—just that dandruff. **Moral:** One speck of dandruff is worth a thousand words—in some situations, and in some cultures.

Here the U. S. ambassador communicated something to this Japanese girl.[1] What he communicated was neither what he said nor what he intended to communicate; he was not even aware of that girl or her reaction. Still, we can say that there was **communication** if we are referring to any behavior that is perceived and interpreted by another, whether or not it is spoken or intended or even within the person's conscious awareness. This concept of human communication, different from many other uses of the word, is the concept we will employ in this book.

Perhaps it is safe to say that most of what is communicated in any encounter between people, even those from the same culture, is not spoken, not interpreted as it was intended, and largely occurs outside of their awareness. That does not mean, of course, that speaking is unimportant or that we should be satisfied with any interpretation that is made of our behavior.

Some writers have extended this concept to the point of stating, as a principle, that it is impossible **not** to communicate.[2] Their logic is simply that if "communication" embraces all human behavior, then it is impossible to not **communicate** because it is impossible to **not behave.** It is possible to avoid certain behaviors, such as speaking, but the very absence of behavior, if behavior is expected, still communicates. Not answering a person usually is a far more powerful "message" than anything that might be said. "No news" may or may not be "good news," but if one is expecting news—a letter, a word of thanks, any response—then that kind of "no news" is also news; it communicates something.

The implications of this view of communication may be discomfiting at first, especially in intercultural communication, where each party is likely to feel more uncertain about how his behavior is observed and interpreted than he would in his own society. Probably it is especially disturbing to persons who like to feel that they have full control of a situation and want others

[1] Some might also feel that the unseen wife "communicated" to the girl, too.
[2] Paul Watzlawick, Janet Beavin, and Don D. Jackson, **The Pragmatics of Human Communication** (New York: W. W. Norton, 1967), pp. 48–51.

to accept them on their own terms. But for these very reasons we need a broad concept of communication when considering what transpires between people of different cultural backgrounds. Without it we will be left with the confusions and protestations that so often have characterized discussions of international and intercultural communication, with each blaming the other for misunderstanding: "That's not what I said," and "That's not what I meant." Without a broader understanding we will continue to try to "improve communication" merely by repeating the same thing in a louder voice.

This word "communication" often is used in many different ways; some persons equate it with **agreement,** saying that two people who disagree about something are "not communicating." But if people are disagreeing and know it, they must be communicating; it seems far more accurate and less pretentious merely to say that they disagree. The word "communication" also is used to mean "understanding," quite apart from agreement. The American in a Paris cafe tells the waiter that he will have the **soupe du jour;** the waiter informs him that it is tomato soup; and the American snaps back, "I know that—I studied French in College." They are having difficulty understanding, perhaps, but they are communicating nevertheless.

Two other uses seem as unhelpful as they are common. One is the use of "more communication" or "less communication" not as a measure of the frequency of speech or other communicative acts, but as an equivalent of positive impact. Just as some people say that one person has "more personality" than somebody else, they may say that a particular individual "communicates more" or "really communicates." The dullest conversationalist "really communicates," too, even though he may seem to be tedious company. This usage is especially annoying when used to describe different societies; for example, Italians "communicate more" than the Swedes. A related use is that which limits "communication" to something that is viewed as positive, productive, or at least satisfying. Thus some people may say that when people stop talking and start fighting, they have ceased to communicate. But a fight is just as much a kind of communication as a speech or a song or flecks of dandruff.

Perspectives

In thinking about intercultural communication, we are consider-ing two of the broadest and most abstract categories we could possibly link together. Like other terms at such a high level of abstraction, the two tend to blend into each other. Much of what is called "patterns of communication" could be—and is, in other contexts—called "cultural patterns." It is not surprising, there-fore, that one writer has said that "culture is communication,"[3] and that others have said that at a certain point, principles of communication and anthropological statements about a culture are identical.[4] Nevertheless, there are important differences in the study of "communication" and the study of "culture;" aca-demically, despite sharing of data and insights, researchers have pursued different approaches, and different contributions have resulted. We would like to begin by presenting a very limited num-ber of non-technical observations or "perspectives" from the eclectic field of interpersonal communication. And, though it will not be easy, we would like to do so without cultural bias.

As just noted, it is often difficult to distinguish between a gen-eral communication pattern and a more limited cultural pattern. Many, or perhaps most, of the learned principles of communi-cation are culturally limited. If these are principles learned informally (such as looking at the person you are talking to) they may seem to be universal because everybody else around us follows the same rules. It is only when we go outside of our familiar territory that we realize not everybody behaves in the same way and that, indeed, good advice at home may be very bad advice elsewhere. If these principles result from academic studies, particularly those carefully controlled experimental studies with impressive neutrality of statistics, we may also feel we have described something basic about "human be-havior." But of course, as social scientists have come to realize, much that is described about "human behavior" does not apply outside the society in which the study was conducted and may not even describe much more than the kind of "college culture"

---

[3] Edward T. Hall, **The Silent Language** (New York, Doubleday, 1959), p. 37.
[4] Jurgen Ruesch and Gregory Bateson, **Communication: Social Matrix of Psychi-atry** (New York: W. W. Norton, 1951), p. 8.

where the study took place. This also seems to be true of some of the grand theories which have gained international recognition. A Mexican colleague, who is a psychiatrist, remarked of Freud, "Freudian theory does not work so well here; he speaks of repression, but we Mexicans remember **everything!**"

We believe that to be sensitive to intercultural communication we must have some understanding of at least rudimentary concepts of interpersonal communication, as well as some understanding of some aspects of culture. A book claiming to fully encompass either of these might be suspect; thus a book attempting to relate both might seem outrageous. But to avoid saying something about each as they are linked together seems, in the middle of the twentieth century, unduly cautious. We begin with a few insights from the field of interpersonal communication.

Six men in a dialogue

We usually identify the person with whom we are talking simply by saying his or her name or perhaps by giving a physical description ("that tall blond guy") or perhaps by describing an activity ("that woman having coffee"). But if we think for a moment, we realize that these perceptions are dangerously oversimplified.

Person **A** does not just communicate with person **B;** he or she communicates with his "image" of person **B,** an image which may change during the communication. And, similarly, person **B** has an image of person **A,** which influences how he speaks to **A** and how he interprets what **A** says. This is most apparent when a person in conversation discovers the identity (or status) of another; for example, in Mexico, where clergymen are forbidden to wear clerical garb in public, many Roman Catholic priests have experienced a dramatic change in a conversation with a stranger who has just told a dirty joke and asks "What do you do?" The response, "I'm a priest," produces a sudden change of expression and a series of embarrassing comments and apologies ("Oh . . . Father, I didn't know . . . why didn't you . . . I hope you'll forgive what I . . . oh, my God!").

To a much greater extent than we may realize, we communicate not with flesh-and-blood people, but with roles, with positions of status, with representatives of the social structure. Across cultures, obviously, this realization is of great significance. Not only are the classifications which influence our communicative behavior likely to be different from what we are familiar with, we are also likely to lack the information and clues which tell us "who is who." If a newly arrived German medical doctor calls upon the mayor of an Indian town, the doctor is likely to talk to **his image of an Indian mayor,** not that particular Indian "who happens to be mayor." But how does the information that "this man is the mayor" assist the doctor in speaking differently than he would to any other person? If nothing else, the recognition of role and status somehow causes us to alter communication, but we may not know how best to alter it. At any rate, the two flesh and blood people, plus the image each has of the other, adds up to "four people" in the dialogue. It becomes even more complex when more changes occur in image and situation; Suppose, for example, the mayor is the doctor's patient or suppose the doctor wishes to beg a favor of the mayor.

We must add at least two (the geometry suggests still more) when we realize that each of these parties has his own self-image, his own self-concept in this particular situation. The doctor is not just another person—he never is. As "a medical doctor," he may wish to be treated in a particular manner, and he has his own image of how he should be seen by the mayor or whomever he is talking with. But in different cultures it is probably difficult for him to know what his image is to those people: another Schweitzer, perhaps—until he learns that the mayor never heard of Schweitzer (which might also alter his image of the mayor); perhaps as "a typical German" or "a typical European" or even a typical "Englishman," depending on the mayor's experience; or perhaps as a miracle worker (it is his skill and not his ethnicity which shapes the image—perhaps); perhaps as an intruder; perhaps as an outcast from his own society ("why has he come **here?**"). It would be very difficult for this visitor, as for any visitor, ever to know quite what his image is; he can only guess, based on the reports he has heard and the behavior which he observes and interprets.

In a mobile society which espouses egalitarian values, such as the United States, persons may wish to minimize the role and status image of themselves and of others. A father may prefer to be thought of just as his son's "buddy;" the president may wish to be thought of as "the voters' friend." Persons from such cultures may like to think of the influence of images and self-concepts as masks, and as essentially harmful to good communication. They may feel that "true communication" occurs only when six men in the dialogue are leveled to the "basic two."

In countless popular American novels, dramas, and films, this conflict between "the real self" and the image has been emphasized to show that the images are prejudicial and distort communication. American psychotherapists such as Maslow and Rogers stress similar views.[5] In communication studies the emphasis on such projects as role-playing exercises, T-group experience, and sensitivity training has also sought not merely to recognize the influence of such images but apparently to do away with them entirely in order to achieve "true communication." The American student of communication is likely to regard "status," "rank," and other categories as essentially harmful to communication. But intercultural communication is more likely to be effective if all "six-plus men" are recognized and accommodated; indeed, those fifth and sixth persons in the dialogue are often more important than the first two.

One of those people

A very strong influence in a person's self-concept and in his image of the other's self-concept is what is sometimes called "the reference group concept." This refers to a larger grouping with which people identify themselves or others, and it often serves as a guide to action and as a basis of comparison. The most obvious of such reference groups are identified by broad semantic categories, including nationality, sex, age, region ("a Texan" or "a Parisian," for example), and race. In intercultural communication, confusions in reference group identification are very common.

[5] See Abraham H. Maslow, **Toward a Psychology of Being**, 2nd ed. (New York: Van Nostrand Reinhold, 1968), and Carl R. Rogers, **On Becoming a Person** (Boston: Houghton Mifflin, 1961).

For example, in Kenya, as in most African nations, there are many tribes, often quite unrelated in languages spoken, physical appearance, and cultural values. A member of the Luo tribe in Kenya may think of himself first as a Luo, secondly as a citizen of Kenya. He may or may not, at times, identify himself as an African, or as a member of "the third world." But if he travels to Europe or to the United States to study, he is more likely to be identified first as "an African" (an extraordinary grouping perhaps comparable to an American being identified as a "Northern Hemisphere Person"), and secondly as a Kenyan. At times he may be grouped as "black" or "Negro." It is unlikely that many persons, apart from those who have visited or studied about Kenya will classify him as a Luo. He is likely to be invited to meetings and parties with people with whom he feels little or no commonality ("the foreign students")—including, perhaps, a Moslem from Morocco, a Coptic Christian from Egypt, a South African white, a political refugee from Angola, and the daughter of an Ismaeli trader from Malawi. Semantically all of these people may legitimately be classified as "Africans," but in terms of reference group identification, it is possible that none of these "Africans" had ever thought of themselves as being members of the same group.

The reference group concept cuts across many basic principles of communication: it may help to explain differing psychological "sets" of people in communication, it is certainly related to self-concepts and images of others, and it often suggests some of the structures which will be imposed upon the fluid process of communication. Moreover, a person's changing reference group identification is often an indication of the influence of communication: our Luo student may come to think of himself as "an African" because he is so often called upon to represent "Africans" and to answer questions and give opinions on matters he had never considered previously.

In rhetorical theory, the reference group identification has always been important. For a rhetorical theorist such as Kenneth Burke, "identification" rather than "persuasion" is the key term in the study of rhetoric.[6] Certainly the facile persuader is likely

---

[6] Kenneth Burke, **A Grammar of Motives** (New York: Prentice-Hall, 1955).

to seek any plausible form of identifying himself with his audience; thus Nixon in political campaigns was alternately "a Quaker," "a former soldier," "a child who knew poverty, too," "an established lawyer," "a Californian," "a New Yorker," and so forth, depending on which identification is more likely to match that of his audience. And the audiences are not likely to feel that these identifications are inconsistent.

It seems that Americans, for reasons to be discussed later, feel rather free to associate and dissociate themselves from different groups, and they may wish to be treated as "individuals" rather than being considered as a member of any single group or even as "Americans." Younger persons, especially, are likely to try to dissociate themselves from their country and to assert their individuality or their commonality with "youth." Perhaps most Americans abroad will remark, "Of course I am not a typical American." And this may be true, for typically most Americans are not found abroad; but it may also be true that to say "I am not a typical American" is a typically American thing to say.

Inappropriate reference grouping has long been noted by sociologists, and the chances of misclassifying unfamiliar cultures are even greater than they are for the same culture. "You Mexicans and Puerto Ricans all seem the same to me," remarks a person who is surely not a member of either group. A third-generation German-American objects to a black political activist, who can trace his family lines back to before the Mayflower, and says "I don't know why you people are always complaining —you have more advantages here than in Africa!" Such irrelevant comparisons are the product of ignorance, and as we are likely to be more ignorant about other cultures than about our own, we must expect to observe many more such reactions in intercultural communication.

As we will note in discussing language and culture, the common word stock may predispose us to make certain groupings and not others. In Swahili the three main racial-social categories are **Mafrika** ("Black Africans," usually); **Mhindi** ("Asian," usually applied to the merchant and professional group of Indian ancestry which has comprised the bulk of the East African business and professional community); and **Mzungu** (usually translated as "European" but including all "whites." Significantly,

"Mzungu" historically refers to the lost "white man" seen wandering around). There are, of course, words for all nationalities, religions, and other ethnic distinctions. In Japanese there are two broad groupings: **Nihonjin,** the Japanese, and **Gaijin,** meaning, usually, "white" foreigner or "Westerner." For other national groups there are specific words but no word which would group **Nihonjin** with other Asians in a way that "Asian" might in English. American categories, of course, are different still. Often they appear to be relatively precise: "third generation Polish Catholic." Rarely is a word like "European" used, but "Latin American" is a net that captures millions. And "Latin," which may have some linguistic value, is more likely to group persons according to imagined emotional behavior. Thus the influence of a person's available word stock may be influential in his choice of reference groups, and his own semantic distinctions are likely to be very different from those of another who speaks a different language.

Not only language influence but the sheer necessity of categorization may make such reference groupings inevitable. The prevalence of deductive reasoning requires broad categories from which specifics may be deduced: in our own culture, so long as we talk and think in terms of Ms. Owen, the coed; Mr. Smith, the politician; and Dr. Russell, the philosopher, we may continue to talk of Mr. Díaz, the Mexican, and Miss Lee, the Korean. Ignorance, too, leads us into false categories: so long as people believe there are tigers in Africa (there are none, except in zoos) or that Africa is mostly jungle (about 5 percent is jungle), we should not be surprised that "Africans" are grouped as basically the same throughout the continent. In intercultural communication our ignorance affects the entire process of communication. Too often we add insult to ignorance.

Sorting things out

The mental processes with which we perceive and interpret human behavior make any analysis of interpersonal communication difficult, since we can only guess how another person is thinking and because we are by no means fully aware of how we ourselves are reacting. Thus for many years communication scholars in a number of related fields have sought means of analyzing overt behavior: primarily speech but, increasingly, nonverbal behavior as well. Any such attempt involves certain "models" or diagrams which represent the structure of the interaction. Many of these identify a speaker or "sender," a listener or "receiver," and many attempt to show with grids or arrows the "flow of communication." Other scholars, while recognizing the need for some structure for purposes of identification, have objected to communication models which are static and linear in form. They argue that communication is a fluid process, "multi-linear" at least ("a speaker" is also a listener—even when he is speaking), and impossible to diagram adequately without greatly distorting what is going on. Even with the addition of a term like "feedback"— that all-purpose word in communication theory—one is assuming a great deal, oversimplifying, and ignoring the process of communication. In the West traditional emphasis given to verbal communication may demand a directional interpretation: Two people "talking at once" suggests "no communication." But in forms of communication which are defined as multi-personal (as in many dances), the parties interact so completely that it is difficult to identify a leader and follower, a sender and a receiver. Such an image is likely to be a better model for intercultural communication than the linear models.

For example, a young girl is likely "to communicate a smile" not as the start of communication or even as acknowledgment of receipt of communication but as a point in the process. The smile originates in several places (his remark, her upbringing, their relationship) and reflects and directs all of these at the same time. If one is at a funeral, one probably does not laugh— but not primarily because of concern for the others' reaction (the feedback?) but because of reasons shared by all members. It may be best not to think of beginnings, middles, and ends, or of senders and receivers.

If communication is process, different persons are likely to impose different structures on the "same process" based on different backgrounds, assumptions, and purposes. The person in a discussion group says, "I am only silent because they do not invite me to speak," but the others say, "we have given up on this person because he never wants to speak though we have shown him through our example that speaking is important." The foreign technical advisor says, "Their childish attitudes made me give up trying to help them," but those who would be "helped" say "his treating us like children makes us wish he would go away." These and other typical patterns illustrate the difficulty of trying to structure the process of communication—except from the individual viewpoints of the persons involved.

Nevertheless, to stress that communication is a process that we enter into is not sufficient for interpreting the process. We need to impose some kind of structure, even though the attempt may result in a chicken-and-egg dilemma—particularly in Samuel Butler's formulation, "Is the chicken the egg's way of creating another egg, or is the egg the chicken's way of creating another chicken?" That is, we are more often interested in guessing intention and reaction than in speculating on which event came first.

So long as we recognize that as participants or observers in the process of communication we are imposing the structure, and that there are alternative ways of giving structure to the otherwise fluid process, we may proceed. Some theorists have referred to this as the act of "punctuating" the process, using the analogy of writing symbols which mark beginnings and endings, questions and exclamations.[7] The analogy seems especially appropriate for cross-cultural communication, since upon first hearing a foreign language we think that the words are all seemingly run together. Only with acquired skill do we learn to perceive beginnings and endings. Similarly with much larger aspects of cultural patterns of behavior, experience leads us to comprehend meaningful patterns.

It is hoped that some of the basic concepts of interpersonal communication, such as self-images and reference groups, will be helpful in providing clues to the structure of the communication process. Even more helpful, when we consider interaction across cultures, will be our awareness of differing value orientations, nonverbal patterns, and structures of argument.

Within the realm of interpersonal communication theory, there is one principle of structure, a principle first proposed by Gregory

[7] Watzlawick, **Human Communication**, pp. 54–59.

Bateson,[8] which we believe to be most helpful in interpreting intercultural encounters. This says that every spoken "message" may be interpreted on two levels: **what** is said and **how** it is said. The "how" is much less precise and includes nonverbal behavior (which could be classified as part of the "what"), vocal inflection (paralanguage), setting, timing, and much more. In Bateson's terminology, there are two aspects of each intended communication: "the report" (the what) and "the command" (the how and why). Like the distinction between "denotation" and "connotation," however, there are basic problems of identification and definition.

Perhaps the distinguishing characteristic is that the "report" is largely verbal and recognized and is the sort of datum that would appear in a printed text. The "how" is largely nonverbal, sometimes paralinguistic, and often is more difficult to describe. Our descriptions of the "how" are likely to be imprecise—"He didn't seem serious when he said it"—but can be made relatively precise ("He said it at a distance of about twenty-one feet with his eyes looking downward and with a voice we would use to communicate embarrassment").

Normally, we expect that these two aspects are consistent with each other, and conventionally the "command" aspect has been treated as a complement of the report aspect. In information theory, which usually conceives of communication as verbal ("systematic") behavior, the command elements of communication may be ignored, or may be classified as functionally redundant elements, or, in some analyses, may be classified as part of the "noise" factor which interferes with the message. That is, many studies of interpersonal communication disregard nearly all aspects of communication except the verbal; communication is rendered into a kind of playwright's script and the analysis begins here. Other studies pay attention to facial expressions, gestures, vocal inflection, to the extent that the actions "say the same thing" as the words; thus the actions are functionally redundant in the sense that if a listener does not hear every word spoken or does not know the meaning of a particular word, he may still be able to understand, or "fill in," on the basis

[8] Ibid., pp. 179–81.

of these nonverbal and paralinguistic expressions. Such expressions may also be regarded as dysfunctional or treated as elements of "noise" (an all-purpose term for any kind of interference in the "channel" which disrupts or garbles the "message"). Thus, a speaker's nervous twitch, his cracking of knuckles, or pacing back and forth while speaking, is noticed to the extent that it seems to threaten the verbal message and make clear reception difficult.

Often if there is a conflict between report and command we are likely to pay more attention to the command aspect, or the nonverbal, than to **what** was said. A mother scolding her child and demanding, "Now, you say 'I am sorry,'" will not be satisfied if the child says "I am sorry" while laughing at his mother. The child can claim, "But I said it, didn't I?" But she may feel that he didn't mean it.

Conflicts between the report and command functions of communication are sometimes noted, sometimes not. Paradoxes can be noted in any newspaper any day: A monument to Joyce Kilmer, the poet who penned "Trees," was built after several dozen trees had been chopped down. Government officials have been found to be violating the law in order to arrest persons for violating the law; and so on. Those who notice such paradoxes may become cynical or at least receive a message quite different from the one intended.

The effect of inconsistency between report and command across cultures is less often noticed by the party who is inconsistent. In many parts of the world, the American Peace Corps volunteer hopes to convey the meaning of idealism, self-sacrifice, and identification with the people he has come to serve. And yet he is often paid a stipend considerably higher than the average earnings of the people he serves, and is provided with supplies, perquisites, and a round-trip ticket—all of which can be seen as quite inconsistent with his espoused values of "sacrifice." Elaborate government aid programs to developing nations are often clearly of greatest benefit to the donor nation. And—as with some inconsistencies observed within a single culture—the reactions abroad are likely to be critical, if not cynical.

But it is at the level of interpersonal communication and not government policy that we wish to be most concerned about inconsistencies between the **what** and the **how,** the **report** and the **command.** Edward T. Hall, following publication of **The Silent Language,** has been credited with an extremely significant contribution to intercultural communication, a contribution which can be interpreted in terms of **report** and **command.** He has stressed that on one level, the report communication can convey one meaning, while on another level—the nonverbal, **command** level—a very different meaning can be conveyed. The result of such inconsistencies is neither "good communication" nor "no communication"; the result might be called "miscommunication": something is communicated, even though it is not what was intended and often it is not what was thought to have been communicated. The Englishman, Jones, and the Mexican, López, are likely to prefer being positioned at different distances from each other: Jones prefers a bit more distance between himself and another person, while López's preference is "too close" for Mr. Jones' comfort. Jones, speaking fluent Spanish, may express in words his feeling of friendship, but by standing away from López he also communicates (to López) aloofness, something very different from his words. López is also friendly and "easy going" in what he says, but as he moves closer to Jones so that he, López, feels more comfortable, he seems to Jones to be "pushy," "aggressive." A kind of dance may ensue, with Jones retreating a bit each time to feel comfortable, and neither is likely to recognize what is happening. Both may feel awkward and uncomfortable even though the verbal content seems relaxed and friendly. Because of Hall's writings, this kind of problem is now perhaps the most widely discussed by students of intercultural communication, but it remains as only one example of report-command inconsistency and there is no proof that spacial pattern differences are the most important barrier to intercultural communication. There is a tempting danger for students of intercultural communication to feel that if a person stands a certain distance from his counterpart, arrives at the appropriate time, and casts his eyes in the right direction, he surely will be effective. Though these elements are important in communication—and so often have been ignored in the past—they are still but part of communicative behavior. Moreover, as we shall consider later, it is even more possible to miscommunicate when all of these behaviors are "correct" while other elements—spoken language and, particularly, values, for example—are inconsistent. It is even possible, as many Japanese have indicated, that the foreigner who adjusts too much and behaves nonverbally too much like a Japanese, is considered quite strange and miscommunicates for this reason!

Actors all

Although we can never be sure what aspects of our behavior will be observed and interpreted in ways not at all intended, most of what we say and do is directed toward particular individuals in particular situations to create a particular interpretation. Not only what we say, but also where and when we say it, how we are dressed, and much more contribute to creating the impression we hope to convey. This suggests a perspective of performance, of consciously acting—with props and costumes in an appropriate setting—for the benefit of a selected audience. The dramatic metaphor is used to provide insight, not to be interpreted so literally that people seem to be calculating and insincere.

It is interesting that in recent years, the "actor-audience" model of communication has been largely neglected, possibly because the sender-receiver, encoder-decoder mechanical models have been stressed. And yet for over 2000 years, the actor-audience assumption was the basis for the study of "persuasion" which was **the model** of interpersonal communication. "Analyze your audience" is the first lesson of rhetoric, followed by "adapt to your audience." This was such a familiar approach to communication that it is odd that it has fallen out of favor in recent years. The social science tradition, by and large, has not emphasized this relationship, perhaps because the ancient notion of a rhetorical "art" evoked a neo-Platonic reaction among some social scientists. As an "art" there has been no progress expected of "science" (and perhaps, too, it is not even an "art" but a kind of knack, as Plato argued, thus receiving the abuse of both artist and scientist). Probably, too, there is a feeling that there is something unjust, dishonest, and demeaning about always trying to adapt to an audience, of always playing a part. For whatever reasons, the performance view of communication largely has been ignored in the mechanical models.

A notable exception is the sociologist, Erving Goffman, whose works have stressed that acting or performance is a part of almost all of our behavior.[9] Like a modern Aristotle, he has sought to describe in general, nonexperimental terms, the strategies of "impression management." Goffman's first and best-known book, **The Presentation of Self in Everyday Life,** provides examples that can be easily recognized: Even though hospital nurses often run out of things to do, either officially or practically, they don't dare sit down or look unoccupied when they have finished their appointed rounds. Because nurses are seen as curative personnel, such "relaxed" behavior would upset the patients; thus they are often required to scurry about looking busy— filling out charts on clipboards, demonstrating their roles as helpers, even though this busyness is largely performance. Their audience demands it and their role as nurses is largely defined in terms of that bedridden audience. A baseball umpire must often decide, very quickly, whether a runner is "out" or "safe," and even if he feels unsure, he must appear to be decisive. As Goffman makes clear, we not only acquiesce to such performances, we expect them, demand them. We would not **praise** a nurse or an umpire who behaved otherwise; we would say they were poor in executing their duties.

Every day we all must make similar performances for similar reasons. We do so out of social necessity, not because we are cynical. And we do so even knowing, sometimes, that our audience is aware that we are playing our role.

The view of communication as performance is extremely important in considering intercultural communication. For one thing, perhaps the most frequent communications across cultures are those of self-conscious performance. A person arriving in another country or welcoming a guest in his own country assumes an extremely predictable role: that of the advisor, the teacher, the student, and perhaps most often, that vague role of 'guest.' Until some routine is established, until the formality becomes more personal, predictable performances are to be expected and understood. Until some routine is established, there are probably more little ceremonies—welcoming speeches, orientation meetings, dinner parties and the like, all quite per-

[9] See Erving Goffman, **The Presentation of Self in Everyday Life** (New York: Doubleday, 1959), and **Encounters** (Indianapolis: Bobbs-Merrill, 1961).

formance centered—enacted across cultures than within our own culture, or at least it might seem so to Americans. Not quite knowing how he is seen in a new culture, the visitor has great difficulty in knowing how to act—serious, casual, or flip; intimate or aloof. And the visitor's cultural background and values are likely to direct even this attempt. Likewise, he does not know how to judge the "audience reaction": "They seemed pleasant, but was that for me, or are they always that way?" Or, "They seemed unfriendly by my standards; is that 'expected,' is that their impression of **me,** or am I in such a state that I cannot tell their real reaction?" Cross-culturally, there is difficulty in interpreting the success of performance.

Standards of acting and even the value of performance are likely to vary from culture to culture, a problem likely to affect Americans, especially. A recent trend in communication education in the United States is manifest in a variety of ways, such as "sensitivity training," or expressions such as "Tell it like it is." While we do not wish to be unduly critical, this trend is really very "American," for Americans are likely to dislike status differences, formality, host-guest roles, and anything that looks like older and therefore (in the American view) more rigid systems. North Americans want to get down to "brass tacks," to "reality," to "business," to "the nitty gritty"—the terms change but this value or value orientation or complex of value orientations seems to have remained remarkably consistent over the years. Such values eschew the idea of **performing.** And yet ceremony, speeches (even in an extremely non-speech oriented society such as Japan), and social amenities of all kinds are expected, even demanded. The American is often unprepared for this, both in experience and in cultural values.

Later we will discuss the difficulty that many non-Americans encounter in dealing with the informality in this country. But briefly we might note here that the apparent absence of performance and ceremony in much of American communication —"Be frank," "Make yourself at home," "Help yourself,"—is equally disturbing for many non-Americans unaccustomed to directives which seem to require performances without rules or standards. It is not surprising, therefore, that residents or students from other countries often appraise the United States as open, free, and friendly, but also as confusing, cold, and cruel.

Our behavior then, often is based on performance for a particular audience, and the form of performance—as well as its value—varies across cultures. One cannot be "just himself," or "do what comes naturally" when he is suddenly in the strange surroundings of a new culture and far away from the familiarity of his own culture.

A functional approach

A young French couple may spend an evening in which they first have a deep philosophical discussion, followed by a violent argument, followed by a long period of silence. The amount of communication between the two has not changed; rather, the **form** of communication has changed. But even in the lapses they are communicating clearly, if not loudly. In the Japanese romantic tradition, a couple may sit together for hours and exchange no more than a half-dozen words while communicating as much and as well as their more verbal counterparts in other societies. Should the young man observe to his fiance, "How beautiful is the moon," he will have communicated a proposal of marriage at least as clearly as his French counterpart would through many more words all related to the romantic prospects ahead. Similarly, college students in the United States complain that they and their parents "never really communicate; we just talk about trivial things." It is not so much that the students and their parents have or have not "communicated"; it is more likely that their respective styles and functions of communication differ, in this case to their mutual dissatisfaction.

Across cultures this problem of contrasting or conflicting functions of communication is especially troublesome. Not only is the word "communication" used so promiscuously as to make it difficult to identify more specific problems of interaction, the form and style of communication across cultures is often so contrastive that, in the more popular sense, people often cannot tell if they are "communicating" or not.

And so it may be helpful to identify at least some broad functions of communication and in the process perhaps suggest other functions which might be added. Characterizing kinds of expression on the basis of apparent or intended function is use-ful for at least two reasons: one, we can often, though not always, find "failures to communicate" when there are different func-tions expected or perceived by the parties involved; and in addi-tion, we may be able to suggest preferred orders and frequencies of the functions in different cultures.

For example, in the U.S. a public speaker is likely to begin a speech on almost any subject with a joke ("a funny thing happened to me on the way to . . ."). He does this partly because he has learned that this is a good way to begin a speech and also to suggest that he is a friendly guy (important in establish-ing his ethos in his own culture, but it may not be important in a host culture). In a culture other than his own, when he tells his joke, he may do so with a "straight face" (in keeping with his culture's standards: "Don't laugh at your own jokes"). But his audience may not be able to tell if this was a joke or not, and it is very likely that, to be safe, his audience will not laugh, for even those who suspect they heard a joke may prefer to seem slow rather than be rude by laughing at a comment that might have been serious. Though part of the problem in this hypothet-ical case is one of value differences, much of the problem may be interpreted as a conflict between the intended and the per-ceived (or those which are expected) functions of communica-tion. In this way it is misleading to blame either this unfortunate speaker or the audience for "failing to communicate." The speaker may say so after the speech, of course, but this simply means he did not get the response he expected and does not know why. The significance of this distinction may be clearer if we consider occasions such as this: A speaker tells a joke which the audience does not think is funny but the people laugh any-way because they understand the purpose of the joke and what is expected of them. To not laugh would be rude and surely would discomfit the speaker just as much as would laughing at some-thing not intended to be funny.

The functional approach alerts us to potential problems in communication. When something intended as small talk, such as "Stop in and see me whenever you are in the neighborhood," is taken by a stranger to be a genuine request, both parties are embarrassed when the stranger does indeed stop by. In school and college classrooms, we expect the transmission of information to be a central function, so that most students take notes on what is said; even if the information is not personally meaningful, it will be functionally useful in answering examinations. But the student who spends six hours a day taking notes on what is said within the classroom rarely takes notes outside of class, even if the information outside is more relevant. The atheist may dismiss most of religion as "mere ritual," while the faithful may or may not stress ritual as a value but may see religious services as serving more functions than ritual alone. A pert English lady calls her new male friend, "Love," but probably if this friend attaches some literal significance to that sobriquet he will feel deceived. In Brazil **dotor** (doctor) may be applied to almost any mature Brazilian as an expression of respect and affection (a cartoon in Brazil several years ago showed a person calling out, "Hello Doctor," whereupon everybody on the street turned around and waved!). To assume that the Brazilian "doctor" is the product of years of professional university training would be to misinterpret the function of that name.

There are several common and important functions of communication which we will describe below and refer to elsewhere in this book.

Small talk. Expressions which show an openness or a desire to enter into a conversation take many forms and have been given several names by communication theorists: small talk, "phatic communion," (a name coined by the anthropologist Malinowski for a more limited function of communication, but often extended to the great range of "small talk") and others. Though this function would seem to be universal, it varies from culture to culture in several aspects. For one thing, the expressed forms are so idiomatic and diverse as to mislead any dictionary-minded visitor unfamiliar with them. Many are even odd gramatical constructions within their own language ("How do you do?"); many are set patterns (as when two people meeting exchange the greeting, "Hello"); and very many are questions and answers, but they are questions which require no thought and answers which meet no test of accuracy (what we sometimes refer to as the "rhetorical" question). Thus many cultures have an expression which is the equivalent of "How hot it is!" but do not have equivalents of "How hot is it?" In the former, the person addressed needs only to agree ("It sure is!"), while in the latter he needs to have more detailed and accurate information. On the other hand, unless one is familiar with the form and function of such patterns, it may seem difficult to answer some questions which are meant to serve this function. English speakers may be surprised to learn that some non-native speakers of English will pause and think about answering a question like "How are you?" or "How are things!" It has taken some Americans in Japan a long time before discovering that in Japan the question "Where are you going?" functionally means the same thing as "How are you?" and requires neither thought nor honesty for a functionally appropriate answer; the standard answer is **"Chotto soko made"**—"Just over there."

Viewed functionally, a remark or question which might seem absurd if taken too seriously ("It looks like it's raining, doesn't it?" said when it is just starting to rain) might be perfectly appropriate, whereas a reply which is honest and accurate might be wrong because it is not what is expected.

Two other aspects of this first function may also vary: (1) the length of time devoted to such functions before passing into a different level of communication; and (2) the frequency with which such expressions are exchanged between the same persons during a period of a day or week. The first of these reflects that even this function may be regarded as serving many additional functions, especially between strangers: Exchanging "small talk" may reveal considerable information about the character and personalities of the individuals, of their language abilities (across cultures, at least), of their desire to talk about other subjects, and may even provide some clues as to which other subjects might be appropriate. Also, in a sense, because the forms are so predictable, easily interpreted, and therefore require so little thought as to content, the persons are able to take in a great deal of information about such traits as voice tones, rate, and volume, which is extremely important in preparing for further conversation.

The length of time taken in exchanging small talk varies across cultures, but the reason is not simply one of convention or custom; rather, this is related to pace of living, many values concerning individuals and activity, and, of course, values associated with time itself. If people from the United States seem to "want to get down to business" more quickly than most other people in the world, it is probably due in part to the American's distinction between the individual and his role or job, and thus we do not have to "test" through small talk the personal worth of, say, a plumber or electrician—for we don't care about such things. Literally, "that is none of our business." In much of the world, however, this distinction is not so clear-cut (see Chapter Four), and so it is important to be able to judge this individual as a person before accepting him in his particular function. Thus another functional conflict in communication occurs when persons from one culture expect and desire to move on to another function, while the persons from the other culture seem to want to remain at the same level of communication.

Similarly, cultural patterns may differ in the frequency of small talk exchanges between the same persons within a given period of time. In the United States, if two friends happen to see each other four times within one day, the extent of their small talk is likely to decrease with each successive meeting, so that by the fourth time or even by the third, almost no comment need be exchanged. In much of Latin America, on the other hand, nearly the same pattern of greetings may be repeated each time ("How are you, how is your mother, how is your father . . ?").

Relating and receiving information. When people travel across cultures, they appear to give more attention to this function than they might at home, which is interesting in itself. This is the function we are referring to when we speak of taking a phrase literally. Usually, instructions or directions on how to get somewhere is the kind of information involved in this function. This, too, is the function most often associated with the popular view of "communication."

There are some observations about this function especially important in cross-cultural communication. One has been suggested several times previously: Information is often **not** to be taken literally, but cross-culturally—particularly if we are not fully confident of the language and especially if we are unfamiliar with customs—we are likely to "take literally" most of what is said, ignoring the functional approach to meaning. Moreover, in a new situation we are sometimes likely to perceive as **information** kinds of behavior which other members of the culture ignore and which we would also ignore in our own culture. Sometimes we are also likely to ignore or be incapable of perceiving as **information** what is intended as information. Partly for this reason, there seems to be some truth in the familiar attitude that newcomers or strangers have a clearer insight into some aspects of a culture than do members of the culture or even foreign residents of several years. The problem, of course, is that the newcomer is never really sure how significant his observations are: They may be different, but that does not make them profound or even accurate interpretations.

This function of relating and receiving information may also serve other functions. When one gives information, for example, he may also be saying something about himself ("See what I know?") and something about his attitude toward the other person ("I know more than you" or "I want to help you"). That strangers often appear to be so curious in a new culture, asking questions about every possible subject, may also suggest that we tend to resort to this form of communication as a substitute for small talk expressions with which we are unfamiliar.

Catharsis or tension release. A mixed category, tension release includes laughter; exclamations of surprise and other emotions ("Oh, wow!"); expressions of anger (swearing); and a variety of autistic mannerisms (such as snapping our fingers when we are trying to think—or have suddenly thought—of something). Of all the functions of communication, this one would seem to be the most instinctive and personal, minimally influenced by language and culture. And yet there are significant differences cross-culturally in the form and frequency of catharsis.

Expressions of anger are instructive of cultural differences. In most languages there appear to be a range of expressions to roughly coincide with the degree of anger to be expressed (or the degree of tension to be released); there are also likely to be differences according to the speaker's age, sex, background, role, and the social setting in which the anger is expressed. And, as with the other functions, this form may serve more than the immediate and apparent function: A person may swear because he or she is angry; a man may swear to show that he is a man—or, perhaps, to convey other information. Moreover, any person who has learned to speak another language probably realizes that foreign swear words are not likely to express his anger as effectively as his native language does. In this sense, it may be more difficult to communicate with ourselves in a foreign language than it is to communicate with others.

As suggested above, it may be especially risky to express some forms of tension in the language of another culture; not only may the speaker be ignorant of the specific social implications of such expressions, his phrase—even if semantically correct—may strike his hosts as being odd, false, a performance.

Cathartic expressions are often confusing across cultures because we are likely to assume that they are universal when clearly they are not. Laughter, for example, in most Western cultures is usually asociated with humor—whether it's nonsensical, clever, gentle, or cruel. In Japan, laughter is often an indication of embarrassment, so that misunderstandings often occur when, for example, a European expresses anger and this anger embarrasses his Japanese counterpart, who then expresses his embarrassment through laughter. If the European is ignorant of this custom, he is likely to become even angrier as a result of feeling he is being laughed at. In Tanzania, President Nyerere sometimes begins a speech with a kind of gentle laugh which is echoed by the audience and then repeated by the President, and so on, until a "laughing relationship" is established. For one accustomed to a Western view of laughing, this performance is most puzzling. No Swahili dictionary will give the meaning of that laughter.

Ritual. Of all of the functions of communication, perhaps none has received as much attention by anthropologists as that of the ritual. There are a number of reasons for this attention: Rituals often express the ethos of a culture better than do most other forms of communication; also, in rituals the outside observer is able—and probably compelled—to remain detached and therefore able to make objective observations; and rituals help to direct the sense of community, the sense of permanence. Originated so long ago, most rituals cannot be explained easily by those who participate in them, and often the explanations are rationales conjectured by participants first confronted with the question, "Why do you do this?" Thus, the advantage of detached observations may carry an ironic disadvantage: While we may be able to collect objective, detailed information on certain rituals, our exclusion might make it impossible to relate this information to our behavior when we are in a new culture.

Nevertheless, visitors are often invited to observe, if not participate in directly, the rituals of their host country. To attend a wedding, funeral, feast, Saint's Day, national holiday, or local festival is usually desired by visitors, since it is something special and memorable and possibly even a candidate for slides or tape recordings for the mechanized traveler. Travel agencies, too, play up many large festivals and encourage tourists to visit during the festive season.

Rituals are likely to be awkward occasions for communication; The visitor feels like an outsider but wants to participate to some extent; he may know how to behave appropriately but knows also that appropriate behavior during some rituals may be very different from the usual day-to-day behavior; he's appreciative of the special food, the dress, the dances, and yet feels that true appreciation is impossible for one who is not a member of the community.

For a resident—in the United States, especially—ritual as a communicative function may be difficult to appreciate in his own country. As will be noted later, values which direct us toward the future, encourage change, or minimize formality tend to relegate ritual, when perceived as such, to a primitive category: "**mere** ritual." In addition, it is often difficult to recognize rituals within our own culture. Thus Americans may think of fireworks on the Fourth of July as ritualistic but may forget that birthday parties (with ice cream and cake, games, presents, candles) are also little rituals for marking ages. And Americans may be surprised when they discover that in much of the world, birthdays are not celebrated.

Deciding what to categorize as ritual is somewhat more difficult than it might first appear to be. What of the dress, music, dancing, and life-style of "youth"? These customs would seem to have great ritualistic value in distinguishing people who like the same music and style of clothing and hair from "the straight people" who are outside of this community. One of the striking things about the "youth revolution" or "the counterculture" of the late 1960s and the 1970s is its universality: that young persons throughout the world could express membership in the same kind of community. Apart from some religious rituals which are similar in many parts of the world, this phenomenon is historically unique. Therefore, on the basis of this functional approach, a shift from the "hippie revolution" to the "Jesus revolution" in the United States does not seem so surprising.

Affective communication. The function of affective (not effective) communication is to express emotions toward another person, and as such it suffers the cultural distinction between "head and heart," **reason** and **emotion.** Even though there are affective elements in almost all other functions of communication, the the ill-definable category of affective communication is useful in examining communication across cultures.

Considerable attention has been given to theory and research on the need for balance between reason and emotion and also to the view that persons, sub-cultures, and cultures which have been deprived of either reason or emotion have stressed the other. Some small-group research, conducted primarily in the United States, suggests that every group discussion will, over a time, produce a balance between "task-oriented" comments and "socioemotional expressions."[10] Advice to administrators often warns against a too business-like attitude which does not show enough concern for the personal feelings of the staff. Aristotelian rhetoric recommends a balance between **logos** and **pathos,** appeals of **reason** and **emotion.** Latin American philosophers have stressed the spirit of **la raza,** with strong affective sentiments as something better than the cold, calculating cultures of Northern European origin, including England and the United States. (The analogy of Ariel and Caliban frequently is cited.) Japanese are fond of comparing their aesthetic and soulful (located in the belly, it would seem) culture with that of "the rational West."

In popular American mythology today, the most affectively typified people are the poor, the humble, the uneducated, the rural and just about anybody "in the good old days." Suburban-

---

[10] See, for example, R. F. Bales, **Interaction Process Analysis** (Cambridge: Addison-Wesley, 1950).

ites even more than their urban neighbors have no "soul," are mechanized, distant, unfeeling. Nearly anybody who is affluent is suspected of lacking human affective qualities, at least in this popular view. In this country, success American-style either requires a lack of feeling or destroys feeling. This is a constant theme in much literature throughout the world, it would seem: It is difficult to find a credible financial success who is compassionate and nearly as difficult to find an interesting impoverished character who is highly "rational." Part of the remarkable popularity of John Kennedy, who would seem to be an exception to this pattern (in much of the world his image towers above Lincoln's), was that he had close family ties, was handsome and witty, and was Roman Catholic, a religion regarded as "irrational" by many Protestants.

Affective communication is the communication of feelings, of honest, heart-felt emotions. And much of intercultural communication is based on goals in which such expressions are minimized, if not discouraged altogether. That is, in business, in technical assistance programs, in foreign study and research work, and in diplomatic negotiations, the conveying of information and the instrumental (see below) functions receive first priority. When a culture's values and reasoning patterns (and even aspects of language) clearly distinguish these, the affective qualities of communication may suffer. Former Secretary of State John Foster Dulles' comment that "The U.S. does not have friends, it has interests" is bitterly remembered by Latin American critics (with Mr. Dulles sometimes called "Mr. Dollars"), as is the rhetorical question asked a number of years ago by a congressional representative, "Now that we have spent billions of dollars in foreign aid, how many friends have we bought?"

Note that the category of affective communication includes insults as well as compliments, dislike as well as love. Perhaps more so than most of the other general functions, affective elements are often expressed nonverbally (hugs, kisses, a pat on the back, an angry gesture), and this accounts for additional problems across cultures. If it were possible to line up cultures on a continuum beginning with the most perceivably expressive, those which seem to be most expressive might also seem to be the most affective. In this case, a hypothetical bookkeeper from

Honduras might seem to have more "soul" than a Vermont Saint.

Instrumental communication. When words or gestures are used as **instruments** in helping to achieve some result, we may identify them as **instrumental.** As in previous categories, such a broad definition of function might seem to include nearly all of what we call **communication.** But in attempting to keep these categories broad enough for a wide variety of uses, we can say that some gestures and expressions are more clearly instrumental than others: Commands and requests ("Open the door," "Do not smoke") especially seem instrumental and quite distinct from other functions, with the possible exception of conveying information. A weather report would seem to be classified as "conveying information," but upon interpretation it may be instrumental in suggesting what kind of clothing to wear, or whether or not to carry an umbrella.

As suggested in the previous category, instrumental expressions are often contrasted with affective expressions: if one's most frequent expressions are highly instrumental, he is likely to be regarded as lacking in feelings. It may be that there is a status differential which influences these two forms when the same goal is intended; that is, a person with authority may legitimately express his role through instrumental communication ("Do this, don't do that"), whereas a person who lacks power in any situation must achieve goals through indirection (flattery, cajoling). Thus in many cultures, the husband is the acknowledged authority in the home, giving the orders and speaking in a less affective style. (By extension, this may be part of the explanation for cultural distinctions between the head and the heart, as the "heart" is more affective and most often associated with the powerless.)

In the Judeo-Christian tradition, the Old Testament God is highly instrumental. Indeed, it would be difficult to find more striking examples of instrumental communication than in Genesis, where God's every word turns into reality. Christ, however, added an affective style, with values on God's love, forgiveness, compassion. In Roman Catholicism in many cultures God remains aloof and instrumental, while Mary is the affective soulful go-between, who intercedes. An interesting study revealed that the style of communication between a male saint and the Virgin Mary in Mexican churches perfectly mirrored communication between a child and his parents in the Mexican home.[11] The author described these parallel differences in terms of instrumental and affective communication.

In intercultural communication the recognition of instrumental or directive communication may be difficult. In time, a child learns that when his mother says "I don't think so" she often means "No;" likewise, across cultures and languages it takes time to learn the functional equivalents for instrumental goals. When a person's ability to speak a second or third language is weak, he is likely, lacking the skills in affective language, to sound more blunt, more directive than he intends. Cultural value differences also complicate the problem: The American's values both of frankness and of minimization of status differences may appear to be too blunt or crude in cultures where indirectness is valued, while they may not be directive enough in cultures where a person of higher status is expected to give commands as if he were an army general. Moreover, ascribed roles according to sex often are reflected in a female-affective style and a male-instrumental style. Compared to many societies, however, American men and women speak in about the same style, and this means that in some cultures the American woman is likely to sound insufficiently affective ("demanding," "aggressive," "masculine" in the eyes of her host-culture counterparts), while the American male may seem too affective (and, therefore, weak, unmasculine).

While there are other functions which could be listed here, our purpose is only to provide a representative and suggestive list of categories. Thus we are including only the six given previously. Any one function is likely to be expressed in other functional styles and interpreted across cultures as having still different functional intents. And these differences reflect and are yet further complicated by the presence of different values, nonverbal behavior, language predispositions, and the other perspectives mentioned earlier. Even this complex composition might be analyzed if a speaker always had one functional intention in mind and could express this function distinct from other

[11] Cynthia Nelson, "Saints and Sinners: Parallels in the Sex-Role Differentiation in the Family of Saints and in the Family of Man in a Mexican Peasant Village," mimeographed, n.d.

functions. However, although we have separated functions for purposes of explanation, most expressions are likely to serve several functions at the same time, and often the speaker does not have a single goal in mind. Even such a commonplace airport greeting as, "Welcome, we've all been looking forward to your visit," may represent the following functions: 1. **Small talk**—a conventional way of acknowledging the presence of another; 2. **Transmission of information**—implying that preparations have been made involving an unstated number of persons; 3. **Catharsis** —it may be that many greetings on occasion result in part from the tension which has developed in preparation and waiting for the visit; 4. **Ritual**—at least in an extended sense of ritual, such as Goffman uses to describe such everyday interactions. 5. **Affective communication**—clearly this appears to be a compliment to the visitor. 6. **Instrumental**—the comment may direct the guest to reply in kind ("I've been looking forward to this visit, too.").

For the sake of brevity, most of our examples have been limited to the expressions of a single speaker or a single interchange between two persons. Using a larger unit of discourse for analysis, such as an hour of behavior, the functional division may be still easier, for we can discover patterns in the expressions of each person and in the total field of communication established between the two.

Confusion frequently occurs when a listener knows the literal meaning of what is said but still is not sure "what it means" and therefore does not know how to respond. An American greets the friend of a non-American in a way that seems insulting; should the non-American ignore this, defend his friend, or add his own insult! The Tokyo housewife tells her dinner guest that there is nothing to eat; should the guest say he isn't hungry, be puzzled since he was invited to dinner, or treat this as conventional politeness? A functional approach to communication alerts us to such varied interpretations of the same "reports."

Communication is still a fuzzy concept, used sometimes to describe intentional "one-way" expressions and at other times used to describe a complex phenomenon which exists whenever persons are mutually aware of the presence of others. Keen scholarly writing does not result from fuzzy concepts, but at the current stage of communication studies it would be worse to be more precise or even to be thoroughly consistent. After all, one basic assumption is that the structural process of communication is considered differently by different persons, and we would like to leave the door open for as many structures as possible, depending on the needs, interests, and knowledge of each reader.

If nothing else, perhaps these perspectives remind us of the enormous complexity of communication, even apart from any differences in the cultural backgrounds of those who are communicating. Now a cliché in the field of communication is the belief that complete understanding between any two persons is impossible, and that misunderstanding occurs to a far greater degree than we usually assume. That we do as well as we do may be cause for some satisfaction. But in the global context today, the knowledge that we do so poorly must be cause for deep concern.

TWO

Encountering differences

Suppose that you're planning to visit a part of the world about which you know very little—except that it is quite different from your own country. You are sophisticated enough to expect that the spoken language and probably some gestures will be different. You know, too, that customs will be different, but you are not sure exactly what this will mean. At least there will be interesting things to take pictures of or write home about. The climate and foods will be different, of course, but these differences are attractions and are not really problems. Such is the would-be tourist's view of a foreign culture.

Suppose you make the trip. From the moment you arrive, your background—culturally, as a foreigner, and personally, as you —will influence everything you expect, a great deal of what you do and do not do, and most of how you later think about what has happened. Communication, as we are using that term, involves expectations, perceptions, choices, actions, and interpretations. Most of the people you meet will be similarly influenced by their own backgrounds, culturally, socially, and personally. If some of the people you meet think you act a little strangely, they may never know whether you are peculiar, or whether most people from your country are strange, or whether all "foreigners" are strange. You will face a similar problem, if it is a problem, in your reactions for some time: Is this person unusually slow, or are all of these people slow? Is this person exceptionally polite, or are all of these people that way? (Both questions might also be reversed: Am I especially fast, or are Americans that way? Am I especially casual or impolite or is that "the American way?")

Most of what you do will be "what comes naturally"—which means what you have always done or seen others do back home. Most of our behavior is outside of our awareness so that "normal behavior" means behavior according to the norms of our culture and not what is done everywhere or done "naturally." Still, to the extent that you are aware of the possibilities of different behavior in the land you are visiting you may be unusually self-conscious of some of this "normal behavior."

Suppose you have flown to the new land. Will you be met at the airport? If so, what—if anything—does that mean? If not, what, if anything, does that mean? Are you dressed properly? Do your greeters expect anything in particular? Should you walk slowly or quickly, smile or look serious (or what if smiling is taken as being serious?), allow others to pass before you or hurry to be among the first deposited on the ground? Will you shake hands or bow or embrace your welcoming party? If your hosts don't meet you, should you head for the hotel or wait around? Well, the number of options accelerate geometrically until at some point you take refuge in the excuse that the flight was long and you are simply too tired to be held accountable for whatever you might do. But even that "excuse" communicates more than its literal truth. It may be taken to mean "leave me alone" or a hint for an invitation to a more stimulating evening.

Cultural patterns and intercultural communication

Communication includes all kinds of behavior. We cannot separate **culture** from **communication,** for as soon as we start to talk about one we are almost inevitably talking about the other, too. But it is possible to distinguish between **cultural patterns of communication** and truly **intercultural** or **cross-cultural** communication, though many writers do not make that distinction. That is, we can talk about American communication patterns without worrying about what happens when a person from another culture visits the United States or an American visits another society. We can say, for example, that some cultures are "ladies first" cultures and others are "men first" cultures, without wondering what happens when two couples, one from each of the two cultures, attempt to go through a doorway at the same time. But it is difficult to talk about the encounters of persons from different cultures without also looking at the patterns within each of the cultures. We should not expect in all cases that what happens will be one pattern rather than another or a combination of both patterns. Often, a third pattern will emerge, and we cannot always guess what it will be by knowing what the "normal behavior" is for each of the parties involved.

In this chapter we consider twelve situations which cannot be properly understood without some awareness of cultural assumptions. In none of the cases is "language" per se the most important problem, though we should appreciate how spoken language would normally complicate things even further. Only the first four cases include an interpretation of the possible causes of problems. In three of these we follow poor Richard in his well-meaning but awkward encounters overseas. In the fourth we ponder the domestic problem of a Brazilian wife who prepares a dinner party for our hapless friend.

In examples 5 to 8 we ask you to think of yourself as being a member of a culture very different from your own. The cultures from which the incidents are taken are not identified, but it is best to assume all are fairly representative of societies often classified as traditional, agrarian, developing nations, third world or non-Western. Such labels derive from different disciplines and emphasize different factors (history, livelihood, socioeconomic realities, and geography) but what they label has at least this much in common: All are likely to be very different from nations like the United States, Canada, England, and most of Western Europe. In these cases you will be trying to sense cultural patterns of behavior which are very different from those with which you are probably most familiar.

In the final four cases (9 to 12) we again ask you to imagine that you are from the United States and are encountering persons from other cultures. Thus these again represent potential problems in intercultural understanding. Three incidents occur outside of the United States, while in the fourth the American is entertaining foreign visitors at his own home.

Poor Richard

Meet Richard, a model American: friendly, easy-going, unpretentious, well-intentioned, practical. But poor Richard inevitably seems to run into problems when he is in other countries. The problems are especially annoying because they so often seem to arise when everything is going well and communication appears to be at its best.

While visiting Egypt, Richard was invited to a spectacular dinner at the home of an Egyptian friend. And what a dinner it was! Clearly the host and hostess had gone out of their way to entertain him. Yet, as he was leaving their home he made a special effort to thank them for their spectacular dinner and sensed that something he said was wrong. Something about his sincere compliment was misunderstood.

In Japan he had an even less pleasant experience, but he thought he had handled it well. A number of serious mistakes had occurred in a project he was supervising. While the fault did not lie with any one person, he was a supervisor and at least partly to blame. At a special meeting called to discuss the problem, poor Richard made an effort to explain in detail why he had done what he had done. He wanted to show that anybody in the same situation could have made the same mistake and to tacitly suggest that he should not be blamed unduly. He even went to the trouble of distributing materials which explained the situation rather clearly. And yet, even during his explanation, he sensed that something he was saying or doing was wrong.

Even in England where he felt more at home, where he had no problems with language, this kind of misunderstanding occurred. He had been invited to take tea with one of his colleagues, a purely social, relaxed occasion. Tea was served along with sugar and cream. As he helped himself to some sugar and cream, he again sensed he had done something wrong.

Assuming that Richard, his hosts, and counterparts all mean well; assuming that Richard is truly sensitive to tensions and misunderstandings, and not simply neurotic; assuming all sorts of things which in actual life experiences are not so simply assumed; and further assuming a good American assumption that these are at least understandable, correctable problems—where shall we look, what questions shall we ask to discover what went wrong?

Dinner. In Egypt as in many cultures, the human relationship is valued so highly that it is not expressed in an objective but impersonal way. While Americans certainly value human relationships, they are more likely to speak of them in less personal, more objective terms. In this case, Richard's mistake might be that he chose to praise the food itself rather than the total evening, for which the food was simply the setting or excuse. For his host and hostess it was as if he had attended an art exhibit and complimented the artist by saying, "What beautiful frames your pictures are in."

The conference. In Japan the situation may be more complicated (or at least the typical Western image of Japan invites mysterious interpretations). For this example we can simply say that Japanese people value order and harmony among persons in a group, and that the organization itself—be it a family or a vast corporation—is more valued than the characteristics or idiosyncracies of any member. While this feeling is not alien to Americans—or to any society—Americans stress individuality as a value and are apt to assert individual differences when they seem justifiably in conflict with the goals or values of the group. In this case, Richard's mistake was in making great efforts to defend himself. Let the others assume that the errors were not intentional, but it is not right to defend yourself, even when your unstated intent is to assist the group by warning others of similar mistakes. A simple apology and acceptance of the blame would have been appropriate. (In contrast, for poor Richard to have merely apologized would have seemed to him to be subserviant, unmanly. Nothing in his experience had prepared him for the Japanese reaction—in fact he had been taught to despise such behavior.)

Taking tea. As for England, we might be tempted to look for some nonverbal indiscretion. While there are some very significant differences in language and language style, we expect fewer problems between Americans and Englishmen than between Americans and almost any other group. In this case we might look beyond the gesture of taking sugar or cream to the values expressed in this gesture: for Americans, "Help yourself"; for the English counterpart, "Be my guest." American and English people equally enjoy entertaining and being entertained, but they differ somewhat in the value of the distinction. Typically, the ideal guest at an American party is one who "makes himself at home," even to the point of answering the door or fixing his own drink. For persons in many other societies, including at least this hypothetical English host, such guest behavior is presumptuous or rude. Poor Richard may object to this explanation, saying, "In other words, English people like to stand on ceremony." If so, he still does not understand. Another analogy may help Richard to appreciate the host's point of view: An American guest at an American party who would rearrange the furniture without being asked, suggest the dinner menu, and in other ways "make himself at home" also would seem to be presumptuous.

In analyzing apparent problems of communication across cultures, it is all too tempting to look first for difficulties posed by language misinterpretations or assume some nonverbal indiscretion. But we have tried to suggest through these brief discussions of Richard's problems that the misunderstanding or misbehavior more likely resides elsewhere, in the subtler but consistent cultural patterns of behavior which become understandable when we appreciate differences in cultural values. Thus what we first need, in attempting to analyze any such situation, is not necessarily more language skill or more information about the mores of a particular culture, but rather an openness to alternatives to our own conventional behavior. If we appreciate the logic of our own actions, we can more quickly imagine alternatives equally consistent with other values. With this in mind, let us turn things around and look at a problem faced by a person who, in another society, must entertain Richard.

The dinner party. Suppose you are the wife of a **funcionario** in the Brazilian government who has just invited Richard, a North

American civil engineer, to dinner. The engineer is helping to supervise the construction of a new bridge in your city, and you do not know much more about him than that. Your problem seems a simple one: which set of dishes to use. You have two sets, and if this Richard wasn't a foreigner and your husband hadn't made such a thing of his visiting, you wouldn't have given it much thought. Should you use the expensive set of imported plastic dishes, or should you use the usual family set of local hand-made, hand-painted pottery dishes? You know that the dinner is "special," but that only makes the problem more difficult.

This apparently innocuous problem, nearly free of what we ordinarily think of as a **communication situation,** is far more complicated than it might appear. By looking at the situation from different points of view, we can easily come up with at least ten different definitions of the situations and related choices.

1. Use the plastic dishes. They are more expensive so they should be used for such a special guest. Richard will be impressed.

2. Use the local dishes. Richard is "imported," too, and probably eats off of plastic dishes every night. He'll like something different.

3. Use the plastic dishes. Maybe he has the same set at home, but that might be all the more reason to use them—it will make him feel at home, which is what you would like the dinner to mean to him.

4. Use the local dishes. The meal will be a local meal, so the dishes should be, too.

5. Use the plastic dishes. Use the best, after all, to show that your husband is a worldly man even if he lives in this city. It's an international sort of dinner, isn't it? Plastic is international, isn't it?

6. Use the local dishes. This visitor probably is staying in some hotel where they use plastic dishes like yours—if it is a good hotel. Show him something of the real **nordestinos.** Be proud!

7. Use the plastic dishes. They are beautiful! Every one is exactly alike! These local dishes are all right, but each is shaped and painted just a little differently and he might notice. Your husband said the dinner should be beautiful, so this means you should use the company set.

8. Use the local dishes. They are beautiful, too. They are nice enough and besides, they might be something to talk about during the meal. You can tell the guest about the Vargas family that makes them.

9. Use the plastic dishes and the local dishes together. This will solve all of the problems—and it will show that you are proud of your country but also have things that came from far away.

10. Don't ever use the plastic and the local dishes together. It will make the local dishes look terrible, and it will seem like you don't have enough of either.

Why doesn't your husband take Richard to a nice restaurant?

Additional comments

The question of which set of dishes to use illustrates how complicated even the simplest choices and actions can be when we encounter the unknown. When a guest comes, even if he is from our own neighborhood, we may have to make some guesses about how to act, but there is a wide area of common expectations and understanding. Where persons from different cultures meet, everything is much more complicated. With a problem like that of which dishes to use, the interpretation of the host and hostess is always somewhat different from that of the guest. If only local dishes or only plastic dishes are used, the guest has no way of knowing that another set was considered. If the plastic dishes are chosen, the hostess may hope that the guest compliments her on the fine dishes; but since the guest cannot know that the dishes were specially chosen, he may be cautious about expressing compliments. He may assume that the plastic dishes are cheap, local, and practical and say nothing about them, disappointing the hostess. But suppose he guesses that these are special and says so with a compliment? If the hostess was only using what she had and was a little embarrassed by her humble plastic dishes, his compliment might make her more embarrassed.

In short, we should remember our first assumption: communication includes all of our behavior; we cannot avoid communicating. Where the interaction is special and there is some tension and heightened sensitivity—usually the case in interpersonal communication across cultures—even the most innocuous behavior may seem charged with meaning.

Test yourself by imagining you are the person described in each of the situations below. Our previous examples gave some indication of kinds of interpretations that are possible, but here we leave the interpretations up to you. There should be at least two or three plausible interpretations of each situation, but as a general rule the larger the number and more varied the reactions, the better. Even if some ways of thinking would not be characteristic of the societies from which these situations were taken, so long as they help us to break out of our own "normal" ways of viewing things, they help to sensitize us to other ways of thinking. In order to encourage as wide a range of interpretations as possible, we have not identified the particular cultures from which these examples were taken.

Cultural patterns within developing nations

A young man. You are a shopkeeper in a middle-sized city in a developing nation, which is characterized by a high percentage of illiteracy. Widespread literacy campaigns began only twenty years ago following independence. As a merchant you are functionally literate in the national language—far more than most of your customers are, but reading is difficult for you. Fortunately, you are much better at mathematics. In your country many languages are spoken. Somebody told you that there were more than fifty languages and you know from experience that you cannot understand the conversations of some of your customers. Three languages seem most important to you: the language spoken by members of your clan; the national language, which you speak fairly well; and the language of the colonial leaders, which is still the language used by educated people, used in government, written on the money, and used in high school and at the university.

Every day or so you notice a young man, about twenty years old, walking past your shop. He always carries a book or a newspaper. You don't know him, but you do notice that sometimes the book or newspapers seem to be written in the colonial language. And sometimes the newspapers are written in the national language. You overheard him speaking to a friend once and he talked the way your clan does, but you don't know who he is. How do you feel about this young man and his books and newspapers?

A gift of a bag of milk. You are a mother of seven children. Your husband is a laborer. He works hard, but with the rising costs and low wages, your family never has any money by the end of the month. You keep hoping and praying for some stroke of luck that will change things. Today you had a little bit of luck. A man from the state capital arrived in town in a truck loaded with plastic bags of powdered milk. You just happened to be there while the man was making a speech about sharing things, about the government and foreign governments, and about things that were not very interesting to you. But then he started giving away the bags of milk. He gave you one! What do you think about as you walk home with your plastic bag of powdered milk? What will you do with it?

Census. You and your wife are out plowing in your field when four young people you have never seen before suddenly appear. They introduce themselves, explaining that they are from the big city. They are carrying big pads of papers and looking around. They tell you that they are doing something called a **census.** A census, they explain, is counting all of the people in your country. They ask you if you are married, where you live, and how many children you have. Who are these people? What should you tell them?

Gathering grasses on the mountain. Your people have always lived on the slopes of this mountain, which must be the most beautiful place in all creation. You have a small farm which you, your husband, and your children cultivate, and, like most of your neighbors, you also have a cow. Your cow, of course, stays in your home. It gives milk and helps to keep the house warm at night when the mountain becomes cold. Your people have been blessed with so many children that the farms seem to get smaller and smaller every few years so there is certainly no room for the cow to graze. Every day you and the other women go out to gather wild grasses to bring home to feed your cows.

One day a man from the city comes and says that the president has a new idea. He says that from now on it will not be necessary for the women to go and gather grass for the cows. He says that every morning the government will send a truck from farm to farm filled with grass. The grass will not cost anything. The women can use their time to do other more important things than gathering grasses.

You and the other women agree to try the new plan. Sure enough, every day the truck comes with enough grass, and as the man promised you don't have to give anything in exchange for the grass. But something is wrong. You are unhappy now. You liked the old way better. Why?

Meet the family. For years you've been writing letters to a pen pal who lives on the other side of the world. Finally you were able to save enough money to visit your friend for a month, living with your friend's family. What a reception you were given at the airport! Your "adopted family" seems so friendly and generous that right away you know you are going to have a wonderful time. Though it is a large family, they live in a big house, spacious enough for them to give you your own room. After unpacking some of your things, you go for a walk with your friend to see a little of the city. When you return to your room, you are startled to see that your belongings seem to have been "examined." Some of your personal items—shampoo and some medicine you brought—obviously have been removed from your suitcase and left on the table. And a fountain pen which you had left on the table is missing. What is going on here? What, if anything, should you say and do?

A date with Mona. You are a young man who has come to this country on a junior-year-abroad program to study history. In one of your classes you become friendly with a beautiful girl, Mona, whose father, you learn, is also very knowledgable about his nation's history. Mona invites you to dinner one evening to meet her family and discuss history. The warmth and friendliness of the family is exceeded only by the significant feast Mona's mother has prepared. You are overwhelmed. You don't have much of a chance to talk to Mona's mother, however, since she, as well as the other daughters, keep out of sight most of the time, and even Mona's father is unable to spend much time visiting with you. Still, you have a wonderful time talking with Mona in the sitting room. A few weeks later, however, Mona invites you again, promising that this time her father will surely be able to talk about history. Again you visit, again an elaborate meal is prepared, again the women disappear after serving the meal, but this time you do talk with Mona's father for a long time. You also have some time alone with the lovely Mona.

You want to reciprocate as best you can, but living alone in a small apartment and not being a particularly good cook makes this difficult. Still, one day after class you invite Mona to come to your apartment for dinner, explaining that you want to repay her kindness and try your hand at cooking some of the local delicacies. You are only half kidding when you tell Mona that maybe she can teach you how to cook properly. But Mona is suddenly angry. Almost crying she says, "I didn't know you thought I was **that** kind of girl!" and she walks away. What went wrong?

A friend of a friend of a friend. While doing graduate work at a university overseas you become very good friends of Mr. Amm, who lives in the same boarding house. You seem to enjoy the same sort of jokes and ways of relaxing in the evenings, but his academic major its unrelated to yours. However, one of his best friends, Mr. Bom, two years older than he, is a major in the same field, and Mr. Amm has often suggested that you meet him. Later you learn that Mr. Bom has been doing research on exactly the same topic as you are, and that he is likely to be able to be very helpful in your preparation for a field study. Since you don't want to bother your friend and don't want to lose any more time in meeting this person, you go directly to where Mr. Bom lives, introduce yourself, and mention your mutual friend, and have a wonderful talk about your study. The next day you visit Mr. Amm to tell him of that meeting and to thank him for telling you about Mr. Bom. Your friend reacts cooly: "Yes," he says, "I heard you both met. I hope your research goes well." His manner tells you that something is wrong, but what?

Make yourself at home. You are active in a foreign student club at your university and have several good friends from different countries. One of them tells you his parents and sister will be visiting, and he asks you if you would like to meet them. You invite all of them to visit your home one afternoon. They arrive and present you with a nicely wrapped gift. You tell them they shouldn't have brought anything, but thank them and proceed to open the gift, which turns out to be a very pretty vase from their country. You thank them again. You sense some awkwardness and realize that you have not offered them anything to drink. "Would you like coffee or tea or a soft drink?" you ask. They all refuse. Things seem more awkward now. But you talk a little about their country, about studies at the university, about the cost of living, and eventually the father whispers something to his son. "I think we must be leaving to return to the hotel," he says. Everybody stands up, shakes hands, and they start to leave. "Please come and visit again," you say as you stand and watch the family walk to the door, open it, and disappear down the hall. Two days later, in a very indirect way, you learn from another friend that the visitors thought you were a rude host. You ask why and you are told, "Well, I heard that there were at least three things you did that were very impolite." What happened?

Concluding remarks

Now and then a problem of misunderstanding across cultures is so dramatic and at such an important level, that everybody takes notice of the problem. This is particularly true if the reasons for misunderstanding seem clear, such as an error in language translation. But most problems, like most of what is called intercultural communication, occur on a level that is both undramatic and yet more complicated. This is particularly true if the reason for misunderstanding lies in conflicts of values. It is quite likely that in many cases, including some of those just described, the persons involved are not fully sure of what went wrong.

To analyze such incidents and to anticipate potential problems in an effort to avoid them or cope with them as they occur, we must become sensitive to some of the cultural influences in communication which, in our own society, we take for granted. We must call into awareness much of what we usually ignore, and must begin to think in terms that may be totally new. We will focus primarily on four themes and the relationships among these: (1) cultural values, (2) nonverbal behavior, (3) language behavior, and (4) patterns of reasoning and rhetorical expression. Of these four, the subject of values may be of greater benefit in anticipating and analyzing "what went wrong" but also "what went right" when communication seems to be at its best. In the next chapter we introduce the subject of values and several ways in which this subject has been approached, and in Chapters Four and Five we present a broad layout of value orientations. Most of the incidents just described can be better understood when the underlying cultural values are understood. We suggest that after reading the next two chapters you return to these cases for a second time. You may return with new insights.

THREE

Something of values

Years ago, John Kouwenhoven wrote a provocative series of essays entitled, **The Beer Can by the Highway; or, What's American about America.**[1] The effort sought to discover common themes among apparently diverse aspects of the culture. The most American form of the skyscraper, for example, was shown to be related to the most American form of music, jazz. In each, when one has finished, one just stops. On a skyscraper there is no elaborate roof, no tower or temple perched atop. Jazz, too, the author argued, stops abruptly when the end is reached. There is no advance warning that the end is in sight, no Beethoven-like elaboration of the conclusion. We might also add that American conversations, in contrast to those in many societies, seem to just stop when they are concluded. Even American friendships are also said to "just stop" when it is felt there is no longer any reason to continue them. An American high school senior wrote in his school yearbook, "Good-bye, I'll never see you again."

The Kouwenhoven idea makes good exercise in studying inter-cultural communication, since any expressive form from a culture

[1] John Kouwenhoven, **The Beer Can By the Highway; Essays on What's American about America** (New York: Doubleday, 1961).

might be selected. A McDonald's hamburger may offer us a rich diet of American values: efficiency, sameness, quantification. **Playboy** magazine has been analyzed to demonstrate a variety of American themes, including, as a colleague noted, standardization and the belief that bigger is better!

The student of values asks the same kind of question: What is Chinese about China, what is French about France, what is Russian about Russia? It assumes that any culture manifests in many ways its special character. Any traveler recognizes this when he says: "How French!" "How very German!" "How Canadian!" But the student of values is interested in what is reflected within the form, and not in the form itself. He is more interested in the value of status differentiation than in differences in form of address, uniforms, titles, or the order of introductions which might express these differences. He is interested more in the value of nature's superiority over man or in fatalism, than in specific prayers, rituals, or responses to technology which might also reflect that value. The student of values seeks underlying principles as categories both for distinguishing cultures and for finding commonplaces among cultures. To borrow an analogy from the transformational grammarians he seeks the deep structure of the culture, which is more significant than the "surface meaning" of more apparent cultural manifestation. And, continuing the analogy, he appreciates that members of the culture are not likely themselves to be aware of this deeper structure and that acculturation derives from a vast number of surface specifics (parental discipline, folk and fairy tales, jokes, homely persuasive appeals and much more). Our analogy stops here, however. The transformationalist believes that at the level of deep structure there are universals common to all languages; in the case of values, however, our emphasis is on differences across cultures. The values theorist thus moves inductively from the specifics to the more abstract general principle but he also moves deductively, for his examination of specifics proceeds within the constructs of some value theory.

Cultures, subcultures, and nations

When we speak of values or value orientations, our focus should always be on cultures, not nations. A nation is a political entity which may contain within it many quite different cultures; similarly, national borders may politically distinguish areas which are culturally identical. The lines drawn in Europe during the last century slicing up Africa into European colonies produced some nations which contain many different cultures, and cruelly divided unified cultures into separate nations. Within the United States, we may say there are different cultures or, as is more commonly said, different **subcultures.**

In an introduction to the study of intercultural communication it would be far more accurate to identify a group in terms of culture instead of nationality. But this is not easy. We are accustomed to identifying areas and societies by national names, so that a more specific referent ("the Nahua culture" versus "the Mexican culture") is confusing or requires explanation. Another reason is that there is much more disagreement about how to identify some cultures than how to identify a nation. There is little agreement on how to identify the subcultures within the United States, for example. For the purposes of this book, therefore, we usually will speak of cultural values by national names ("American values").[2] However, these should be interpreted as referring to those values that seem dominant within that society and which are most often associated with that society. The values approach we will follow, explained later in this chapter, accommodates variations in values in any society. Indeed, it is an assumption of this approach that every society probably contains, at any one time, alternative or even competing values. In short, the national identification is primarily for convenience, a point of reference, for dominant values in a nation. Other alternative values are to be expected and must be dealt with in a more detailed examination.

In this book we will say little about communication between different cultural (or subcultural) groups within a single nation. Much of what we discuss in this book is relevant to that subject, but relations within a nation and communication between per-

---

[2] The word "American" is a term we will use often, but with some apologies. Many persons in Middle, Central, and South America, as well as in Canada, resent the appropriation of the term by the United States. They may say, quite rightly, that they are **Americans,** too. Unfortunately the **United States** does not lend itself to a convenient adjectival form, at least not in English. (Even if it did there are other "United States" in the world, including **The United Mexican States.**)

sons from different nations are not fully comparable. Readers are free to extend our presentation to matters of race relations or even the generation gap within the United States or any other nation, but in doing so they must also add other considerations.

Keeping in mind these general distinctions between cultures, subcultures, and nations—as well as the problems entailed in labeling and the goals of our study of intercultural communication—we may proceed with our analysis of cultural values.

An analogy

An analogy from Gestalt psychology may help to clarify the character and limitations of a values approach. If a person is shown this `.˙.` he is likely to perceive a triangle and not three distinct dots. One explanation is that people seek to organize, to grasp the whole, and, in that seeking, to simplify. Most persons say that the dots form a triangle, but they also admit that "there is no real triangle there." The values approach is similar; values or value orientations are perceived as the organization of data, attempts to grasp a whole pattern, and also as abstractions from discrete bits of evidence that give shape to that pattern.

This same analogy suggests risks in the values approach. One is that of limitation or simplification. Depending on what elements of a culture are given special attention, different configurations of values may be suggested. For example, the Japanese **kimono** is cut in the same shape for men and for women, and in the Japanese language the same title, **San** (equivalent to Mr., Miss, Ms., or Mrs.), is used in addressing men and women. Given this limited data, we might speculate that Japanese people value the equality of the sexes in social roles, but it takes little data to discover how erroneous this interpretation is. Another risk is that which allows the Gestalt principle to be used in projective tests, such as the **Rorschach.** There is a very great danger of projecting onto another culture what the observer expects, be it a projection of his own culture or an image formed from travelogues and history books.

Definitions

"A value system," Ethel Albert writes, ". . . represents what is expected or hoped for, required or forbidden. It is not a report of actual conduct but is the system of criteria by which conduct is judged and sanctions applied."[3] The "system of criteria" Professor Albert speaks of is rarely explicit within the culture. Rather, as she put it, a kind of Socratic midwifery is required to draw from the culture what is there but unrecognized in its broad patterns. As she notes, few languages have a general term equivalent to **value,** and while some rules of conduct may be explicit ("You must always . . . ," "You must never . . . !"), most value interpretations must be abstracted from diverse sources. These include child-rearing patterns, folk tales, linguistic data, tacit codes of social interaction, law, and much more.

The value of informality so characteristic of much of the United States, for example, is revealed in many forms: verbally, in such expressions as "Don't stand on ceremony," and "Make yourself at home;" non-verbally, as in the preference for casual clothes (tuxedoes may be rented if needed), and the relative lack of calling cards and company lapel pins; in forms of address, with the preference for first names and awkwardness toward titles; in architecture, with the loss of parlors and the increase of recreation rooms in homes, or the change of bank architecture from Greek temples to the friendly neighborhood savings and loan.

The range of sources which may contribute to determining the patterning of values is so vast that clear distinctions between values, cultural patterns, and communication patterns may be only arbitrary.

According to Clyde Kluckhohn, an anthropologist who has written extensively on value theory, about the only defining point about values which is generally agreed upon is that they have to do with **normative** as opposed to **existential** propositions.[4] That is, values have to do with what is judged **good** or **bad,** right or wrong. Statements based on values describe the ideal, the standards by which behavior is evaluated; they do not necessarily describe the actual behavior. Statements about what is true and false are commonly labeled **beliefs.** This distinction between

[3] Ethel Albert, "Value Systems," in **The International Encyclopedia of the Social Sciences,** vol. 16 (New York: Macmillan, 1968).
[4] Clyde Kluckhohn, "Values and Value Orientations in the Theory of Action: An Exploration in Definition and Classification," in **Toward a General Theory of Action,** eds. Talcott Parsons and Edward Shils (Cambridge: Harvard University Press, 1951), 390–406.

beliefs and values, Kluckhohn is quick to point out, is not always easy to maintain.

> What "must be done" is usually closely related to what is believed to be "the nature of things"; however, beliefs about "what is" are often disguised assumptions of "what ought to be." Moreover, the values of the group, when institutionalized and internalized, have for members of the group, a practical kind of existential validity.[5]

The self-fulfilling prophecy also functions to render some values into social facts. If a society values a woman as a housekeeper and mother, as expressed in the statement, "The woman's place is in the home," as a matter of **fact** as well as of value a woman's place will be in the home.

It is helpful to try to distinguish values from **preferences.** Preferences are the sort of thing that poll takers are so often surveying: the preferred political candidate, the woman most admired, or the brand preferred (market research). Within a single culture we expect differences, and without asking we may never be sure of what or whom is preferred at the moment. But because values lie much deeper, they are more difficult to ask about directly. If we could survey values, we would find fewer differences than we find in preferences. On a U.S. college campus, there may be many preferences in choice of majors, but the values underlying all of the preferences may be similar—the value of education or even that of getting away from home.

One difficulty with defining values is that of time-span. Fads and fashions are best regarded as preferences, however enduring or classic they may seem to be at the time. But what of the value of the nuclear family? What of countless morals in folk and fairy tales? These change, too. (A cartoon in **The New Yorker** shows a "hip" father reading the end of a fairy tale to his child: **"And they lived happily for some time."**) The concept of values must be based on a wide time-span, just as that of culture, which in so many ways is an amplification of values, must also be. We would like to be able to say that what Toqueville observed and predicted of the United States in 1831 still holds true. We would not like to be obliged to date and index—as Korzybski urged

5 Ibid., pp. 389–90.

the General Semanticists to do—every generalization about a culture. Even in periods of rapid social change, of considerable borrowing from other cultures, the tenacity of cultural values demands our appreciation. But what of the theme in Toffler's **Future Shock,** that large segments of societies are changing so rapidly that the impact of change is analogous to the "culture shock" one experiences in traveling to another quite different society?[6] To many value theorists, perhaps, Toffler has over-stated his case or, perhaps, has simply projected his own American value of change onto societies where it is not applicable. We will return to this question later in the book, but for now we should acknowledge that the criterion of endurance, which in the past has been basic to the value concept, must be reappraised.

Systems

We must remember when speaking of a **culture's value system** that "the system" exists more in the mind of the observer than in the culture itself, even though our descriptions of values do not always make this clear. This may be more apparent when we realize that any number of systems may be applied to the same culture, each with its own consistency, purpose, and applicability. The description of value orientations presented in the following chapter is one such system. To appreciate its use and limitations, we should first briefly consider other approaches, which should help to distinguish our approach in the following two chapters while also clarifying the concept of cultural values.

Cultural interpretations of basic needs. Some scholars, notably biologists, zoologists, and many psychologists, have sought to describe human behavior in terms of biological and psychological universals.[7] Individual and cultural behaviors are interpreted within this framework, providing a common denominator for all societies. Some such systems are hierarchical, requiring that certain needs be satisfied before others, while other systems are simpler listings of "basics," which can be symbolized in many

[6] Alvin Toffler, **Future Shock** (New York: Random House, 1970).
[7] See, for example, Konrad Lorenz, **On Aggression** (New York: Harcourt, Brace and World, 1966), and Desmond Morris, **The Naked Ape: A Zoologist's Study of the Human Animal** (New York, McGraw-Hill, 1967).

forms. Food, love, recognition, territorial rights, and stimulation, among many others, are basics which have been assumed to be universal and thus are a basis for comparing societies.

Dorothy Lee has written a sharp criticism of this approach stressing two main objections.[8] One is methodological, as she argues that such lists tend to generate still more lists until they become unwieldy; moreover, there may be little common agreement of what is to be considered **basic.** Her second objection is characteristic of a cultural anthropologist: she believes that the concept of **value** itself is a better **base term** than **basic needs** or **primary needs.** She feels that it is more accurate to say that a person's needs arise from the values of his culture than to say that the cultural values stem from his needs. She illustrates this by showing that in the United States there is a **need** for privacy (reflected in private rooms and private cars, for instance), which, she says, arises out of other values of independence and individualism. As the mother has needs for her own privacy— free time to live her own life—she inevitably but subtly inculcates the same needs in her child. But none of these needs is biological or universal. They arise out of a culture's values.

Universal values. What we might call the **universal values approach** appears to be the oldest of the five approaches described here, and should be familiar to persons aware of **The Rhetoric,** by Aristotle, or nearly any book on public speaking. The person preparing his speech is urged to analyze his audience and adapt to their values. Thus, in this approach classifications —apart from national or cultural identification—of persons are provided, along with the values assumed to be characteristic of such persons. Thus we are told that young people value challenge and idealism, while old people tend to favor the past and are distrustful of change. Similarly, we learn of the values of the rich and the poor, the alienated and the "true believer," and so on.

Unfortunately, the strength of this kind of approach is also its chief weakness. We may be impressed that so many of the insights of **The Rhetoric** continue to seem applicable today in many cultures quite distinct from each other, as well as being

[8] Dorothy Lee, **Freedom and Culture** (Englewood Cliffs, N. J.: Prentice-Hall, 1959), 70–77.

distinct from the Athens of Aristotle. But this also means that we cannot directly apply these universals to distinguish among cultures. This writer has discussed aspects of **The Rhetoric** with students in several very different societies: the United States, Mexico, Tanzania, and Japan. In each case, students affirmed that Aristotle's descriptions—even the age classifications—were very astute and descriptive of the broad groups described. Obviously these similarities totally ignore more significant differences. The problems lie in the incompleteness of such descriptions and in the abstract language in which the observations are presented.

In a later chapter we will return to the intention and form of **The Rhetoric** which may suddenly become relevant again in our age. The person entering another culture may have to adapt to the values of his audience, too, but for guidance he will require a more specific and comprehensive view of values.

Value lists. The most frequent means of presenting values is through simple lists. The Boy Scout oath is a kind of list of values for a scout, and lists of values for a culture can be as stark and abstract as that of the scouts. We may read, for example, that Americans value equality, fair play, progress, and self-reliance, often without reading any explanation of how such values function or how they are related. Like other explanations that are "clear only if known," such a list may be convenient and seem accurate to someone familiar with the culture described, but it may be misleading to someone who has no other information to rely upon.

There are other disadvantages, too. A culture which has been researched extensively (usually by many different sources), is allotted a much longer list than one that has not received so much attention. The lists may be accurate, but they do not necessarily provide enough clues or questions for speculations about the less-studied societies. A related problem is in the language of the values. Terms may be fashioned or taken from a culture's history to characterize certain values, but in attempting to compare societies (as in trying to adjust to a different value system when entering another society) there may be no common means of comparison. Two examples from representative lists of American values may illustrate this problem: **Puritan morality** often is cited as a value or cluster of values which influences thought and action in the United States. What do we do with such a concept when we wish to describe comparable or alternative values in Finland, Romania, or Iran? (Note that although it is dangerous to expect values in different cultures always to correspond, that is not our objection here. When values are stated only from the point of view of one society—and often in a word without equivalence in other languages, it is difficult to make the comparisons which are needed for adaptation or accommodation.) Cleanliness does not so often appear in lists of values in the United States; used in an expression like "Cleanliness is next to Godliness" or rejected by members of "the counterculture" as an undesirable trait to be identified with, cleanliness may deserve such attention. In past sociological surveys of desired traits in prospective marriage partners, "cleanliness" has ranked very high in the United States; in parallel studies in Mexico it has ranked relatively low. Should cleanliness be included in a list of values in the United States? If so, how should we distinguish between that value here and "cleanliness" in a nation like Japan, where cleanliness has aesthetic and spiritual significances far different and much more evident than in the United States?

Yet another limitation of such lists is that of generalizing about the culture. A culture and a nation may be different entities, and within each we may find variations in the importance of some values. A list of values is likely to describe only those of the majority and usually those which have been recognized for many years. To assume that such values characterize nearly all in a society is risky, particularly in pluralistic societies and in those undergoing rapid social change. But if we are told only to be cautious about generalizing, we are left without guidance for analyzing the values of people not included in our generalization. The introduction of a term like **subcultures** may be helpful, but then similar problems arise when we try to spin out more lists for each subculture.

Value orientations. In an attempt to improve upon the previous approaches, Florence Kluckhohn and her associates at Harvard developed the concept of **value orientations**.[9] In this approach, it

[9] Florence Kluckhohn and Fred Strodtbeck, **Variations in Value Orientations** (Evanston: Row, Peterson, 1961).

is assumed that there are universal problems and conditions which men in all societies face and only a limited number of solutions to these problems. Each of these possible solutions is called a **value orientation,** and we can expect to find variations among these even within a single society. As a social scientist, she believed that these orientations could be tested empirically, with the orientations operationalized in hypothetical situations and presented in questionnaire form. The results would give in rank order the dominant and minority value orientations within the culture tested. Her initial research was based on five sets of value orientations. In this book we have retained these, with a slight modification in one case, and extended the list to a total of twenty-five, each with three variations.

An example from Kluckhohn will serve to illustrate this approach. Every society must consider the relationship between a person and his environment. One possibility is for a person to see himself as the master of that environment, with nature viewed as something to be exploited. Another possibility is the reverse of this: for the person to see himself at the mercy of natural and supernatural forces. Yet a third possibility is for the person to view himself as a part of nature, neither master nor slave, but as one who must live in harmony with his surroundings. With these three possibilities, hypothetical problems with possible solutions or responses which correspond to each of the alternative value orientations can be posed, surveys can be taken, and the results can be computed and analyzed. The result is the value orientations for that society listed in rank order, from most characteristic to least characteristic.

But there are problems with this approach. One, which does not directly concern us in this book, is that of operationalizing the orientations and testing them through surveys. The particular situations proposed are crucial in the interpretation of the orientations and if the method is to be used for comparative studies it may be difficult in some cases to find comparable situations for very different cultures. Of course, the system of orientations can be used merely to provide a vocabulary and point reference for discussion or for application other than questionnaire surveys. (This in fact will be our approach.)

A second limitation resides in the deductive nature of the approach. Our criticisms of the value lists are largely criticisms of the inductive method, starting with specifics and then generalizing to the culture. Here we encounter other problems precisely because the approach arises not out of specific situations in cultures, but out of abstract notions of basic problems with a fixed number of solutions. How does one decide what problems to pose? Which solutions and how many solutions should be included? Are we not likely to project our own system of evaluation by proceeding this way? What of the aesthetic bias, so frequently a problem in abstract deductive approaches, which may lose in accuracy and applicability what it gains in symmetry and consistency? (Should all problems have exactly three solutions?)

We cannot avoid these questions, but having recognized them we should have a clearer notion of our limitations. The question of what problems or categories to propose remains a good question—but those selected are not pure inventions. Each of the value orientations presented in Chapters Four and Five arises from empirical data obtained from many cultures. The greater danger is not that of hypothesizing irrelevant categories but in not including enough. Since the scheme is not intended to be exhaustive, this is not a major problem; one is always free to add more or, if desired, to combine categories or to ignore some entirely. The bias of consistently posing three alternatives for each set is a more serious problem yet, but here again the problem is not so much that of creating an artificial category (in order to always have a total of three) as in the phrasing of those categories, with the possibility of leaving unrepresented a culturally viable orientation.

Despite these problems, the advantages should be apparent. We have a structure and vocabulary that can be used as a standard for comparing different cultures and for describing variations within a single society. This may be the basis of devising questionnaires or interview protocols, or it may provide the matrix into which isolated observations about a culture may be fitted. It may be used to interpret changes in values in the history of a society and to project future value changes.

The approach in this book. To conceptualize the range of values considered in the following two chapters, it may be helpful to think first of three intersecting spheres: **self, society,** and **nature.**

Their intersections provide three additional categories: **family** (between self and society), **human nature** (between society and nature), and the **supernatural** (between nature and self).

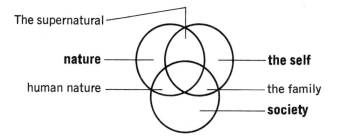

No claim is made that the first three mentioned are primary and the second three are derived, though an American might arrive at that conclusion. That is, the configuration of salient American values may give much more stress to self than to family, and, one writer suggests, more to nature than to society.[10] The supernatural might be viewed as an area of competition between self and nature, with family more of a reflection of society than the other way around. If so, this appears to differ considerably from most societies in the world where family is likely to command much more attention than either self or society, with each of these being interpreted through the family. In any case, these spheres are suggested only to show their relationship with each other and as major topics under which specific value orientations are discussed. As in any attempt to isolate and label values, our distinctions are admittedly arbitrary. Only some cultures would attempt to distinguish the supernatural from nature, for example. Moreover, the subjects discussed under any one category (or within any of these six spheres) can also apply to other categories, and thus we again must warn against rigid applications of this format.

What we have tried to do is to take the basic concept of value orientations, discussed previously, and rearrange and expand it. To the original five sets of value orientations proposed by Florence Kluckhohn, we have added twenty, for a total of twenty-

[10] Edward C. Stewart, **American Cultural Patterns: A Cross-Cultural Perspective** (Pittsburgh: Regional Council for International Education, 1971).

five sets. We have also retained the three variations for each set, which thus yields seventy-five value orientations to consider. As we have mentioned, there are obvious risks in limiting the variations to three and, indeed, there is no empirical basis for allowing no more or less than three variations for every consideration. However, to offer only two variations suggests a dichotomy that invites misinterpretation for each position, and to extend the number to four or more would make our "introduction" hopelessly unwieldly.

In the following two chapters we will discuss these variations in value orientations in greater detail. In the remainder of the book we will continue to refer to the role of cultural values as they function in nonverbal behavior, in house structure and family patterns in various cultures, in language, and in the ways in which we reason and express our arguments. We have allotted more space for our discussion of values than for any other topic considered in this book. Not only do values pervade all of the other topics, they also may provide the best guidance for understanding and adapting to other cultural patterns of communication.

A chart of the value orientations discussed in Chapters Four and Five appears below. In referring to the chart, keep in mind the following: 1. All variations may exist in any one society. 2. While those orientations listed in the left-hand column are those often attributed to the United States as a culture, there is no necessary relationship among all of the values in either of the other two columns. 3. This outline is neither definitive nor exhaustive; to be applicable to specific communication between persons from particular cultures, further refinement would be necessary.

SELF

Individualism—interdependence

1. individualism	2. individuality	3. interdependence

Age

1. youth	2. the middle years	3. old age

Sex

1. equality of sexes	2. female superiority	3. male superiority

Activity

1. doing	2. being-in-becoming	3. being

THE FAMILY

Relational orientations

1. individualistic	2. collateral	3. lineal

Authority

1. democratic	2. authority-centered	3. authoritarian

Positional role behavior

1. open	2. general	3. specific

Mobility

1. high mobility	2. phasic mobility	3. low mobility, stasis

SOCIETY

Social reciprocity

1. independence	2. symmetrical-obligatory	3. complementary-obligatory

Group membership

1. many groups, brief identification, sub-ordination of group to individual	2. balance of nos.1 and 3	3. few groups, prolonged iden-tification, sub-ordination of the member to the group

Intermediaries

1. no intermediaries (directness)	2. specialist intermediaries only	3. essential intermediaries

Formality

1. informality	2. selective formality	3. pervasive formality

Property

1. private	2. utilitarian	3. community

HUMAN NATURE

Rationality

1. rational	2. intuitive	3. irrational

Good and evil

1. good	2. mixture of good and evil	3. evil

Happiness, pleasure

1. happiness as goal	2. inextricable bond of happiness and sadness	3. life is mostly sadness

Mutability

| 1. change, growth, learning | 2. some change | 3. unchanging |

NATURE

Relationship of man and nature

| 1. man dominating nature | 2. man in harmony with nature | 3. nature dominating man |

Ways of knowing nature

| 1. abstract | 2. circle of induction-deduction | 3. specific |

Structure of nature

| 1. mechanistic | 2. spiritual | 3. organic |

Concept of time

| 1. future | 2. present | 3. past |

THE SUPERNATURAL

Relationship of man and the supernatural

| 1. man as god | 2. pantheism | 3. man controlled by the supernatural |

Meaning of life

| 1. physical, material goals | 2. intellectual goals | 3. spiritual goals |

Providence

| 1. good in life is unlimited | 2. balance of good and misfortune | 3. good in life is limited |

Knowledge of the cosmic order

| 1. order is comprehensible | 2. faith and reason | 3. mysterious and unknowable |

FOUR

An outline of value orientations: Self, family, society

We have divided our discussion of the value spheres into two chapters. Although both are closely related, this chapter concentrates on those value orientations derived from observations of social structure and social interaction here categorized broadly as **self, family,** and **society.** In the following chapter, we turn to a discussion of **human nature, nature,** and the **supernatural,** and in so doing we blur the conventional distinction between values (what is thought to be good) and beliefs (what is thought to be true). The distinction between the chapters also reveals another difference which we find interesting. While in this chapter it is relatively easy to identify dominant orientations within a culture with which we are familiar, it is more difficult to do so in Chapter Five (on human nature, nature, and the supernatural). Indeed, in many cases we may find that all seem to be equally appropriate within a single culture, depending on the situation in which they come to play. We will say more about this at the beginning of Chapter Five and again in Chapter Ten when we discuss rhetoric and reasoning.

Cultural patterns of communication and potential conflicts in communication resulting from intercultural encounters are frequently mentioned in our discussion, but even more often they are implicit or left open to be discovered in specific cases. Thus although we are primarily concerned in these two chapters with a discussion of cultural differences, and not specifically inter-cultural communication, the extensions to communication should not be ignored. Finally, we must stress once more that all of the value orientations in this chapter and those presented in Chapter Five are related; only in a conceptual scheme such as this would they be so sharply distinguished. Moreover, note that orientations which, for convenience, appear under one heading may also apply to other categories.

The self

"Self" is an important word. We carry with us a sense of who we are and what we should be and what we want to be, and if our behavior does not always match our image we may say, "I am not **myself**," or "Excuse me for last night, I was not my **self**." In the literature of psychology, the word **self** occupies an important place; we speak of self-concepts, self-images, self-actualization. In everyday codes of behavior we may praise the man who is selfless and admonish the one who is selfish or self-centered. We may credit environment or circumstance for an individual's action or we may say that he has only him**self** to blame.

The meaning of self, how an individual is classified and dis-tinguished from his family and society differs considerably across cultures. Many of the orientations described under the headings of family, society, and human nature—as well as orien-tations not represented in this chapter—could be included in appraising a culture's view of the self. Here we will consider four sets of value orientations:

Individualism—interdependence

1. individualism	2. individuality	3. interdependence

Age

1. youth	2. the middle years	3. old age

Sex

1. equality of the sexes	2. female superiority	3. male superiority

Activity

1. doing   2. being-in-becoming   3. being

Individualism, individuality, interdependence. A national flag is probably the worst place to find appropriate expressions of its culture, but in the case of the stars and stripes, some values of the United States are graphically depicted. With the thirteen stripes marking the nation's original colonies, and the field of stars counting out the additions to the union, the U.S. flag marks its nation's growth through quantification from a fixed beginning. This is also important in the American's personal assessment of self—and we will have more to say about this later. What interests us here, however, is the sense of **individualism** symbolized by the individual stars. Each state, large or small, old or relatively new in its addition to the union, is given an identical representation in the field. Politically, the idea of each state being independent but equal may be outmoded, but as a model of values related to the self, the image is closely analogous. What marks individualism in the United States is not so much the peculiar characteristics of each person but the sense each person has of having a separate but equal place in society. Occasionally in political documents the possible exceptions to this rule are enumerated as they are rejected (. . . regardless of race, creed, previous condition of servitude, sex . . .). To such explicit categories we could add the implicit ". . . regardless of length of membership, family position, occupation, age." This fusion of individualism and equality is so valued and so basic that many Americans find it most difficult to relate to contrasting values in other cultures where interdependence, complementary relationships, valued differences in age and sex greatly determine a person's sense of self.

Individuality is different and appears to be much more the norm in the world than United States-style individualism is. Individuality refers to the person's freedom to act differently within the limits set by the social structure. Compared to the United States, many other cultures appear to be much more tolerant of "eccentrics" and "local characters." This confusion of one kind of individualism with individuality at first appears paradoxical: We might suppose that a society which promises apparently great personal freedoms would produce the greatest number of obviously unique, even peculiar people, and yet for more than a century visitors to the United States have been struck by a kind of "sameness" or standardization. As one writer interpreted it, U.S. freedom allows everybody to be like everybody else.[1] As Riesman described it, this is an "other-directed society" in which nearly all guides for behavior are found in the behaviors of others.[2] Yet another interpretation is suggested by the analogy of the stars in the flag: be accepted by others, unite with others; equality or a kind of standardization is essential.

This leads to another observation where we find that much of the salient political rhetoric does not correspond to facts: While the individual (glorified as "the rugged individualist") is praised, historically individuals in the United States have made their achievements in loose groupings. What is different here (see also FAMILY: **authority**) is that the independent U.S. self must never feel bound to a particular group; he must always be free to change his alliances or, if necessary, to move on. Periodically in the United States, popular criticisms are directed toward the individual too bound to a group ("the organization man," "group-thinking," supporter of "the establishment"). Cultures better characterized by values of individuality are likely to lack this kind of independence from the group, as well as individual mobility. Thus it may be that such cultures allow for greater diversity in personal behavior in order to give balance to the individual vis-à-vis the group, whereas the United States, characterized by loose groupings and high mobility, does not.

For the child growing up in the United States, these values of equality and independence leading to individualism are introduced and reinforced in many ways. At a very early age—too early from the point of view of persons in many other societies—children are encouraged to make their own decisions and to contribute their suggestions for the plans of the entire family. What foods to eat, where to go on vacation, even whether or not to "join the family" on special occasions are frequently posed as

[1] Stewart, **American Patterns**, p. 69; also Florence Kluckhohn, **Value Orientations**, p. 23.
[2] David Riesman, **The Lonely Crowd** (New Haven: Yale University Press, 1950).

individual choices. If a group decision is made, it may be determined by a "vote," with children and parents having or appearing to have equal parts in the vote. Important broad social changes in the United States, too, are related to this principle, even when they appear to run counter to cherished American institutions; thus the college drop-out, the divorcee, the gap between generations, and even the lack of gun control laws, all may be rationalized directly or indirectly in terms of these values.

Another expression of the distinction between individuality and individualism may be seen in attitudes toward voting. Votes are individual, but the majority (or plurality) rules, and those in the minority feel obliged to support—if sometimes begrudgingly —the winning candidate. Compared historically and throughout the world at present, there are remarkably few people in the United States who refuse to go along with the outcome of voting. An enormous number of decisions are put to a vote, a procedure which maintains individualism and equality and in its effect requires eventual subordination to the will of the majority.

With the risk of pushing the flag analogy too far, we might look at the Japanese national flag for a contrast to both individualism and individuality. A single red circle on a field of white represents the value of national unity and, indeed, as the circle represents the sun, it expresses permanence and the past, as well. **Conformity to or identity with the group**—the family, the organization (business or school), and the nation ("the national family") is the dominant value. In Japan few decisions are put to a vote: The consensus of feeling is sought, so that if there is a vote it is more a formality than an instrumental act. Individual expressions of opinion are few, and traditionally the person who "stands out" is not praised. Interdependence and harmony within the "circle" are the values and, to many foreign observers, the regulations on behavior which maintain these values are incredibly complex. (To the average Japanese person, too, there is a feeling that one **must** be Japanese in order to understand and thus act appropriately. In Japanese the same word may be used to express understanding, acceptance, and proper behavior. This is in striking contrast to the United States, where it is thought that anybody can become an American, and, as Hall says, where foreigners are regarded as "underdeveloped Americans.")[3]

The Japanese language also contributes to the maintenance of this pattern, for it is difficult to utter a single sentence about human relations without having to select appropriate pronouns which reflect or determine the particular relationship of speaker and listener, including both relative status and degree of intimacy. (Many Japanese people have reported they feel more free and more "individualistic" when speaking another language, such as English, where "I am I and you are you" regardless of how we are related in conversation.)

Here we will use the term **interdependence** to identify the pattern where the self is largely determined by a person's current relationship to others in the social structure.

Three alternative individualization categories are thus appropriate: individualism, where each self is regarded as equally independent but voluntarily allied with others for specific purposes (characteristic of the dominant values in the United States); individuality, where persons are interdependent and more strictly limited and shaped by more specific social categories, such as age, sex, family, tribe, and yet within these constraints are allowed individual freedom of expression and behavior; and interdependence, where a person's concept of self almost always involves a consciousness of his place in society and his relationship to another or others with whom he interacts.

Age. The meaning of age is as old a concern as the riddle of the sphinx. There are obvious cultural differences in what is considered too-old-to or too-young-to marry or rule or fight: Brief news items (usually from far away places) in almost any newspaper daily demonstrate some of the more obvious cultural differences ("Sixty-year-old Man Marries Twelve-Year-Old Girl"). But the more subtle valuations of ages should be noted. What is important about age values is not the actual or even relative ages but rather the characteristics which are assumed to accrue with these ages.

A youth-valuing culture (including the United States) values —along with some degree of maturity—vigor, idealism, and a

---

[3] Hall, **Silent Language**, p. 9.

freshness that is thought to be dissipated with age. Economically and socially, the "youth market" dictates fashion, language, and tastes in popular culture. "Experiences," rather than "experience," are valued; typically the American desires the opportunity to have many and varied experiences, and these are usually only possible and judged meaningful while one is still relatively young. Jacket blurbs on novels boast of the author's many experiences. Fathers strive to give their children opportunities and experiences they themselves did not have. A slogan of the late 1960s warned youth not to trust anybody over the age of thirty. Psychiatrists report increasing cases of young people who have burned themselves out while still in their teens and clients who feel they are has-beens before they are yet forty. The social environment which nurtures the values of youth is one of constant change, with new freedoms and new kinds of experiences available every year. So accelerated is the change that a U.S. sociologist in 1970 defined the span of a generation for persons of college age or younger as less than four years.

At the other extreme are the values of age and experience. The value of age has traditionally been the dominant orientation of most cultures in the world, for the elders of societies were the repositories of knowledge as well as the locus of power and authority. Where age is valued it is likely to be expressed in special forms of address—for any old person, regardless of position.

Not much need be said about the middle alternative except, in Aristotelian fashion, that it may be valued as it avoids the excesses of both alternatives. In fact, if not as a value, the middle years are the most productive.

The influence of age values on a person's concept of his self and how he is perceived by others is very important. Upon entering another society one may be puzzled by the degree of respect or indifference he finds as a result of local value orientations toward age. Rhetorically, one who is praised as "old, and therefore wise," in his own culture may elsewhere have to claim to be "mature but still youthful." Or in seeking community support, one may find that the support of one elder is worth much more than the combined enthusiasm of all the young. Politically, too, age values must be reckoned with: Leaders in the fights for independence (in Latin America in the 1940s and in Africa in the 1950s) more frequently have been young men, though these cultures traditionally have valued age. (The same was true for the American Revolution in the Eighteenth Century). And it seems clear that much of the extraordinary appeal of John Kennedy among people in developing nations was that he was young (and stressed his youth and its accompanying values) and therefore offered hope for changes in U.S. foreign policy.

One final observation is that there are obvious limitations to a person's ability to adapt, for age is a matter of fact as well as of value. A person cannot so easily "become" older or younger than he is when he enters a society where a person of a different age might enjoy advantages.

Sex. The previous observation about limits of age adaptability is even more obviously true for values toward sex-role differences. Intercultural organizations such as CARE have in the past had a policy against sending women abroad to represent the organization because most societies are overtly male dominated. In more recent years, CARE and other organizations with similar policies have run into their own cultural conflicts between local demands for equality for the sexes and foreign realities where the sexes are not equal.

Since it is difficult to find practical examples of modern matriarchal states (though they exist among many tribes in Africa, Asia, and elsewhere) we will briefly consider only the other two alternatives.

Male superiority sometimes takes two divergent forms, though both include the distinction between appropriate behaviors for men and women. In one form, perhaps generally true of non-Western societies, the woman's role is to serve the man—including, often, doing hard physical labor, deferring to his judgments, and socially subordinating herself in such ways as walking behind him and eating after he has eaten. The romantic tradition of the West, of course, is somewhat different: While the man may have the authority, he treats women as the weaker sex and has evolved a pattern of social amenities such as standing when a lady enters the room or holding a door for her. In this variation, as much contemporary women's literature has reminded us, women are treated much like children—weak, immature, less intelligent, more emotional. In either case there are many activities that are limited to men and others that are the exclusive province of women, but the specific activities vary considerably from culture to culture.

Equality of sexes is still an exceptional value in the world, and some might argue that even where it is claimed as a value it exists more as a goal than a fact. But in any case, the value would be that there is no particular role distinction that results from sex difference, that any kind of work or relaxation may be enjoyed by men or women, and that friendships will include persons of both sexes and not of the same sex only. Because sex equality, like any equality, is widely regarded as a **modern value,** many societies claim it, offering such proof as equal rights in voting, educational opportunities, and representation within the social and political establishment. But for the student of intercultural communication it helps greatly if he can avoid thinking that any of these value orientations is better or more modern than others. The Women's Liberation Movement in the U.S. in recent years, for example, is quite consistent with other American values of individualism, equality, and independence and has been accepted largely in those terms. In many other societies, however, the goals of women's liberation are contrary to the total cultural patterns and are likely to be rejected just as any other foreign value in isolation would be.

Activity. The activity dimension is one of the first five sets of value orientations which Florence Kluckhohn proposed and attempted to test empirically. These categories now have found a place within the literature and thus, unlike most values categories, there is some comparative data for activity orientations in several cultures.

The **doing** orientation of activity values is undeniably a U.S. orientation. Conventionally, an American identifies himself in terms of his activities (professions or occupations, normally). Even very small children are frequently quizzed on what they want to **be** when they grow up—meaning what do they want to **do**. English language family names are typically those of doers: Baker, Smith, Carpenter, for example. While there are obvious differences in the status attached to kinds of activities, objectifiable and practical **doing** activities are more highly valued than sentient activities, in which it is difficult to see what one does: Inventors are more praised than poets; doctors of medicine rank higher than do doctors of philosophy. This aspect of the **doing** orientation appears to run counter to both historical and most current cultural evaluations of activities, in which a person who works with his hands usually is held in less esteem than is one who works with his head.

Part of the intercultural folklore of Americans is the surprise (and assumed delight) of the host nationals when the U.S. ambassador, technical advisor, or professor rolls up his sleeves and pitches in to **do** something, while his counterparts remain unwilling to soil their hands. This appears to be a modern variation of the schoolchild's object lesson which unfavorably compares the gentlemen of Jamestown with the pioneers of Plymouth.

Very closely related to this value of doing are those sentiments of change and progress, and the confidence that "where there's a will there's a way." Thus where one from a doing culture encounters societies that seem backward or underdeveloped he is likely to attribute the cause to laziness in one form or another. Doing is also closely tied, at least in the experience of the United States, to an emphasis on youth and energy for obvious reasons.

Being-in-becoming at first appears to be an awkward category, and there is a suspicion that Kluckhohn proposed it to provide a third term (with doing and being) for reasons of conceptual consistency. But upon closer examination it proves to be functionally descriptive. Kluckhohn identifies this category with the outlook of the artist, who, through his endeavors, seeks to discover himself rather than change the world. Where the aesthetic component is basic (and not, as in the United States, regarded as nonessential or even opposed to what is practical) we may expect to find this value orientation more prominent. Similarly, where the culture views man as in search of self-discovery or fulfillment, the value orientation becomes vital. Thus there are obvious religious, philosophical, and psychological overtones in this value orientation, and its importance in cultures may be initially sensed through these sources.

Stewart equates the **being** orientation with Maslow's concept of self-actualization and characteristics of his peak experiences, which are valued in themselves without comparison to other standards.[4] The activity orientations of many, perhaps most, non-

---

[4] Stewart, **American Patterns,** pp. 32–33.

Western or traditional societies are better characterized by these latter two terms than by the doing orientation of the industrialized, change-oriented doing societies. Life is an organic whole, people are people, and it is human to embrace life—which frequently, to the doers evokes ambivalent reactions of envy (for the other's simplicity, spontaneity, and sheer humanity) and pity (for the other's unwillingness to alter his condition and improve). The film version of **Zorba the Greek** adapted from the novel by Nikos Kazantzakis portrayed the dramatic encounter between a young Englishman ostensibly from a doing orientation and the Greek, Alexis Zorba, ostensibly of a being orientation: The resolution of their life styles appears in the mutual **being-in-becoming** mode, as the Englishman says: "Zorba, teach me how to dance."

The family

Acculturation, like life itself, is born of the family. Nearly every significant element of culture is introduced to the individual through the family. In the theory of transactional psychology, each person carries within him a microcosmic family, enabling him to act as a child, parent, or adult and to regard others similarly.[5] In society at large, the family model can be applied, even without making a Freudian interpretation. Parallels between religious concepts and the modal family structure of a culture, too, are not difficult to make (God, the father, the mother Church). Thus the four categories discussed in this section can be extended easily to the sphere of society and applied equally in an interpretation of the "self."

Relational orientations
1. individualistic	2. collateral	3. lineal

Authority
1. democratic	2. authority-centered	3. authoritarian

Positional role behavior
1. open	2. general	3. specific

Mobility
1. high mobility	2. phasic mobility	3. low mobility, stasis

[5] See, for example, Eric Berne, **Games People Play** (New York: Grove Press, 1964), or Thomas A. Harris, **I'm OK, You're OK** (New York: Harper and Row, 1967).

Relational orientations. Using Florence Kluckhohn's distinctions, we describe a continuum from the individualistic orientation, in which a family may be only slightly more than a biological necessity, through the collateral orientation, where the family identification is still strong but membership is much more limited in generation and in numbers of relations, to the lineal orientation, where one identifies with a wide and very old extended family.

The meaning of "identification" here involves more than taking the family name. In cultures characterized by the lineal orientation, such as traditional Japan and China, the identification may require the taking care of graves of ancestors and obeying the wishes of parents long since dead. It will also require taking care of parents in their old age and the expectation that their children will do the same. In sharp contrast, a person in a culture characterized by an individualistic orientation, such as the United States, is generally spared these obligations, this being the value shared by the older as well as younger members of the family. Impersonal institutions, such as insurance and retirement plans, are entrusted with the care of the elderly.

The individualistic orientation in the United States exists with other value orientations, such as individuality in self-concept mentioned previously, relatively high mobility, the doing activity orientation, independence within social reciprocity, and others. Not surprisingly, innovations in the family structure are most easily introduced here, such as communal living arrangements, adoption of previously unrelated children—even by single persons, and group marriage.

The collateral orientation is distinguished from the lineal by its relative lack of historical consciousness. A person may be able to trace his ancestory back many generations, but he may do so without particular reverence or even relevance to his own life. The extended family, typical of the collateral orientation, includes uncles and aunts and distant cousins who may share such a deep sense of relationship that their separation from each other is felt as keenly as that of husband and wife or of child and parents. Part of the problem of relocating Indian refugees who were expelled from Uganda in 1972 was that their concept of family was much broader than that of the government authorities in nations where they were to be temporarily provided for, and thus they preferred to remain in refugee camps with uncles and cousins rather than to be separated through relocation.

Family identification is more than a definition of family or a feeling of family. It also describes networks of interpersonal communication and gives direction to the achievement of any number of tasks. If money is needed or something must be purchased or repaired, a person in a collaterally oriented culture most likely thinks first of asking for help among his relatives rather than seeking some outside person or institution. In its worst forms it leads to the nepotism characteristic of so many of the "developing nations." The North American is likely to feel that he has achieved less (is less of an individual) if he gets a job through his "family connections" or if, after about the age of twenty, he or she lives with parents or even a brother or sister. In cultures characterized by the alternative orientations, the reverse may be true.

The relational orientation also is reflected in speech patterns. Often metaphors for relationships express this clearly. When President Kennedy visited Mexico in 1962, he spoke of the relations between the two nations as those of neighbors, friends, allies, and partners. These are words of an individualistic orientation—relations based on proximity or agreement, not blood. Months after Kennedy's visit this writer presented Mexicans (in Mexico City) the same sentences with those terms left blank to be filled in. The Mexican respondents supplied words of a collateral orientation: brothers, sisters, and cousins.[6] A more elaborate collateral metaphor for friendship was expressed by a Tanzanian friend who wished to extend his greeting to another's wife. He put it this way: "Say 'Hello' to my sister-in-law." The collateral metaphor can extend to political abstractions, too. Tanzania's word for "socialism," as coined by President Nyerere, is **Ujamaa,** literally "family-hood," and intended to express traditional African values of working together and sharing.

Authority. The establishment and maintenance of authority exists in all societies and throughout nearly every institution

[6] John Condon, "Value Analysis of Cross-Cultural Communication: A Methodology and Application for Selected United States-Mexican Communications, 1962–1963" (Ph.D. diss., Northwestern University, 1964).

in society. For convenience and because of its primary impact on other social organizations, we will treat the question of authority within the FAMILY category.

We will consider three patterns: The first we may call the **democratic** oriented family or organization where ideally the authority figure is obliged to solicit the opinions of all members and act according to their wishes. The second is an authority-centered pattern, where actual authority does not reside in an individual but rather in some more abstract or general form, such as religious beliefs or the family name. The third is an authoritarian pattern, where an individual (the father, usually) makes the important decisions and the others are expected to obey; the authority role is by ascription and thus there is nobody else who can adequately serve as the authority. Within specific families, of course, it is not uncommon to find aspects of all of these patterns.

Margaret Mead has distinguished the U.S. family from the British family in a way that corresponds to two of these patterns.[7] She has written that typically in England the father is the head of the household, and that no one questions his authority. Thus the father speaks at the table from the position of authority. Since it is unnecessary to establish his authority through arguing, the father may understate his opinions; the children, seen but not heard, listen attentively and in growing up come to imitate the authority style of father. In the U.S., however, families are more democratic or child-centered, and since the children may do more of the speaking, dinner-table conversations bear the characteristics of children's talk: exaggeration, loud voices, discontinuity. The result, Mead suggests, is that American children grow up with no other model than themselves and become only older children. (The **childlike** if not **childish** style of people from the U.S. has been mentioned by many foreign critics.) British adult speech is likely to strike some Americans as stuffy; U.S. adult speech is likely to strike some Englishmen as noisy, exaggerated, childlike. And it all can be traced, so the argument runs, to the authority at the dinner table.

[7] Margaret Mead, "A Case History in Cross-National Communications," in **The Communication of Ideas,** ed. Lyman Bryson (New York: Harper and Row, 1948), pp. 209–29.

The distinction between authoritarian and authority-centered values should be noted. In the former pattern, authority is tempered by the particular characteristics of the authority—thus his (or her) commands are to be obeyed without question, however foolish or whimsical they may appear. Appeals to this kind of authority may be of a wheedling, whining, personal kind, or may often be directed through another individual who is personally closer to the authority. Thus in cultures characterized by this pattern, the mother often serves as the go-between for children and father. Father may be gone often from the house, may be irritable or inebriated when at home, or apparently unpredictable in his behavior, without weakening his position as authority. (The imaginative study of communication in a Mexican church mentioned in Chapter One—contrasting prayers of thanks and petition before male and female statues—revealed that the communicative behavior exactly mirrored communication in most of the homes in that Mexican community.[8] The male deity, like the father, was treated as remote and unpredictable; the statue of the Virgin Mary, in contrast, received much more affective, persuasive communication, much as the mother at home would receive from her children in her role as intermediary between the children and the remote father.)

In the authority-centered pattern, commands and instructions are likely to be far more predictable, consistent with (and justified by) whatever structure or faith the authority is entrusted to represent. It is possible to argue with this authority figure in terms of the institutions he represents and to try to show that an alternative course is more in keeping with the teachings of the Bible, the true Marxist philosophy, the traditions of the clan, and so on. As implied, where this is the form of authority in society, schisms or divisions may arise.

We will return to these authority distinctions in Chapter Seven, in discussing family housing structures.

Positional role behavior. The three patterns described here range from a pattern where there is no necessary role behavior appropriate to age and sex, to one where there are very specific rights and obligations within a family as determined chiefly by

---

[8] Nelson, "Saints and Sinners."

sex and relative age. The middle pattern describes a balance, where rights and obligations exist as a general kind only, neither completely fixed nor completely free. Since these distinctions have already been anticipated in other value orientations (SELF: **individualism—interdependence, age, sex;** and FAMILY: **positional role behavior**) and will be refined in later patterns (SOCIETY: **social reciprocity, group membership, intermediaries**) we will limit our discussion.

At one extreme we find a large segment of the United States where there is no particular expected role significance to being older or younger or, increasingly, to being male or female. Many reasons for this should be clear from other discussions of value orientations. At a simple level, the differences may be noted in the beginning small talk stages of conversations where Americans rarely inquire if a stranger has brothers and sisters. To do so would seem at least irrelevant and possibly too personal.

Japan represents a culture characterized by the opposite variation. The oldest son is expected to maintain the family name and endeavors (the farm or business, for example) and is primarily responsible for supporting his parents in their old age. (Not surprisingly, many girls are reluctant to marry an oldest son, for this will mean that she must obey not only her own husband but his parents as well.) There are also very specific obligations and rights of the older daughter, and younger sons and daughters as well. While such social obligations are well known among students of Japanese culture, not so well known are the stereotypic personality characteristics associated with relative age and sex. So close is this fit that Japanese people readily guess even a stranger's position in his family by observing his behavior, and will even more easily guess his personality by knowing if the person is an oldest daughter, second son, and so on. The Japanese language reflects and may be presumed to help direct these distinctions, for there are separate words for "older brother" and "younger brother," and "older sister" and "younger sister," but no words for "brother" or "sister" alone. (These are also extended metaphorically: a waitress in a restaurant may be signaled by the customer's calling **"onee-san,"** "older sister.")

The middle alternative may characterize cultures in transition from position-role variation and much of European and Latin American societies. Here we find rather clear but general kinds of expectations for a person by virtue of his age, sex, and position in his family, but compromises and alternatives are possible. Just as a ruler may be a king or a queen, depending on the sex of the older one, a business or even a farm may be run by a man or a woman. (By contrast, in Japan if there is some family enterprise to continue and there is no oldest son, the husband of the oldest daughter may be adopted into the family, changing his name, so that the male will retain the authority. Male adoption also is followed by childless families who wish to maintain the family lineage.)

Mobility. Technological changes have obviously influenced mobility, but mobility as a value is not found in all societies where the technological possibilities exist. Switzerland is a good example: A person must reside in a city for a period of fifteen years before becoming a "citizen" of that city and only thereafter may proceed to citizenship within the nation. The United States today presents the opposite extreme; the norm appears to be constantly shifting in an effort to better oneself. U.S. expressions such as "the man on the go," or "let's get moving" reflect this orientation. Between these extremes are those values we may call **phasic mobility,** the value of limited or periodic movement (for some specified gain, such as money or education or "experience") with the expectation of returning to our place of origin. Thus while a migrant worker and a business executive may superficially resemble each other, their values are likely to be different: the migrant worker knows where his home is and where he will return to; the mobile executive's home is where he hangs his hat, and his choice of a location for retirement is likely to be whatever location attracts him along the way.

In intercultural encounters these distinctions may be very important; the person who travels abroad as a student or adviser or worker is likely to be judged in terms of the values of mobility of his host culture. The traveler may expect to be appraised as a "seeker" or as someone "broadening his horizons," but may find he is mistrusted as an escapist or even one exiled from his community. (Note that "exile" as a form of punishment is meaningless in societies like the U.S., where moving is valued.) Students who travel from stasis-valuing cultures in order to study abroad encounter serious problems upon re-entering their cultures; for whatever they have gained in studies they may have lost in personal contacts and identification with their place of residence. In direct contrast, many U.S. college-age students would prefer to leave home to attend a college of lower prestige than to remain at home and attend a superior but local institution.

Society

Values, while internalized in the self and introduced through the family, mostly arise in society. The value orientations which are presented here share two characteristics. They are likely to be more explicit than most of the orientations previously described (taking the form of sayings about how to treat a neighbor, in rules of etiquette and proper behavior, and in some cases being codified in explicit laws). Also, they may take divergent orientations for family and nonfamily behavior. For example, politeness and formality may characterize nearly all relationships in society outside of the family but never within the family; or the concept of **private property** may be the dominant value orientation in society at large, but within families, **community** or **utilitarian** values—as with the family car—may dominate. To the extent that the first characteristic is true, discovering these values is somewhat easier than discovering others. We can ask direct questions about obligations, about group membership, formality, the use of go-betweens, and about property rights. However, to the extent that the second characteristic (the divergence of family, friends, and nonfamily patterns) is true, special caution must be taken in stating the context. Some foreigners in Japan, for example, who have made the great effort required to learn Japanese and who have tried to conform to the obvious Japanese values of formality, have learned too late that they alienate would-be friends by always being sure to say "Thank you." (By Western standards, the Japanese equivalents of "thank you" are overused—in public; the expression is almost never used within the family.)

In the sphere of society we will expand our list to six sets as follows:

Social reciprocity

1. independence	2. symmetrical-obligatory	3. complementary-obligatory

Group membership

1. many groups, brief identification, and subordination of group to individual	2. balance of 1 and 3	3. few groups, prolonged identification, and subordination of the member to the group

Intermediaries

1. no intermediaries (directness)	2. specialist intermed. only	3. essential intermed.

Formality

1. informality	2. selective formality	3. pervasive formality

Property

1. private	2. utilitarian	3. community

Social reciprocity. Social reciprocity refers to the process of give-and-take in interpersonal communication, both formally and informally. The alternative variations presented here are: (1) independence, where the value is to avoid as many commitments and obligations as possible, all being seen as threats to freedom; (2) symmetrical-obligatory, where a person has obligations primarily to equals or institutions with whom he has established some contractual base; and (3) complementary-obligatory, where, in a sense, a person is forever indebted to others (and he, himself, is a recipient of such debts), **especially those of superior or subordinate status.**

What appears to be a small request in one society takes on broader implications in another. In the United States a request to do a favor may imply no necessary reciprocation. We may give a gift without any expectation of receiving one in return, a value epitomized in countless children's Christmas tales. In some cultures, however, the expression that "one good turn deserves another" may literally state the rules of social inter-action.

The second and third patterns stress the importance of the obligation of returning, in kind or worth, what has been given, be it an actual thing or a favor. The difference is in the relative status relationship of the parties involved. In the pattern of complementary-obligatory values, the interaction valued is between unequals, what in Latin America is often called the **peón-patrón** relationship. The landowner or boss or patron has certain obligations to his tenants, employees, or **peones,** and they in turn have obligations to him. Failure to meet these obligations, of course, can alter their relationship and thus such systems are difficult to stop because the mutual obligations have accrued over a long period of time. In governments, including many city governments in the United States, the patronage system is of this kind. Since persons in the United States largely value the **independence** variation, a word like patronage often has a negative connotation.

In the symmetrical-obligatory pattern, the sense of obligation is present, but interactions are more valued between equals, such as in the old European pattern of international marriages of royalty to help guarantee smooth political relations between the states.

At times the United States has acted in national foreign policy in keeping with its own independent value orientation and consequently acting counter to the values of complementary-obligatory relations.

Symmetrical-obligatory value orientations, while not quite as objectionable as complementary orientations, also tend to be rejected by Americans. The faith in the series of checks-and-balances in government, and the suspicion of "too cozy" or "incestuous" relationships among business corporations (interlocking directorates) or between church and state, industry and the military, may be taken as forms of negative valuation toward the middle alternative. In many societies, of course, such as in most of Latin America, such interdependent relationships are a matter of course. There may be criticism in individual cases, but not at the level of values.

Elsewhere in this book we will find it convenient to combine the last two orientations under the label **interdependence** and contrast this with the remaining alternative, **independence**.

Group membership. While characteristics of family structure and values find obvious parallels in social group membership, there are other value orientations which apply to groups and friendships apart from family structure and values. Such factors as the number of groups with which a person identifies, his length of association with those groups, and his obligations within those groups appear to be correlated positively. Thus we find at one extreme in this dimension of values: (1) affiliation with a relatively large number of groups, relatively brief and frequent changes in such affiliation, and the emphasis of the individual over the group. At the other end of the continuum we find (3) affiliation with a relatively small number of groups, relatively long identification with those groups, and subordination of the individual to the group. Between these alternatives is an attempt at a balance in these characteristics. Frequently characteristic of this middle position is that the individual exercises greater personal freedom in selecting group affiliation than would be the case of the third position, but a much greater range of obligations and length of affiliation than is the case with the first position.

In most traditional societies where mobility is limited and social change is slow, an individual is identified with groups in an ascriptive manner. He is, in effect, born into social groups and remains a part of those limited groups throughout his life. Contacts with strangers are likewise limited, and thus serious or prolonged encounters with strangers are rare. Likewise it is not common for such an individual to evaluate a friend or associate by separating his talents or abilities from his personality as a whole, any more than one does in evaluating a brother or mother or father. Each is who he is, what he is, totally. For these reasons, friendships or alliances are not based as much on specific functions or abilities as they are on "the complete person," including his "inner self," not just his outward manner.

This description is very different from one made of friendships and group affiliations in many urban, industrialized societies characterized by more facile mobility, both physical and social. A person in such a society, such as in most of North America,

England, and Western Europe for the most part, a person is encouraged to "make friends" or "establish contacts" of the kind that best suit him. We may regard such associations as "functional friendships" and, as such, friends may be shared. (At the other extreme, of course, sharing friends is no more possible than "sharing brothers.") Friendships and less personable associations are likely to be segmented: My co-worker may not be my drinking buddy; people I get together with for old times' sake may soon prove to be tedious company because we no longer have anything in common. Judged severely, such friendships may be superficial, as in the Kleenex analogy: Use your friend and throw him away, and up pops another. Viewed more positively, the pattern allows the value of a wide circle of friends, and a well-rounded, flexible personality.

From a values perspective, the studies of groups by U.S. social scientists are culturally limited, as mentioned in Chapter One, for they are mostly posited on the latter group-membership or friendship assumptions. Task-oriented and socioemotional matters are, in a very American fashion, distinguished. Indeed, most such experimental studies are of task-oriented groups, which reflects a sub-theme of this orientation that task achievement takes precedence over human relations. In following the social scientific dictates of isolating or randomizing variables, most such studies must be of strangers, little known or unknown to each other and equally unfamiliar with the experimenter's task. In the world today such groupings are atypical and thus a person who studies communication must be cautious when extending some hypotheses of group interaction to cultures which represent quite different values.

Intermediaries. Miles Standish is chiefly remembered for what his emissary was told by Priscilla: "Speak for yourself, John." Ever since, Americans have been urged to speak for themselves and avoid enlisting or serving as go-betweens. Very closely tied to values of informality and individualism, this directness in human interactions is highly valued in the United States. The alternative of using an intermediary to smooth the way and prevent potentially embarrassing confrontations is likely to be judged by Americans as an inconvenience and at times as a sign of weakness or lack of courage. Persons who seem to seek out the role of go-between for some arrangements ("the match-maker") may be viewed as meddlers.

It therefore comes as a surprise to some Americans to discover that in much of the world go-betweens are essential for the smooth functioning of human relations. A brief mention of some of the functions intermediaries perform may help to show why they continue to be so important and how their role relates to other value orientations. A go-between may provide a human bond or guarantee that an agreement, be it a marriage proposal or a business deal, is entered into and will be maintained in good faith; a paper agreement or words exchanged between strangers may be seen as less binding. Similarly, the go-between maintains certain obligations toward and extracts comparable obligations from those he serves. Should the marriage or business deal fail, the parties must reckon with the go-between. And if there is some point before such a failure when the parties have ceased talking to each other, it is the go-between who can listen to each and report to each in an attempt to patch things up. Where a society does not provide for this particular role, more specialized agents, such as counselors or lawyers, may be required to serve these same functions. As Goffman has noted, the go-between not only is privy to information from both sides, he may be selective in what he reports, usually giving the impression that he favors one party (the one he happens to be talking to at the time) more than the other.[9] Obviously such a factor in the communication process is impossible without such an intermediary.

We suggest these alternatives for valuing intermediaries: (1) the value of direct interaction without recourse to intermediaries; (2) a preference for technical or specialist intermediaries only; and (3) intermediaries regarded as essential for most important transactions. It may sometimes be difficult to distinguish between an intermediary as such and the casual assistance of a friend or expert called in to supplement what the parties alone cannot do for themselves, such as the role of lawyers in preparing contracts or lawsuits. It may be possible to appraise the actual cultural value of the go-between by empirically discover-

[9] Goffman, **Self in Everyday Life,** pp. 149–51.

ing the range and number of transactions which call for an intermediary.

The middle variation of technical and specialist intermediaries is especially interesting as a transitional stage. The United States is moving rapidly in this direction with the increasing acceptance of specialists for many kinds of human encounters: counselors of all kinds, therapists, consultants—including the increasing number of those in international trade and business, dating bureaus, employment agencies, and many more specialist go-betweens whose function seemed unnecessary even recently. It may also provide the future value orientation for societies which have valued go-betweens of a more personal kind, such as the neighbor, aunt, or prominent community figure who served as a matchmaker. The change can be seen where that role becomes increasingly ceremonial (as is the best man, bridesmaid, or godparent in the United States), rather than instrumentally essential.

Formality. The three alternatives for this value dimension require little explanation. At one extreme is the value of informality: Formal codes of conduct, titles and honorifics, and politer forms of speech seem at least unnecessary and frequently disruptive to "real" communication. In sharp contrast, the value of formality allows for smooth and predictable communication while avoiding risks of awkward or embarrassing encounters. A variation of these is the compartmentalization of formality, which we have called **selective formality,** for interactions which may be dignified by that formality. Though what is treated formally may vary across cultures (many Japanese wives never call their husbands by their given names, for example), all societies seem to allow for both formality and informality in specific relationships. Even in a largely informal-valuing culture, such as the United States, formal deference before judges and high-ranking political officials is called for. The difficulty in communicating with persons from other cultures is in knowing to whom and on which occasions one should act formally or informally. Often it is difficult to state the rules, even when describing our own culture.

North Americans are likely to assume that informality is essential in sincere human relations. They are likely to feel uncomfortable with titles (and assume others feel the same way): "Don't call me Professor, call me Harry." Psychologically, American men who seem too polite may be considered feminine, or "sissy-like." This in turn seems bound up in a certain distrust of intellectuals and "fancy" language. Thus formality often is distrusted as a mask.

There are many anecdotes about the clash of cultural styles and many jokes which express stereotypes about formality or informality of another culture. Chicago's Mayor Richard Daley, who, like other U.S. politicians, has used his unique informal style symbolically for political gain, said in a farewell speech to Britain's Queen Elizabeth and Prince Phillip, "Next time you come, bring the kids." And there are stock jokes about English would-be lovers who never get anywhere because they are waiting to be introduced. But it is no laughing matter when persons with different cultural values toward formality meet and each annoys or offends the other, one seeming too cold and reserved and self-conscious about his position and the other seeming brash and impudent by imposing an intimacy that has not yet developed.

Language resources, as well as culturally based habits in the use of language, influence these value orientations. Romance languages and Teutonic languages have retained a distinction in pronouns for the formal **you** and the intimate or friendly **you,** and a shift to or from informality may be signalled through the change in pronouns. ("We know each other well enough," one German may say to another, "Shall we switch from **Sie** to **du?**") English has long since lost this distinction. As mentioned previously, Japanese and, to a much lesser extent, Chinese and Arabic have a much more elaborate system of pronouns and honorifics to indicate the social relationship and appropriate degree of formality between the parties communicating.

Here, as elsewhere, while we must acknowledge the possible influence of language on values, it would be unwise to assume a causal relationship (compare, for example, formality-informality value orientations in English spoken in the United States or Australia with that spoken in England or Liberia).

When we look at aspects of nonverbal behavior in Chapter Six, we will see that formality and informality extends far beyond spoken language to areas of dress, stance, seating behavior, and other nonverbal expressions. We may note here that even where the basic orientations toward formality and informality may be very similar in two cultures, how the values are expressed, both verbally and nonverbally, may differ considerably.

As mentioned in the introduction to this section, social context must be considered when appraising cultural values toward formality. Japan again provides an excellent model of possible misinterpretations: Not only are public and intimate (family) relations sharply distinguished in speech (expressions of thanks, apology, and appreciation are usually inappropriate within a family or unnecessary among close friends) nonverbal formality and informality is similarly split. The businessman may be expected to wear his dark suit and tie when meeting the public, but in his neighborhood or even on a train during vacation he may strip down to his underwear! Goffman has also commented on formality and informality distinctions in what he calls **regions.**[10] A resort, he notes, may impose norms of informality on its guests, so that even strangers greet each other informally as if they were friends. A team of repairmen in a formal setting, such as a schoolhouse or a church, may act self-consciously about discrepancy between their informal behavior and the aura of formality exuded by the setting. Since cultures define appropriate behaviors of formality and informality in comparable settings in different ways, we must be careful in our generalizations toward either end of the formality-informality continuum.

Property. North Americans are likely to think of property as virtually an extension of the self. In times of conflict it may be the seizure or destruction of property which provokes a stronger reaction than violation of human rights or even loss of life. As noted, life, liberty, and property were initially considered as God-given rights in the U.S. credo. But this view, represented by the private orientation, is not universal. At least two other orientations toward property characterize values in many other societies. One of these is what may be called **utilitarian,** where property is seen as having value only as it is useful and used. Americans may be familiar with this view in the philosophy of Henry George and his "single tax" theory, which has appealed to both conservatives

[10] Ibid., pp. 106–140.

and liberals within the United States and, significantly, has been much more widely praised outside of the United States. The third variation we identify as **community,** where neither personal claims of ownership nor right through usage are relevant. Land, again, provides the most familiar model, as expressed in the laws of many societies where the land belongs to all—or to God, transcending all who tread upon it—with laws permitting the leasing of land but never the ownership.

There is a story, no doubt apocryphal, told of President John Kennedy and Mexican President Adolfo López Mateos when the two met in Mexico in 1962. While riding together in a car, President Kennedy noticed the beautiful wrist watch which the Mexican President was wearing and Kennedy complimented López, saying "What a beautiful watch you have." Immediately the Mexican President removed the watch from his wrist and handed it to Kennedy saying, "it is yours." Kennedy, embarrassed by the offer, tried to decline but the Mexican President explained that in his country when a person likes something he should be given it—ownership being a matter of human feelings or need and not private possession. Kennedy was impressed by this and received the watch with the greatest humility. A few minutes later, President López turned to the U.S. President and said: "My, what a beautiful wife you have," whereupon Kennedy replied: "Please take back your watch." Facts aside, the encounter expresses the meeting of two kinds of property values, **private,** in the case of the U.S. President and **utilitarian** in the case of the Mexican leader.

One should not expect that where the utilitarian values are strong that everything is given away freely. A North American is likely to say to a guest, "Make yourself at home," meaning for the guest to act as if he were back in his own home. In Latin America—and in many societies—an expression like **"Está en su casa,"** has a slightly different nuance: **consider this your home.** Visitors to many societies have reported awkward experiences of having been given something immediately after praising it. In one instance a visitor was aware of this attitude about possession and was thus extremely cautious about what she praised, deciding that the safest thing to compliment the hostess on was the rice served at dinner. When the guest left, she was presented with a five pound bag of rice.

The Philippines is often cited as a culture where values toward property are strikingly different from those of private possession so characteristic of the United States and most of Western Europe. What is so often mentioned is the counterpart of the above examples with the **visitor's possessions** being freely shared by the hosts. The visitor who has his belongings examined or "borrowed" without having offered them is likely to become very upset and place the worst judgment on the situation: His hosts are nosey, rude, even thieving. This kind of reaction reveals the depth of values toward property and possession.

Land, as mentioned above, often provides a model of cultural values toward other possessions as well. Land has existed long before man tread upon it and will continue to exist long after man is interred in it, and there can never be more—or less—of it. Consequently, even where values of private property are dominant, some areas of land, such as parks or beaches, may be set aside for the **community,** and there may be encouragements to distribute land to those who will use it, reflecting the utilitarian values. Even in a culture like the United States, characterized by values of private property, the other orientations exist in national parks, and in homestead and land-grant college acts, and so on. Where community values are dominant, on the other hand, there may be laws prohibiting the ownership of any land, and the use of the land may take a communal form—as in cooperative farms or clan or village farming areas. To talk of owning land may be regarded as ridiculous (like owning sunshine) or blasphemous ("buying out God").

As we have mentioned several times before, reactions within a society, including the so-called "counterculture" of youth in the United States, often provide insights into the dominant values of the culture. This is evident in the youth movement in the United States and its perspective toward values of ownership. Many communes have attempted to eliminate the idea of ownership and even do away with the use of money altogether.

Finally we may note that political-economic ideologies are largely formalized extensions of these value orientations. In theory, at least, these three value orientations correspond to the philosophies of capitalism, socialism, and communism respectively.

FIVE

From values to beliefs: Human nature, nature, the supernatural

Many of the value orientations discussed in the previous chapter seem, within a culture, to be so widely shared that they are rarely questioned or even recognized as anything but universal. And therefore when some of the values are challenged and alternatives sought, as during a period of rapid social change or social introspection, the result is shocking. In the United States during the 1960s and 1970s, the causes and clichés (**women's liberation, the generation gap, dropping out**) were all directly related to many of the social values discussed in the previous chapter. As noted, some of the changed views involved not so much a radical shift in values as a further extension of basic values, but they were extensions regarded by many at the time as going too far. And if some proposals seemed radical at first, they served to reveal the gap between professed values and the social realities.

Most of what we will consider in this chapter is different: Whether or not man is basically good; whether things are always changing or whether such changes only reveal how much things remain the same; whether life itself can be comprehended or is ultimately mysterious. These are moot questions, the stuff of philosophical arguments ancient and modern, sometimes profound and sometimes banal. These questions about human nature, about nature, and about the supernatural are as much questions of belief as they are questions of values. And it may be that it is easier for people to recognize—or even hold to—contrasting beliefs than to appreciate contrasting values.

Even within the sphere of "human nature," with value orientations most related to those of the self, the family, and society, we may feel uncertain about what we believe and what society has taught us. Any magazine rack will supply a reader with arguments that man is rational, that he is irrational, or that he should trust his intuition. Stories of evil men intrigue us at least as much as stories that seem to prove that man is basically good. Classics and scraps of ancient texts seem to demonstrate that man has not changed much throughout the millennia, while some news items seem to show that we are changing so fast that we hardly know ourselves. We are offered advice on finding peace of mind through selflessness or through spiritual transcendence, but the advertising that pays for all of these stories promises us happiness through more material nostrums. That we often fail to see inconsistencies in these would seem to reveal a characteristic difference between these values and those we have already considered.

Human nature

If the label "human nature" sounds old-fashioned, we may accept the same area of interest under the labels of psychology, sociology, or anthropology. The semantic distinctions are not so important in themselves, but they imply differences in ways of knowing, and these in turn revolve around the very questions of this study. That is, the study of **human nature** as a social **science** may be possible only if we assume rationality, consistency, and the possibility that man can change as well. It is not surprising, therefore, that the study of human nature as a science emerged in cultures that expressed this view of man. In our consideration of human nature, the following four sets of value orientations are of primary interest:

Rationality

1. rational	2. intuitive	3. irrational

Good and evil

1. good	2. mixture of good and evil	3. evil

Happiness, pleasure

1. happiness as goal	2. inextricable bond of happiness and sadness	3. life is mostly sadness

Mutability

1. change, growth, learning	2. some change	3. unchanging

Rationality. Though outsiders may not always appreciate this fact, man in every culture "thinks." What interests us here is not the expressed form of that thought (see Chapter Ten), but the cultural assumptions of rationality. It is not a matter of statues erected in the name of **reason** or names given to philosophical eras, such as "the age of rationality," but a much humbler notion. If man is "reasonable," then he can be "reasoned with." He can be shown alternatives with the expectation that he will choose the best. He will adhere to criteria and standards which will be accepted by other reasonable men. He can learn.

A culture's emphasis on formal education is a fairly good index of its assumptions of rationality, though of course the form and content of education will vary. The belief in universal education affirms the belief in rationality and where societies deny such education to segments of the population (as to women or certain minority groups) the culture is likely to entertain the notion that these people are not fully rational—that they are inherently stupid or emotional and always have to be told what to do. And the self-fulfilling prophecy may work to perpetuate this notion.

Fortunately it is not necessary to prove that man is rational to maintain that value. Evidence for the value of rationality is found in many forms. Reasons given for actions may be required to be logical and identifiable as logical, and not based on possession by a spirit or hunch. To this extent, at least, the value of rationality is a democratic one: It must be subject to the judgment and appraisal of others. And similarly, it follows that language must play a part in rational values: What is "rational" cannot also be ineffable. It may be, too, that these two characteristics have been combined to give writing an advantage over speech, for until very recently, written material has been subjected to a closer examination by a much wider group of judges than spoken words have been.

What is rational may be shown through comparison with the other alternatives, intuition and irrationality. Intuition is not subject to the same kinds of judgments as rationality; it springs from the person and not an impersonal set of standards. It is interesting that types of persons who have been designated as non-rational are often credited with special powers of intuition or prescience. The "woman's intuition" is a celebrated notion in many societies otherwise characterized as valuing male superiority. The madman, too, in many societies is given credit for flashes of brilliance or, like Cassandra, special powers of foresight. (Note, too, the equation of insanity, stupidity, and the inability to speak which is found in the folklore of much of the West.)

Any of the rationality value orientations may be cited by a spokesman for his society (a poet or philosopher) as a means of distinguishing his culture from others. It is not uncommon to hear that "you people are rational, but my people are not," or vice versa. Rationality may be admired but so may intuition and irrationality. Fear of power, too, may involve different evaluations of "rationality," since one can fear the computerized, impersonal army machine as much as the mad despot. The old dualisms of **mind** and **body** or **mind** and **soul** may also be expressions of differing values of "rationality." Thus in the United States at midcentury the black man has embraced **soul** as a superior value to the white man's overintellectualization. Or, a United States example which suggests the rank order of these orientations, is the 1964 campaign slogan of Senator Barry Goldwater: "In your heart you know he's right," pun intended, of course. For many voters the slogan was countered by humorist Art Buchwald's rejoinder, "But in your head. . . ."

The values of rationality (and intuition and irrationality) are closely tied to concepts of HUMAN NATURE: **mutability** and to most of the categories in **NATURE** and the **SUPERNATURAL**. Before leaving this discussion, however, we should note another significant variation within these first two alternatives: the conception of what is to be included within the sphere of rationalization. In much of the West, perhaps today in most societies, there may be a pattern that claims a dualism of things that can be known through reason and things that cannot. Many Christian sects have held this view ("faith and reason" see **SUPER-NATURAL: knowledge of the cosmic order**) but comparable dualities may be found in any culture which retains very traditional ways of acting alongside the most modern patterns.

We will return to a consideration of these value orientations in Chapter Ten, when we discuss rhetoric and reasoning.

Good and evil. Since values are the subject of cultural interpretations of **good,** this dimension of human nature could well be the starting point for describing all cultural value orientations. It could also be the summation of many other values. As Kluckhohn pointed out when proposing these three alternatives, by adding the factor of change, we can double the number of alternatives,[1] including both **good but corruptible**—expressed so often to describe the innocence of children—and **evil** or **sinful**—with the promise of salvation, as in the orthodox Christian concept of original sin and salvation. But a culture and the dominant theology within it do not always express the same values. Puritan morality may have formerly stressed the sinful image of man, but contemporary U.S. values generally are not so severe. At the least they allow for change, be it through spiritual salvation or through improving the social environment and education. The appeal of the message of human goodness, as in Anne Frank's remarkable testament, suggests an even more optimistic notion. The Pope and others have warned us that the devil is real, but for most Americans the image of the devil is only that of the cartoonist's imp who whispers in one ear while an angel whispers in the other.

We should be especially cautious in assigning any of these orientations to a culture, because the dichotomous thinking pattern, often described as **Western** (or **Aristotelian**), is epitomized

[1] Florence Kluckhohn, **Value Orientations,** p. 17.

in the good versus bad distinction. That is, in the logic of every-day speech patterns we may tend to judge every situation as being **good** or **bad.** This criticism suggests that it is not the subject matter so much as the way of thinking about almost anything that leads to this polar distinction.

The nature of man's goodness and evil obviously cuts across many other value orientations. Again, in the United States the **doing** orientation has been reinforced by Puritan assumptions of evil: The person with nothing to do is seen as easily getting into trouble; an idle mind is the devil's playground. This notion is still widespread, and gives impetus to the support of club activities, scouting, and even homework to keep young people busy and therefore out of trouble. Americans are likely to be discomfitted by seeing people who don't seem to be doing any-thing but are still "moral" and happy. But even excessive activity may not be able to alter an evil that is basic: The road to hell is paved with good intentions.

What constitutes goodness in man further complicates the discrimination among these orientations. Honesty, in any of its several meanings, may or may not be an important constituent in the concept of good. In Mexico there is the famous story of Diogenes visiting Vera Cruz. Someone notices he is crying and asks if it is because in all of Vera Cruz he could not find a single honest man; Diogenes sighs, "Not just that—somebody stole my lantern!" But neither telling lies nor some kinds of thievery may be cultural criteria of badness of man. Albert's study of rhetoric, logic, and poetic in Burundi, for example, reveals the great value in that culture placed upon skillful deception in talk-ing oneself out of accusations.[2] Even in the United States a comparable value is expressed in the Br'er Rabbit stories which originated in Africa; the clever rabbit is not bad for his decep-tions; indeed he is admired for and rewarded by his deceptions. Abraham Lincoln may be a model of the good man because he walked a mile (or was it five?) to return a penny (or was it a book?); but an adult in the United States who would do the same today would probably be regarded more as a fool than a good

[2] Ethel Albert, " 'Rhetoric,' 'Logic,' and 'Poetics' in Burundi: Culture Patterning of Speech Behavior." **American Anthropologist** (Special Publication: **The Ethnography of Communication**, 1964) vol. 66: no. 6, pt. 2, 35–54.

man. How does one interpret a culture's valuation of good and evil in the heroics of **Robin Hood** or **The Godfather,** for that matter?

Orientations toward human goodness or evil may take many forms: openness or suspicion toward strangers; optimism or pessimism about new social enterprises; and assumptions in such institutions as schools, where it is tacitly assumed that a good education produces good people. Like rationality, good and evil in man may be differentiated along regional, ethnic, cultural, or other lines of **we** and **they.** The local people may be seen as basically good but easily corrupted if they leave the village and go to the wicked city. In ethnocentrism, of course, a person's own culture may be regarded as basically good while that of another —often the most visible or nearest one—is regarded as basically bad. Or individual families within a culture may be distinguished between the good people and those with "bad blood," particularly where the lineal orientation is prominent (**Family: Relational Orientations**). The person with a social scientific attitude is likely to equate such orientations with those of prejudice, fear and threat, and ignorance. This may be a mature outlook toward man, but he should also keep in mind that at the level of values, not all cultures should be assumed to express that same kind of maturity.

Happiness. Just as there are many conceptions of happiness, cultures differ in their expectations of happiness in life. In the United States, with our assumptions of progress and the perfectibility of man, happiness is likely to be viewed as a practical goal—even **the** goal—in life. Life, liberty, and the pursuit of happiness we are promised. In popular sentiment of the **Peanuts** characters of Charles Shultz, "Happiness is—" all sorts of simple things around us. For many decades, U.S. movies have been distinguished from films of other countries largely because of the characteristically American happy ending. Too much "thinking" may be regarded by Americans as being in conflict with happiness, much as the word **serious** conveys both the meaning of thoughtful and the opposite of happy. Of course, "in every life a little rain must fall," but "every cloud has a silver lining"—and not the other way 'round.

The opposite orientation is represented by older Christian views of life as a veil of tears through which one must pass be-

fore going to his "reward." This orientation is still widely represented in the United States; while for some people "good works"
are an attempt to provide happiness on earth, for others they are
primarily the ticket to salvation. As implied in most of these
examples, the religious dimension is difficult to separate from
these alternatives. Where there are beliefs of reincarnation or
spiritual salvation, earthly happiness may not be expected. It
seems that in the Judeo-Christian tradition the rise in earthly
pleasures is regarded by the orthodox as a threat to spiritual
values. Too much earthly happiness may be judged decadence
and this, in turn, will invite God's wrath; images of Babylon and
Rome, among other civilizations, will be cited, paralleling Adam's
punishment when he tasted the forbidden fruit.

Many societies, including those with a strong Buddhist influence, are likely to hold views of happiness which differ from
both of these orientations. While Buddhism has many sects, some
even resembling Christian fundamentalism, there is a strong
theme of the inseparability of happiness and unhappiness. Just
as such antonyms as life and death, male and female, require
an opposite in order for each to be meaningful, happiness is
meaningless without its opposite. The familiar **yin-yang** model expresses this unity. Thus seeking happiness will surely bring
unhappiness not because God meant this life to be one of sadness but for reasons which are at least as psychological as they
are philosophical or theological. Alan Watts, a former Episcopa-
lian minister converted to Zen Buddhism, wrote extensively of
this for "Western readers," particularly in his long essay, **The
Wisdom of Insecurity.**[3] He cites the analogy of the drowning man
who is doomed only if he fights his condition and gasps for
breath; to survive he must learn to accept, to float. Characteristic
of this view of happiness and sadness is the emphasis on accepting events without complaining or fighting back, of adjusting
one's feelings to circumstances rather than altering the world.
The value should not be equated with surrender or "fatalism,"
but regarded as another mode of achieving happiness. R. G. H.
Siu, in another context, quotes Chuang Tze's parable:

[3] Alan Watts, **The Wisdom of Insecurity** (New York: Pantheon, 1951).

Cinnamon is edible, so the cinnamon tree is cut down. Ch'i oil is useful, so the Ch'i tree is gashed. On the other hand, a sacred oak, whose wood was good for nothing and accordingly spared, said to the axman in a dream, "For a long time I have been learning to be useless. On several occasions I was nearly destroyed, but I have now succeeded in being useless, which is of greatest use to me. If I were useful, could I have become so great?"[4]

Before leaving this brief discussion, we should note the factor of luck or unexpected good fortune. We can hope that a stroke of luck will bring happiness without assuming that such is the promise in life or the result of individual efforts, and without believing that it is a necessary complement of misfortune. Galjart, in writing of rural development in Brazil, includes this hope as one of the three defining characteristics of what he calls "the patronic syndrome in traditional culture" (comparable to our "complementary obligatory pattern").[5] That is, along with the personal influence of the **patrón** and the saints is "the assumption that any real improvement in one's socio-economic situation depends . . . on favours granted by secular or super-natural powers or on a stroke of luck." This kind of happiness, then, is more personal than societal, rare and fleeting rather than pervasive, and seems most consistent with the "being" relational orientation. In contrast the expectation of **happiness if you work for it,** as in the U.S. pattern, corresponds more to the doing orientation, while the midposition of unified happiness and unhappiness as reflected in the virtue of acceptance seems most congenial with the being-in-becoming orientation.

Mutability. Few values or beliefs are more important than that of the possibility of change in the human condition. Here, clearer than elsewhere, the self-perpetuating, self-fulfilling nature of values and beliefs is manifested. If man is to change, he must come to accept the possibility (and value) of change. If "some

---

[4] R. G. H. Siu, **The Tao of Science: An Essay on Western Knowledge and Eastern Wisdom** (Cambridge: The Technology Press, MIT, and New York: Wiley, 1968), p. 132.

[5] Benno Galjart, **Itaguai: Old Habits and New Practices in a Brazilian Land Settlement** (Wageningen: Center for Agricultural Publishing and Documentation, 1968), p. 85.

people never learn," it may be that some people are convinced that they cannot learn and change. Much of educational philosophy, particularly that represented by the social sciences, is based on the assumption that learning and change are not only possible but practically inevitable. Social and political structures, too, reflect and influence these orientations toward or against change, that man can become something better than he has been or that man is what he was meant to be. And yet, even in the most change-valuing societies such as the U.S., there is little convincing evidence to support or refute the view of significant human changes, except as one seeks that evidence consistent with his beliefs. Rhetorically, **change** is one of those commonplaces where the persuader seeks proofs for any position. That is, in seeking to persuade others, one can find **proofs** that man does not change (perhaps quoting the ancients to show that they were not very different from us in fundamental ways) and proofs that man has completely changed (perhaps quoting from the latest scientific developments or from statistics on population density, transportation, and so on).

The three variations suggested here require little explanation. The value of change (in the positive sense of learning and maturity, not regressive change) is obviously found most in societies that have experienced change. Gross technological changes, however, may be less important than widespread educational and social changes, such as literacy or birth-control programs, which both depend upon and contribute to the assumptions of change. Where technology produces a sudden surge of information, as in radio and, still much less frequently, television broadcasting, the implicit content is **change oriented.** The much-talked-of **revolution of rising expectations,** often resulting from information about life in other societies, is of this kind. A **Sears and Roebuck** catalogue, in this sense, is potentially more revolutionary than **The Quotations of Chairman Mao.** Moreover, the explicit content of much of the most popular information is likely to promise change —particularly self-change or improvement, however shallow or specious the information might be. We may regard **The Power of Positive Thinking** as a cultural model of American assumptions of change, but also note that in translation this book, as well as hundreds of other how-to books, have had a widespread appeal in nearly all parts of the world.

In direct contrast to change-oriented assumptions are a series of possibilities which (1) may regard any change as threatening; (2) may minimize any change as only superficial; or (3) may allow the possibility of change for some segments of the population while denying it to others. Depending on the emphasis and interpretation, we can identify such a society with either the second or third orientations listed above. Taking these three in order, we have at the extreme the **closed societies,** characteristically vertical, ascriptive, and authoritarian or authority-centered. Information will be regarded as the enemy, and any change as threatening. The second form is less severe but difficult to maintain over a period of time; changes perceived initially as superficial may turn out to have deeper consequences. Extending education to women, for example, may at first seem unnecessary but not particularly harmful until it begins to influence marriage patterns and changes in traditional role behaviors. The third variation may appear in forms of elitism, in extreme cases in caste or racist structures which say, in effect, "**those people** can never learn, but **we** can change and progress." (South Africa is currently the most obvious example.) Clearly, to allow **those people** the opportunity to learn and change is threatening: What if they do as well or better than the chosen people?

Political and philosophical models may be especially revealing of change values. The continuum from radical, liberal, conservative to reactionary is essentially a continuum of values or changes. Likewise, the seeking of a utopia or the longing for a return to a Golden Age are reflections of the values of change.

Finally, since so much of intercultural communication—both intended and accidental—relates to the value of change, we must stress again the importance of these orientations. In so many cases every day, as in development programs, the very differences in cultural orientations toward change are the reason for communication and are at the root of misunderstandings and frustrations that are likely to characterize that communication. A **Peace Corps** or other technical-assistance program may be sent ostensibly to encourage innovation or to "help them to help themselves," that is, to help them change in a certain way. But the volunteers, or "experts," may quickly discover resistance not to a particular technique or program, but to the larger value of change itself. The result is frequently frustration for both parties.

Nature

Technology, which derives from an exploitation of the forces of nature, has created environments which are, paradoxically, **unnatural**. The lone scientist at the South Pole may be more comfortable in his outpost than his family is back home in "the temperate zone." We often have more light at night than during the day, and we may become chilled in summer in air-conditioned rooms. Transportation's best routes now seem to be above or below the ground, though man was not made to fly and burrow. Even today's most serious illnesses now seem to be largely "man-made"—luxurious ills many of them—and unnatural.

We are taught to be **objective** about nature, which means in part to treat nature as an object over which we exert control. But just as the separation of self from family is largely a cultural distinction, the separation of man from nature and nature from the supernatural is likewise culturally influenced. Only a small part of the world would regard ecology as a **modern** notion. Assumptions about nature will necessarily involve man's view of himself and his gods, but our discussion of the sphere of nature will stress the following sets of value orientations:

Relationship of man and nature

1. man dominating nature	2. man in harmony with nature	3. nature dominating man

Ways of knowing nature

1. abstract	2. the circle of induction and deduction	3. specific

Structure of nature

1. mechanistic	2. spiritual	3. organic

Concept of time

1. future	2. present	3. past

Relationship of man and nature. Man's relationship with nature is closely allied to man's view of himself and the supernatural. (Though we will distinguish nature from the supernatural, Kluckhohn, who first proposed these three orientations, combined the two.) Here two alternatives may be likened to a master-slave relationship, one with man the master of nature, the other with nature in control of man. The middle alternative is that of man and nature in harmony or, some would say, inseparable.

In the United States today, the view that man dominates nature is unmistakable. Countercultural values—as in the ecology movement, which follows the **harmony** orientation—help to emphasize further the pervasive value of man in control. Space exploration is probably the most dramatic endeavor based on this value, and the excitement that surrounded the moon launches was mostly of a technical kind: "How can we?" not "Why should we?" Americans may speak of "conquering space"—an incredible expression—without a second thought. Buckminster Fuller's image of "spaceship earth" no less than his city-covering domes also reflect this value even as they appeal to members of the U.S. counterculture, who otherwise assume a more modest posture toward nature. Monsoons and germs, earthquakes and mosquitoes are equally subject to man's control. Perhaps it is not even so much a matter of domination and control that is valued, but the spirit of **challenge** that most attracts us. Our proudest achievements, our greatest folk heroes are frequently those who challenged, conquered, or exploited nature. We admire those who can "harness the power of the river" or "tame the wilderness," not only within the United States but anywhere. For many in the United States, the Israelis are to be admired primarily because they claim to have "made the desert bloom."

Nevertheless, nature is not always regarded, even in the United States, as a noble opponent in battle. When we speak of "nature's way" we usually mean something supportive of life. Only in irony is that view of nature mocked ("Death is nature's way of telling you to slow down"). Mother Nature is kind and wise. And this orientation, less prominent in the United States, is perhaps the closest we come to the image of man in harmony with nature, our middle orientation. Nature is a part of man and man is a part of nature. Where this is the dominant orientation, nature is better regarded as animate, if not human, but certainly not "objective." Thus a farmer may have feelings about his fields and the crops they will bear which are akin to his feelings toward human conception and birth. (See Hall's description of the Taos' reaction toward plowing the soil in **The Silent Language.**[6]) Harmony is an appropriate metaphor for the relationship, too, because of the harmony found within nature: the harmony of the seasons, of the planting cycle, of the movement of the stars. For the ancient Greeks, as for most agricultural societies today, the ideal in life was to discover the pattern of nature, imitate it, and live in harmony with it. In Japanese art forms, such as gardening and flower arrangement and **haiku** poetry (characterized not only by its metrical form but its essential reference to the season), harmony of man and nature is an unmistakable value. Even today the well-schooled Japanese flower arranger may apologize to each flower as she bends it into place.

The third orientation, which is the view that nature overwhelms man, is also found in the United States, even though it appears to be the opposite of the dominant U.S. value. What is especially interesting is that our speech patterns here elevate nature to the supernatural: **acts of God.** It is as if we assumed that nature can be predicted, controlled, exploited, but the unpredictable, uncontrollable, and unexploitable must be greater, hence **supernatural.** Nevertheless, the U.S. attitude toward "acts of God" is very different from those where this third orientation is the dominant value. For Americans there is nothing impious about being insured against "acts of God." Elsewhere, as in the Middle East generally, to anticipate the future harvest, may be unthinkable or might invite misfortune.

Implications of these orientations for intercultural contact and understanding are intriguing. It seems clear that cultures which have developed in part because of their sense of mastery over nature will attempt to assist "underdeveloped societies" which frequently hold tenaciously to one of the other two orientations. A survey of such cultural contacts will reveal that these orientations are not easily changed by the introduction of technology and "know how," for the values are a part of all aspects of a cul-

[6] Hall, **Silent Language,** p. 79.

ture. We might also consider the reverse situation, where, as in the recent ecological movement, persons in societies which have valued man's power over nature turn to other cultures for a new appreciation of man's harmonious relationship with nature.

Ways of knowing (perceiving, describing) nature. Long before a student completes high school he has some notion about the importance of things he will never see, from atoms to vitamins, and about vital processes, such as the blood's circulatory system, and genetics. He has a general image, though it may be vague, of evolution, world geography, and the solar system. As a child he asked questions his parents could not easily answer: Who made the world? Why do people get sick? After a few years in school he is likely to be reciting the answers to comparable questions. His educational development is likely to be a process of increasing abstraction, so that when he specializes in some subject in college, much of his most salient vocabulary is so abstract that only other specialists in the same field can understand him. When he tries to explain thermodynamics or cognitive dissonance in more concrete terms, he is likely to warn that he is oversimplifying his explanation. Such an outlook expresses the value that the best way to know and describe the stuff of this world is through abstractions.

In contrast, consider the world view of a mother in West Africa who has never gone to school. She is all too familiar with sickness, but she may be sure there are no germs because she has never seen one. If she is feverish and the doctor comes, she may prefer an injection to a pill, since she can feel the impact of the needle and see the medicine going into the blood, whereas a little pill just disappears into the stomach, which is not where it hurts. New York, Paris, Rome she may never have heard of, so they must lie somewhere beyond the next village. She knows what she has seen and experienced; what is **real** to her is not abstract.

In the circle of induction and deduction, abstractions are valuable as they organize and show relationships among specifics. Concrete evidence tests and, where necessary, modifies the theory or calls for additions or deletions of abstract concepts. It is the ideal of contemporary scientific thought, though in practice it may take a form closer to one or the other variations.

The U.S. assumptions may be closest to the central position but not directly because of its scientific basis. In the long evolution of philosophy from Bacon through British empiricism and American pragmatism, we have learned to be suspicious of the abstract. The man from Missouri is our model American when he says "Show me." We are likely to be distrustful of theories unless we can be given an example or two. On the other hand, we assume some patterns of laws which underlie the examples and are distrustful of interpretations that seem too obvious. A Korean may tell an American that eating ginseng root will make him virile, explaining—as if the reason were not obvious enough —that the root is shaped like a phallus. Probably the American is unimpressed: If the root is potent the reason exists in far less obvious explanations. The Western resistance to acupuncture provides another good example, for not only did the traditional Chinese system not appear to conform to any widely accepted scheme of the human body, there was something about sticking needles into bodies which was too specific to be trusted immediately. (The same line of reasoning could be followed in appraising U.S. attitudes about chiropractors and others.)

U.S. descriptions of the nature of things are likely to take the form of mixed metaphors, combining rather specific human actions with abstract concepts. "Conquering space," mentioned previously, is one example: Mary McCarthy, in writing of the language of U.S. soldiers in Viet Nam, described a similar style of mixing action with abstractions, ("Got to get Charlie's infrastructure").[7] We make war on poverty, ignorance, and disease; our reaction is specific ("Do something"), but the subjects, if they are worth acting on, are abstract.

Anglo-European cultures have often been distinguished from "Eastern" cultures along the lines of valuing abstractions or specifics. Compared to a German or French interpretation of "reality," the British and U.S. values may seem relatively more specific because of their empirical basis. Chinese valuations may be even more specific but not so much as those described in Japanese thought. Such distinctions will be considered in greater detail in Chapter Ten, when we discuss rhetorical forms and reasoning patterns.

[7] Mary McCarthy, **Viet Nam** (New York: Doubleday, 1970).

The assumptions in these orientations are never far from the surface expressions of our thoughts. It can be extremely difficult for a person who describes reality in abstract terms to talk with a person who voices more concrete conceptions. A nutritionist who attempts to introduce a dietary supplement in a society where reality is primarily physical may have a terrible time, for the most important realities of vitamins, and other nutrients, may have no meaning whatsoever for the people with whom he or she is talking. Honest questioning, "What is a vitamin, what does it look like?" may send the visitor farther into abstraction, ever more distant from this common sense world and farther away from the point of the explanation in the first place. A common tendency in attempts to adapt such descriptions is for the expert to talk down to the listener, as if talking to a child. Or, alternately, the expert may begin to sound more and more like a magician than a scientist. If the purpose of the nutritionist's visit was simply to introduce some new product this may not be so serious, but if the goal was to change cultural habits and beliefs about food and health, then both the childlike and the magical explanations will be self-defeating.

Structure of nature. Directly related to the views toward nature is the structure of the natural world. Of the three alternatives considered here—mechanistic, organic, and spiritual, the first is most familiar to persons in the United States, though attractions to the middle alternative have been shown in more recent times. A mechanistic nature clearly encourages the most tinkering with the machine and usually follows a thinking pattern of cause and effect, or **if-then** reasoning. The most familiar analogies of physics or chemistry, as well as popular models and metaphors describing human behavior, are mechanistic. Thus artificial satellites provide models for natural ones, and the computer is proposed as a simplified model of the human brain. In Western philosophy, the mechanistic view of nature has been dominant since Newton and is very much a part of analytical thought: taking the machine apart, examining its components, and reassembling and perhaps improving upon it.

If the above orientation likens nature to a kind of machine, such as a clock, the organic orientation might be likened to attitudes toward plants. The caution about some forms of examination is well expressed in the warning not to pull up the carrots to see how they are growing. Any intrusion into the natural world has repercussions which cannot so easily be anticipated by talk of cause and effect.

The spiritual conception of nature is different still. We may be cautious about tinkering with the universe, not because of its organic unity but because of its spiritual design: testing or questioning is considered destructive and blasphemous. Much of Christian thought prior to the Renaissance reflected this orientation, as all works of man were to glorify God and not examine His works. None of the classic seven liberal arts reflects the mechanistic orientation, where the closest natural subject of study was astronomy, safely removed from man's prying hands.

A friend in Kenya of the Kikuyu tribe seems to have been able to maintain all three orientations. As a guide in the Nairobi game park, he is keenly aware of organic nature, as in the balance which governs the great animals. But he is also aware that sometimes herds must be cropped by the game officers to maintain that balance in the light of limited resources and the encroachment of man. Thus he speaks in public and acts in ways consistent with the mechanistic orientation. Several years ago he made a bet with a friend that man would never go to the moon. His explanation, too long to repeat here, was spiritually conceived (the man professed to be a Christian): that God has His reasons for putting man on the earth and not on the moon. Citing legends as proof, he was sure that if man ever did go to the moon God would destroy the earth.

Concept of time. "Time talks," as Hall says in **The Silent Language.**[8] But also, time is how you talk about it. The division into seconds, minutes, hours, days, weeks, months, and years is so widely accepted that we are likely to forget that these are only categories of a system, consistent and useful, but not self-evident or "natural." A similar case is the division of time into "past, present, and future": These concepts, as Whorf argues, may simply be influences on our thinking of the tense markers of verbs found in most European languages, including English, but not in all languages.[9] To try to be more precise about per-

[8] Hall, **Silent Language,** 128–45.
[9] Benjamin Lee Whorf, **Collected Papers on Metalinguistics** (Washington, D.C.: U.S. Department of State, Foreign Service Institute, 1952).

ception of time is to blur these commonsense notions. Talk about the "present" and it is already past. And the future never comes.

Here we are interested not so much in the semantics of time as the **values** of time. Assuming some validity to the past, present, and future distinctions, where does a culture place its greatest emphasis? Obviously all three alternatives must receive some attention in every society, but as Kluckhohn argues in her first presentation of these value orientations, one is likely to dominate.

In the United States, the future seems to be valued the most. The shift by immigrants from the Old World to the new, the founding of a nation, and the Westerning that followed surely contributed to this value. (Again we should remember that this is not an isolated value; it exists only in its relationship with many other value orientations.) The stress on youth and achievements ("onward and upward," each son better than his father), the value of controlling one's own destiny (which requires planning ahead, saving for a rainy day), and the optimism that the future will be bright (despite laments for the passing of the good old days) are all a part of this orientation. There are special categories in which age is valued, of course: old recipes, but not so much old remedies; family position may be influenced by the past (the D.A.R.—Daughters of the American Revolution, for example) in some parts of the United States (the older parts!), but there is much less enthusiasm for saving an old building than for erecting something new. General Electric's slogan expresses the spirit of most of the nation: "Progress is our most important product." The U.S. child typically has little concern for or knowledge of his family beyond those he has known personally, and a word like **ancestor** sounds archaic to American ears. What was termed the **counterculture** of the 1960s and 1970s was characterized by a greater concern for the present than the future (dropping out and turning on), preferring "happenings" to more anticipated and controlled events, and celebrating as culture heroes those who seemed to value the present.

Those cultures which may be described as predominantly valuing the present are likely to be those also characterized by the being or being-in-becoming variations of the activity dimension. What is important is what is happening now. It is not that the future never comes but that it inevitably comes—so that **mañana** will be the same as now. The past, too, is not denied or forgotten; more likely it is interpreted as a more distant present.

Societies which place greater value on the past are similarly misinterpreted if they are regarded as ignoring the present or the future, or as rejecting change. Japan has had a reputation as a culture with an extreme emphasis on the past ("ancestor worship"), but it is also a society influenced by the philosophy of evanescence, of all things. (This is epitomized in the magnificent Ise Shrine which is dissembled and rebuilt in exactly the same way every twenty years.) Perhaps **conservative,** in the sense of conserving what was good in the past rather than anticipating something better in the future, is a more satisfying name for this variation than **past-oriented.**

In cultures which value tradition and take great care to preserve and pass on their heritage we should expect other expressions of these values. In age orientations, older persons may be valued more than youth; the lineal relationship orientation, phasic or low-mobility orientations, and formality may be expected, as well.

Differences in the concepts toward time often are among the first value differences sensed by a person in a new culture. He is likely to sense a difference in the pace of life, so that things seem too slow or too fast. (Those in the host culture, of course, may have the reverse perception of the visitor's pace.) He may be overwhelmed by efficiency or dismayed by delays. What appear on the surface as minor irritations may be fundamental blocks to major social changes, not to be overcome by temporary speeding up of the work force. This is particularly notable in proposals for development schemes in so-called underdeveloped nations. When foreign investors and advisors with money in hand urged Tanzania's President Nyerere to undertake certain development programs, Nyerere was reluctant—primarily because of his philosophy of socialism and wanting the entire nation to move ahead rather than risk the formation of small elites who would benefit most from the programs. Part of his explanation in rejecting some ideas was in terms of time, saying that the Africans have lived more or less as they do today for thousands of years, and for them there was no great hurry to change things. Only the foreign advisers seemed to be in a hurry.

The supernatural

Since Comte, Western scholars have removed the supernatural from the realm of scientific questioning and have become (as scholars) agnostic about questions of the supernatural. Religion and science seem poles apart except where the wonder of nature itself seems to invite religious appreciation. A writer such as Teilhard de Chardin is notable today precisely because he seeks to bring theology and science together. Elsewhere and in earlier times, a person who would distinguish the two would be singled out, as Galileo and a host of "martyrs of science" have been.

Specific aspects of religious beliefs cannot be treated in this survey, though the literature of proselytizing provides some of the oldest and richest sources of information on the encounters of cultures. (The information available on Bible translation alone is extremely valuable to students of intercultural communication, an area quite apart from religious interests.) We will limit our discussion to four sets of value orientations which closely parallel the issues previously raised.

Relationship of man and the supernatural

1. man as god	2. pantheism	3. man controlled by the supernatural

Meaning of life

1. physical, material goals	2. intellectual goals	3. spiritual goals

Providence

1. good in life is unlimited	2. balance of good and misfortune	3. good in life is limited

Knowledge of the cosmic order

1. order is comprehensible	2. faith and reason	3. mysterious and unknowable

Relationship of man and the supernatural. The parallels between these value orientations and those of the man-nature relationship are quite clear and, as noted, were originally combined by Kluckhohn. Both are expressions of man's power or impotence, but it is useful to distinguish man's relationship with nature from his beliefs relating to the supernatural. While in many cultures such a distinction may not be appropriate, in others including the United States, England, and Northwestern Europe, the two diverge. In the United States, for example, man views himself as the master of nature but in turn maintains a kind of junior partnership with God. The latter relationship is explicit in expressions like "God helps him who helps himself," and is even clearer in that genre of popular biography, film and songs with such titles as "God Is My Co-Pilot," "Somebody Up There Likes Me," "Have You Talked to the Man Upstairs?"

One of these three variations, then, asserts that the ultimate power in all acts is outside of man's control. Man proposes, God disposes. This is the ostensible value of the United States ("In God We Trust"), but it is not always expressed in action. Americans seem not to mind what kind of a god a person believes in, so long as he believes in something above himself. In actions, man may act "like God," but at the level of **values,** such an orientation is untenable, much to the confusion of many foreign visitors who immediately sense the gap between expressed values and behavior.

A much clearer expression of the orientation which subordinates man to his deity is found among Moslems. Indeed, many critics including Moslem critics believe that it is this value that has stultified change in Moslem cultures for centuries. When an Arab says "God willing," as in "God willing, I will see you tomorrow," he is likely to mean it quite literally: only if Allah sees fit will we be here when the sun rises. And **M'sh'Allah,** "God Willing," is a part of almost every greeting and farewell. It is not surprising, then, that one seems to be treading upon God's domain when asking a devout Moslem to anticipate the future.

In Latin America (and among Copts and other Christians in the Middle East), the overall orientation is similar, but the specific pattern is quite different. Man's relationship to God is much more personal, frequently mediated by patron saints or the Virgin Mary. (One explanation for the lack of success of Protestant missionaries in Latin America and in the Middle East is that by discouraging the veneration of saints they have "eliminated the middleman," so to speak. This is as disruptive of communication with the supernatural as the loss of intermediaries would be within the social order.) In this personal form, divine assistance is actively negotiable: a person may strike bargains with his patron saint, offer gifts, or even inflict physical punishments on the **Santo.** In comparison with North American Roman Catholics, who reflect their **individualistic** relational orientations in their faith, the Latin American Catholic reveals the **patronaje** of **collateral and interdependent** orientations. If the North American believes "God helps those who help themselves," the Latin American believes "God helps those who help God."

The middle orientation, simplified as "pantheism," does not distinguish clearly nature from the supernatural. God or the gods are present in all things, and thus is likely to conform to the "harmony with nature" orientation described previously. Traditional Japanese values of harmony with nature find their supernatural counterpart in Shintoism, sometimes described as a religion without dogma. Spirits dwell in rocks, trees, and mountains, and for this reason identification with the land has been as much a social force in Japan as it has among many North American Indian cultures which share comparable beliefs.

The third alternative places man at the center of the universe, however arrogant or humble that position may make him. "God" may be regarded as the prime mover who set things in motion for man, the position of the deistic "founding fathers" of the United States, or even that role may be regarded as unnecessary.

This position may be urged following a revolution in a nation, particularly if the old order which was toppled had been supported by a powerful clergy. Here as elsewhere it is important to remember that official political values, as stated in a constitution or revolutionary songs and art, may not be matched by the actual values of the citizenry. Here, Mexico provides an excellent example: The revolutionary Mexico of some of the murals of Diego Rivera or of the constitution is not the Mexico of most conservative Mexicans.

We conclude with two observations about variations of these orientations within a society. First, in many societies these may be asserted as distinguishing older from younger persons, the educated from the uneducated, etc. The young college student, for example, may say that his grandmother still believes in such-and-such, but that he and other "modern" people do not. A second problem is a semantic one: The same orientation may be called **reverence** by one who holds the value and **superstition** by one who does not. Similarly, it may not always be easy to determine the strength of these orientations from language habits alone. As indicated earlier, "God willing" may be meant to be taken literally or may have little more to do with an omnipotent deity than does the God in "Good-bye."

Meaning of life. "What is the meaning of life?" Societies offer competing answers, including the three below. Distinctions are never clear-cut, but the differences may be appreciated by observing what goals are established in childhood, what kinds of persons are admired within the culture, what reasons are given to support choices of actions, and how members of one society look upon those of another.

Though persons from the United States may sometimes deny it, **material wealth and physical well-being** seem to be much more valued in the United States than are **spiritual** or **intellectual** goals. "The pursuit of happiness" means, for many Americans, the opportunity to secure property and material comforts. Material rewards may be regarded by many as proof of divine approval, of course, just as God is on the side of the winning army, but these are not signs of dominant spiritual values. Intellectual goals, too, if not opposed to material goals, may at least be interpreted through material standards (as in the appeal to go through college in order to earn more money). A capitalistic system with its attendant advertising and consumer consciousness is frequently blamed for dulling the mind and starving the soul, but we must realize that such a system arises out of cultural values at least as much as it influences those values. Even in those segments of U.S. society where the alternative orientations might be expected to dominate, as in educational and religious establishments, materialism—including quantification—may serve to rank one university or church over another. Thus the number of college facilities or books in the library, or the number of converts or missionary schools may be cited as evidence of superiority.

It becomes even clearer when observing a person with a strong materialistic orientation entering a society where spiritual values are dominant. It may be difficult for the visitor to comprehend how a poorly dressed, apparently underfed person can command respect. This feeling is well expressed in the cynical challenge, "If you're so smart why ain't you rich?" During the period of the cold war with the U.S.S.R., much of the domestic U.S. propaganda arguing for U.S. superiority was expressed in terms of comparative materialism—how long a U.S. factory worker had to work to earn a pair of shoes compared to the time required in Russia.

Purely spiritual goals in life depend a great deal on one's concept of man's place in time and in the divine order. If there is life—or lives—after death or before (as in concepts of **karma**), the spiritual dimension will be much more important. India today provides the most outstanding example. The interpretation by visitors that "life here is not valued" (or, more telling, that "life is cheap") may be that of one from a material-valuing society directed towards a society where spiritual values are pronounced. The pattern appears to be that such comments more frequently emanate from "developed nations" and are applied to "underdeveloped nations." Self-immolations, and other acts of suicide, where they arise from a culture and not as reactions to personal frustrations, are likely to indicate that spiritual values transcend material values. Perhaps the more revealing question is not "what is the meaning of life?" but "what is the meaning of death?"

Intellectual values vary in importance across cultures, but we are not aware of any culture which could be said to rank this orientation first. Life's goal as the search for truth seems to be celebrated more in the praise of the dead philosopher than in society's living gad-fly. As a relative position, however, the educator, writer, philosopher, or scientist may be shown to be of different ranks in different cultures.

Providence. Edward Stewart has called attention to a distinction made by George Foster of limited and unlimited **good.**[10] Foster says that characteristically among peasant societies in

---

[10] George M. Foster, "Peasant Society and the Image of Limited Good," **American Anthropologist** 67 (April, 1965): 296; the concept of the "limited good" is treated at length in Stewart, **American Patterns**, pp. 63–65.

the world the "good things" of life—including health, love, honor, as well as land and wealth—are considered finite and thus in limited supply. " 'Good,' like land, is seen as inherent in nature— there to be divided and redivided if necessary, but not to be augmented." This means, among other things, that one person's gain may be viewed as another's loss, and this in turn may produce an ambivalence about benefiting, or a need to conceal such improvements from others in the community. This interpretation is very consistent with social pressures and sanctions, including the distinction between **shame cultures** and **guilt cultures.** (In the former, pressures to conform to the norms of the society are explicit and exerted from without, while in **guilt** cultures, there is an internalized sense of "wrong" so that one who feels guilty punishes himself. It is not always easy to make this neat distinction.) In parts of Africa, to cite one example, a villager might be reluctant to replace his thatched roof with a corrogated metal one; he might fear that something evil would befall him (such as his house burning down). And it might so happen, possibly being attributed to a curse, but accepted as punishment for having usurped a part of the limited good of the community.

The opposite view, well expressed in the U.S. culture, is that of good limited only by man's imagination and will. Time-tables are frequently published to remind us of all of the diseases which medical science has conquered and which anticipate the cures or prevention of other diseases by certain other dates. Similar announcements, by no means limited to the United States, report the steady increase of material goods among the population, the steady rise in income and standard of living, and so on. It remains implicit that happiness, love, friendship, and less material blessings are also increasing.

In contrast with the view of limited good, this orientation encourages each person to display his successes with the assumption that others can then follow his example. A person may, of course, actually be expressing his sense of superiority, but he can rationalize that he is helping to promote the general good.

Our middle position finds expression even in the United States among those who are distrustful of gains because they are likely to be balanced by some kind of loss or misfortune. For some people there is a kind of divine balance sheet on which good fortune is recorded so that it may be balanced by some calamity. Conversely, bad luck or hard times are taken as guarantees that blessings will be bestowed later. The ledger may be balanced in an after-life or in lives of off-spring, but in any case God is just and nobody will receive more than his share of good fortune or misfortune. This philosophy is often supported by stories of a man who has wealth but not health (John D. Rockefeller, for example), in notions that poor people are really happier than the rich, and in myth and literature portraying the predestined fall of great men.

Knowledge of the cosmic order. A scientist in Germany is deeply moved by the incredible patterns of organization he finds in every form of creation, from the smallest cell to the solar system. He writes a book in which his scientific descriptions provide proof of a divine order. A farmer in Peru is very sensitive to the phases of the moon, the cycles of the seasons, and other patterns in nature which guide his sowing and harvesting. But he is far more awed by the unpredictable: the trembling of the land that plunges mountains into the sea, the drought or blight that withers his crops, or a sudden illness that carries away his son. These are mysteries, he says, that cannot be explained. At Notre Dame University a theologian repeats to his students the message of St. Thomas Aquinas: Man requires **faith** as well as **reason.**

These are the models for the three value orientations pertaining to knowledge of the supernatural and the cosmic order. In the first variation, it is not necessary to conclude that a supreme mind created such organization; one may reject teleological explanations and remain impressed that there is an order, a consistency which is predictable throughout the universe. This, of course, is a basic assumption in any scientific attitude. In the contrasting orientation, too, it is the unpredictability, the mystery, which is more important than religious interpretation based upon the mysterious. The middle position, familiar in the West through Thomistic philosophy, allows a wide area for **reason** (hence the assumption of consistency, predictability) but at some point draws a line and calls for trust or acceptance (**faith**) of what is beyond man's limited powers of reason.

The broad relationships between these attitudes toward knowledge of the cosmic order and other orientations in the nature and supernatural spheres readily suggest themselves, but we should not expect consistent parallels within or between cultures. For example, it may seem that in a society whose dominant man-nature orientation is that of man over nature would also follow the SOCIETY: **formality/informality** orientation of regularity and predictability in some divine plan. And yet this would not appear to be the case with the Ismaili sect of Moslems, for example, or many Mormons in the United States, who value man over nature but adhere to the second or third variations above.

There is also the matter of socioeconomic systems which follow one orientation, and religions (particularly syncretistic faiths) which follow an apparently inconsistent orientation. In northeast Brazil, for example, much energy may be expended in "harnessing the power of Amazon," pushing back the frontiers of the **sertão,** and generally following the national motto of **Orden e progreso** ("order and progress"). But the worker who bulldozes the hills into a factory site one day may take part in propitiating the sea-goddess **Irmaja** the next. Spiritism, with its dominant values of mystery and acceptance, claims the largest number of believers in the land of **order and progress.** Japan, too, with its much touted **economic miracle,** based on values of rationality, dominance of nature, and the expansion of an unlimited good (culminating in Prime Minister Tanaka's plan to "restructure the Japanese archipelago") retains its values of mystery: Almost no building, large or small, is undertaken without the consultation of priests and **uranaishi,** who determine the proper orientation to avoid evil. And thousands of Japanese would-be businessmen and engineers jam the shrines at the time of college entrance examinations to pray for luck and to carry home their talismans.

Conclusion

Value orientations are abstract constructs. They are useful only when tempered by an "as if" caution: people in culture X act **as if** they believe that materialism is more important than spiritual concerns, **as if** older persons deserve more respect than younger ones, **as if** intuition is a better guide than reason. Applied with caution, as a framework in which revealing questions can be asked and a great variety of specific behaviors can be related and organized, value orientations can be most helpful.

Value orientations are meaningful only in combination, not in isolation. To identify and discuss values or value orientations, we must treat each individually, but we will be misled if we expect that what they represent can be so individuated. Any change in one area can produce a number of disruptions and adjustments elsewhere. The automobile has meant far more than, as Marshall McLuhan suggests, "wheels as the extension of the foot"; it is also a vehicle to extend individuality, to alter man's relationship toward nature, and to initiate whole new patterns of sexual behavior. Similarly, to appraise a culture's assumptions about human nature is to say something about a person's view of himself and his gods.

Value orientations are incomplete, biased, and reflective of the purposes for which they were invented and for which they may be applied. Such are the limitations of labeling anything, but the significance is even more apparent where there is no standardized system and where the referent is as amorphous as the term, **culture.**

While we have stressed value orientations in these two chapters without always relating them explicitly to cultural patterns of communication and to encounters across cultures, we must not forget such applications. Throughout the remainder of this book we will be looking at the relationship of communication and values, in aspects of spoken language, nonverbal behavior, and patterns of argumentation and rhetoric. Before moving on, however, the reader might do well to return to the cases presented in Chapter Two. Hopefully a greater understanding of cultural values will lead to more and clearer insights into the causes of such problems in intercultural communications.

Before concluding this chapter we wish to consider two additional questions about intercultural communication in general. Must differences in the cultural values of persons communicating inevitably lead to misunderstandings, frustrations, and alienation? Certainly from what has been said thus far this is a reasonable guess. Apparently in any culture, people tend to select as their friends those who most resemble themselves in beliefs, preferences, and styles of communicating. But to some degree, at least for some people, there is also an attraction to such differences in values and a special satisfaction in relationships that are complementary. In such relationships a person often experiences the opposite of what has been anticipated above; he may discover new aspects of his personality or even the joy of expanded consciousness and emotional growth. This is not an uncommon experience among young persons who study abroad or those who work abroad among Peace Corps or other volunteers. Perhaps it is most likely to occur among persons who are emotionally and situationally "free," in the sense of having relatively few fixed obligations to specific cultural institutions at home. Conversely, frustrations may be much more likely when a person in a new culture must finish a certain task within a limited time, whether the task be a business deal or completing a college degree that will satisfy the folks back home. And yet even those observations must be tempered by cultural considerations. The Japanese Peace Corps, for example, has the lowest drop-out rate of any such organization, and yet the Japanese volunteer is relatively far more task-oriented and relatively much less socially conscious about his host culture than his North American counterpart.[11] His satisfaction to a great degree resides in discharging his responsibilities to the satisfaction of his sponsor. The U.S. Peace Corps volunteers, in contrast, are urged to return before their allotted time if **they** feel they are not satisfied with their situation. Of course, personality differences, apart from cultural differences, must play a role in determining whether encounters with other cultural values lead to satisfaction and growth or frustration and alienation.

A second question must also be raised: Where persons from two different cultures come into contact, does the communication largely follow the patterns of one culture or the other, or is some third pattern likely to emerge as a synthesis of the two? The answer to this question also seems to depend on which cultures are involved, the personalities of the individuals, and also on the particular setting and kind of situation which charac-

[11] These observations were made, in conversation, by Mr. O. Muro, former director of training, Japan Overseas Cooperation Volunteers.

terizes such interaction. We merely raise the question here to warn against assuming too much when persons with different cultural values communicate over an extended period of time. After we have discussed aspects of language and culture, non-verbal patterns across cultures, and different patterns of reasoning, we will return to this question and the speculation about an emergent third culture.

We will also see if it is possible to distinguish the relative importance of value differences when compared with other differences in spoken language, nonverbal patterns, and modes of reasoning. Thus this chapter marks not the end of our discussion of values but the beginning.

See what I mean? Observations on nonverbal communication across cultures

The U.S. Secretary of State and the Japanese Foreign Minister signed the reversion of Okinawa agreement in 1972 in a ceremony that was simultaneously telecast in the United States and Japan. The Japanese signed with the traditional ink brush, befitting such an important document, and the U.S. Secretary signed with a series of fountain pens which would later be distributed as mementos of the event. In the United States a commentator remarked that modern Japan apparently still used some "primitive tools," while a Japanese commentator expressed astonishment that the American fountain pens wrote so poorly they could safely be used only once and then discarded.

The British professor of poetry relaxed during his lecture at Ain Shams University in Cairo. So carried away was he in explicating a poem that he leaned back in his chair and so revealed the sole of his foot to an astonished class. To make such a gesture in a Moslem society is the worst kind of insult. The Cairo newspapers the next day carried banner headlines about the student demonstration which resulted, and they denounced British arrogance and demanded that the professor be sent home.

The Russian Premier made a good-will visit to the United States. In order to symbolize friendship between the two nations, the Premier gestured broadly, his hands clasped above his head in a traditional Russian gesture of friendship. Many Americans who saw the action did not get the message. Many thought he was imitating a boxer who had just knocked out his opponent.

Many people believe that the language of gestures is universal. Many people believe that one picture is worth a thousand words, the implication being that what we see is ever so much clearer than what is said. Many people believe that communication means speaking and that misunderstandings only occur with speaking. Many people believe that smiling and frowning and clapping are purely **natural** expressions. Many people believe that the world is flat.

The subject of study that is called **nonverbal communication** is quite new as an academic subject, is interdisciplinary, complex, fascinating, and of great popular appeal. It is too broad to explore in depth in a short chapter in this book. **Nonverbal communication** is, first of all, a **non**-subject: What it does **not** include is much clearer than what it does include. And even what is not to be included is not always agreed upon. The following are some of the topics which have attracted the attention of the student of intercultural communication:

1. hand gestures, both intended and self-directed (autistic), such as the nervous rubbing of hands
2. facial expressions—such as smiles, frowns, yawns
3. posture and stance
4. clothing and hair styles (hair being more like clothes than like skin, both subject to the fashion of the day)
5. walking behavior
6. interpersonal distance (proxemics)
7. touching
8. eye contact and direction of gaze, particularly in "listening behavior"
9. architecture and interior design
10. "artifacts" and nonverbal symbols, such as lapel pins, walking sticks, jewelry

11. graphic symbols, such as pictures to indicate "men's room" or "handle with care"
12. art and rhetorical forms, including wedding dances and political parades
13. somatypes of bodies; ectomorphs, endomorphs, mesomorphs
14. smell (olfaction), including body odors, perfumes, incense
15. paralanguage (though often in language, just as often treated as part of nonverbal behavior—speech rate, pitch, inflections, volume
16. color symbolism
17. synchronization of speech and movement
18. taste, including symbolism of food and the communication function of chatting over coffee or tea, oral gratification—such as smoking or gum chewing
19. thermal influences, such as influences of temperature on communication, sensitivity to body heat
20. cosmetics: temporary—powder, lipstick; permanent—tattoos
21. drum signals, smoke signals, factory whistles, police sirens
22. time symbolism: what is too late or too early to telephone or visit a friend, or too long or too short to make a speech or stay for dinner
23. timing and pauses within verbal behavior
24. silence

Because of the rapid increase in research and publications in this vast subject of nonverbal communication, it is not necessary for us to try to survey the whole field. Excellent books on the subject are listed in the Bibliography at the back of this book. Our purpose in this chapter simply is to point out some of the characteristics of the nonverbal which are of special importance in intercultural communication.

If we take "communication" to include potentially all behavior, then clearly most of communication will not be what is spoken or written. Birdwhistell, who deserves most credit for awakening interest in serious nonverbal studies, has estimated that at most only about 30 percent of what is communicated in a conversation is verbal. His estimate is based on two persons from the same culture speaking their native language.[1] Since so much intercultural communication takes place with at least one of the parties speaking a second or third language or both speaking through an interpreter, it seems safe to assume that across cultures we may rely even more on nonverbal behavior. Add to this the point that most of us are totally unaware of what we are communicating by our own "normal" behavior (and that a person from another culture is likely to be unusually conscious of that behavior, often without properly interpreting it), and the importance of the nonverbal dimension increases even further.

Nonverbal behavior is undeniably important in communication, within a culture or across cultures. It seems far more important than most people ever thought until very recently. But also beware of placing too much of the burden of understanding or misunderstanding on gestures, interpersonal distance, and other such aspects of the nonverbal. This would be as exaggerated an emphasis today as was the near absence of concern for nonverbal behavior until two decades ago.

Characteristics of nonverbal communication across cultures

Although the term **nonverbal** communication indicates a contrast with spoken or written language, many of the significant differences between these modes of expressions are overlooked. It will be helpful to call attention to some of the most apparent differences before proceeding further.

1. Unlike spoken languages, which, as nearly everybody in the world knows, differ from place to place, there is a common notion that most of the topics included in the nonverbal area are universal, **natural,** and not learned.

2. Unlike spoken language, which is based on a comprehensible **system,** nonverbal communication may or may not be so systematized. Currently, most academic studies of nonverbal behavior assume that, like spoken language, they are learned, that they conform to some system ("the silent language"), and

[1] Ray L. Birdwhistell, **Kinesics and Context** (Philadelphia: University of Pennsylvania Press, 1970).

in time will yield something like a grammar, syntax, and vocabulary. Still, present scholars are hesitant to state rules or even the parts of silent speech. To put it simply, nobody knows very much about nonverbal communication in any society, let alone its function across cultures.

3. Unlike spoken language, there are no dictionaries of nonverbal behavior, with the exception of a few monographs of hand gestures and at least one appendix to a dictionary (Italian) also of hand gestures. If we hear a word in a foreign language that we do not know, it is possible to check a dictionary or a book of phrases and get some approximate idea of what the speaker may have meant. We cannot do this with the nonverbal.

4. Unlike spoken language, where if the speaker says something we did not hear well or did not understand we can ask him to repeat or clarify what he said, with the nonverbal it is extremely difficult to ask for clarification. It is possible, though odd, to say to a speaker, "You just smiled this way and moved your head like that: What did you mean?"

5. Unlike spoken language, which is used as often to conceal thought as it is to express thought and which people largely control for their own purposes, much nonverbal behavior seems impossible to control. Of course we can look "happy" when we are not, we can look interested when we are bored, and we can control—to some extent—many nonverbal expressions to convey some feelings that may not be fully sincere. Indeed, most of us do so to some extent nearly every day, but we cannot control everything. We cannot usually control blushing, sweating, a rapid heartbeat, eye-pupil dilation, and we know we can't.

6. As a result of the above, we must expect that at least some of the time our nonverbal behavior and our spoken words may not seem to match. A visitor from another culture may breach etiquette or violate some deep-seated taboo, and we are shocked. Our shock registers, but we may try to keep on talking as if nothing had happened. For example, a person from a largely noncontact culture (where there is relatively little touching of persons) enters a culture where people are constantly embraced, poked, stroked, and patted: Descending the ramp of the airplane our noncontact friend begins his prepared greeting, "I am happy to be in your country," but before he finishes he is crushed in

the embrace of his host. He finishes his words, which say one thing, while his nonverbal reaction may shout the opposite.

Where there is such a contradication between what is said verbally and what is expressed nonverbally, the observer is likely to trust the nonverbal over the verbal. "He **said** he was happy, but he **looked** quite unhappy; so I am sure he was not happy."

The verbal and the nonverbal

William Condon has produced some very revealing studies of the relationship of speech patterns and nonverbal movement.[2] Using a very high-speed motion picture camera with sound, Condon has been able to analyze the speech and movements in minute detail, capturing in a single frame the expressions of a fraction of a second. What Condon believes he has found is extraordinarily important, if true: that speech and gesticulation are totally synchronized, with speech calling the tune, and movement (from gross gestures and body shifting down to the blinking of the eyes) dancing to it. His resulting hypothesis is that no gesture, not even an eye blink, is random. Each movement is synchronized to speech. (At the most obvious level, this is easily demonstrated. Gesture appropriately pointing your finger and saying "You must **stop!**" You will find that your gesture stops with the end of the word, "stop"; it is very difficult to do otherwise and, if it can be forced, it looks very strange.)

The synchronization of speech and gestures can also be recognized when watching a movie that has been dubbed, with the voices of the actors in the original film being substituted by actors' voices in a second language. Most people seem to prefer to hear the original language and read subtitles in translation. One explanation is that the sound of the original—including tone of voice, vocabulary, and sentence structure—is more appealing. Condon's interpretation points out that a dubbed film is "out of sync"; not only words and lip movements, but all of the other movements are off as well.

Condon believes that our gestures and movements are synchronized to the voice of whoever is speaking. We dance to the rhythm

[2] William S. Condon and W. D. Ogston, "A Segmentation of Behavior," **Journal of Psychiatric Research** 5 (1967): 221–35.

of our own voices when we are talking and, as listeners, we dance to the tune of the speaker's voice. If this view is correct, the non-verbal difficulties of communication in another culture, particularly where the language and language rhythms are different from our own, should be far greater than ever appreciated. Not only must we learn to hear and express the new sounds in new rhythms of another language, we must also learn to blink and twitch in a new rhythm!

Speech and body movements, then, may be related through synchronization. But there are other relationships which are less subtle. Nonverbal signs may, at times, serve as a substitute for speech. This is obvious enough within a culture, as where a hand signal to "come here" may substitute for those words. But across cultures the patterns of substitution may be more complicated and may follow a pattern different from that of our own culture.

Not so long ago, designer Henry Dreyfuss published a massive **Symbol Sourcebook,** containing some 8,000 graphic symbols which **Time** magazine in a review called "universally comprehensible."[3] The goal of the book, as admirable as ambitious, was to provide a set of graphic symbols that would be immediately understandable to persons regardless of spoken language or cultural background. The **Time** reviewer was impressed, and commented with illustrations from the book:

> Who, for example, can fail to understand such representational symbols as these widely used warning against thin ice and falling rocks? . . . Packages can be shipped—and protected—in any language, too. These symbols instruct shippers and cargo handlers to "keep frozen" and "keep dry." Equally clear are labels that depict a broken goblet ("fragile"), a crossed-out hook ("use no hooks") and a package separated from the sun by a heavy diagonal line ("protect from heat").[4]

As a step in the direction of creating a universal graphic sign language, these illustrations cannot be objectionable. But to say that such pictures are immediately recognized by all persons without instruction is quite another matter.

[3] "Sign Language," **Time,** April 3, 1972, p. 33.
[4] Ibid.

The "keep frozen" image, for example, is a stylized penguin. It takes a particular Gestalt to mentally distinguish the field from the image, another Gestalt to reassemble the broken lines into the shape of a bird, and some education to (1) recognize the bird as a penguin, (2) know that a penguin lives in cold climates, and (3) perform the exercise in synecdoche which tells you that this bird picture represents coldness. An individual must be taught all of these steps. He could get as far as the last step and conclude that the package contained a penguin. It was exactly that chain of reasoning which led a postal clerk in India to interpret the box symbol as a "broken goblet" and then toss the box in the air—puzzled as to why anybody should be mailing broken glassware.

At about the same time the Dreyfuss book was published, the United States launched a satellite destined for the periphery of space with the hope that it would be intercepted by sentient beings. The satellite contained a graphic image, a line drawing of a naked male and female from the front, a chart showing the fourteen pulsars of the Milky Way, and a diagram of the solar system. Intelligent creatures out there, it was hoped could "read" this and decipher the return address. No reply has been received, so far as we know, but if one comes it must be sent by very intelligent beings, since only a very small percentage of earthlings could similarly interpret most of that message.

Persons who have worked with films and posters in cultures very different from their own, are familiar with the misinterpretation of nonverbal graphics that were not obvious to the people who made them. In Karen Carlson's excellent study of the persuasive wildlife appreciation campaign conducted in Kenya by international conservation groups, it was pointed out how some films were misdirected, even those accompanied by a sound track in a language understandable to the viewers.[5] Even these are based on conventions of film making (not to mention different value assumptions) which are enigmatic to most of the school children lucky enough to see them. Conventions of foreshortening, three dimension representation in two dimensions,

---

[5] Karen A. Carlson, "The Kenya Wildlife Conservation Campaign: A Descriptive and Critical Study of Intercultural Persuasion." Ph.D. dissertation, Northwestern University, 1969.

color symbolism, size perspective also must be learned, somewhat like learning to read and write words. The literature in culture variations in perception has greatly increased in recent years
since the early work at the turn of the century, and the student
particularly interested in this field is directed to read further
in this fascinating area.[6] Our point here is simply that we cannot
assume that such nonverbal symbolization is universally recognized. Much of it may be easier to learn, but that is a different
matter. It is also a matter that if followed far enough leads us
back to ideographic writing symbolisms and thence to the discovery that eventually these become more difficult to learn than
phonetic symbols.

For a moment, let us consider two opposing approaches to
learning about nonverbal behavior. One is of the kind we have
just mentioned, the idea that there is something simpler, more
direct, more universal about the nonverbal than the verbal. If
this were sufficiently true, we should be able to go far in discussing the cultural aspects of nonverbal communication in general.
And, in fact, there is enough universality to unspoken human
expressiveness to be encouraging. At least we can guess that a
woman who seems to be crying **might** be sad, while if she told
us so in a language we didn't understand we might have no idea
of what she meant. And yet we know of many examples, some
within our own nation, where the nonverbal seems to be as unnatural (or **learned**) as the verbal is. To be sure of the meaning
of a particular hand gesture or even certain facial expressions
we may have to observe many similar examples in varying contexts, and we may have to ask some people questions as well.
This second method, similar to that of a linguist seeking to
identify expressions in speech, requires much time, many comparable examples, and careful attention to detail. One who follows such an approach is likely to be suspicious of the isolated
but dramatic anecdote. Most persons seriously engaged in communication in another culture or with persons from another
culture, however, seek neither anecdotes nor detailed analyses.
So we will suggest following the slippery path down the middle,
considering ways of interpreting nonverbal behavior which are

[6] M. H. Segall, D. T. Campbell, and M. J. Herskovits, **The Influence of Culture
on Visual Perception** (Indianapolis: Bobbs-Merrill, 1966), pp. 60–66.

neither as casual and impressionistic as the one, nor as rigorous and time-consuming as the other. The digital/analogical distinction will be of some help here, and the relationship of nonverbal behavior to value orientations may be yet more helpful. We will also briefly note areas of nonverbal behavior which are not so easily related to broader organizing patterns, matters that may simply have to be learned just as a foreign language is learned.

Digital and analogical

The computer has served as a model for aspects of human communication for many years now, sometimes clarifying, sometimes distorting our understanding. One of the simpler and more useful metaphors to come out of such comparisons is the distinction between digital and analogical modes of expression, paralleling those two types of calculators.[7] For most people today, the word "computer" probably refers exclusively to digital computers. The distinction is mainly this: Analogical computations and expressions of results show a parallel (analogy) between **what** is calculated and **how;** in digital computations there is no such necessary correspondence. The movement of the hands of a clock, or the beads on an abacus, are analogical calculations and expressions; the speedy activities of what we usually think of as modern electronic computers are digital. Another way of thinking about the difference is this: With little or no training, one can guess at the meaning of many analogical forms, since in their form they bear some resemblance to what they stand for, but to interpret a digital expression requires a knowledge of the abstract and arbitrary system on which it is based. Roman numerals are thus more analogical than arabic numbers (we still must learn the meaning of I and V and X and C) but there is something more analogical about roman II than arabic 2, and even something more analogical about XX than 20. This example reminds us of another distinction, very important in describing communication: just as roman numerals are more cumbersome than arabic numbers for more complicated calculations (since the numerals must always retain their analogical pattern), most

[7] Watzlawick, **Human Communication.**

analogical expressions are less convenient for refinement and precision than digital expressions. Writings systems, mentioned previously, are excellent examples of this difference. A system of ideographs or 'picture writing'—such as Chinese characters —bears some resemblance in the shapes of many of its characters and the meaning of those characters. The character ⊔⊥ means "mountain" in Chinese or Japanese, and it is easy to see something mountain-like about that character. Spoken Chinese is completely different from spoken Japanese, but both use similar symbols (originally Chinese) and thus many of the same characters can be understood by people of both cultures. In contrast, languages which write in a phonetic alphabet use a digital form of writing, in which there is no necessary parallel between the writing system and the referent. (It was on this basis, apparently, that Marshall McLuhan speculated that different systems of writing will influence ways of thinking, since the symbol-referent relationship is strikingly different.)[8]

Learning analogical expressions is frequently easier and faster **initially** than learning the abstract form of digital expressions. But there is a catch, at least in the case of writing systems. To learn a set of ideographs, such as Chinese characters, means having to learn to write different "pictures" for every referent, often involving combinations of other characters to express abstract concepts and items not easily visualized. With a phonetic alphabet, even one as clumsy and inconsistent as English, once the abstract principles are grasped, progress is swift. Indeed, a person can learn to "read Spanish" in an hour or two, though of course he may not know what those words mean unless he also speaks the language. To learn to write Chinese or Japanese takes many times the effort, and unless one constantly is reading and writing he is apt to forget many of those characters.

What we have said about the digital and analogical in writing systems may apply in our consideration of nonverbal expressiveness in general. Spoken language, with the possible exception of some onomatopoeic words and, apparently, some underlying phonetic symbolism which has been shown to be similar across languages, is exclusively digital. Paralanguage—inflection, tone

[8] Marshall McLuhan, **Understanding Media; The Extensions of Man** (New York: McGraw-Hill, 1964), Chapter Eight.

of voice, volume, rate—seems to be a mixture of digital and analogical. There is no demonstrable analogy between a question and an upward inflection at the end of a sentence, for example, but we do sometimes s-t-r-e-t-c-h our words ("h-e-l-p!") to parallel our feelings at the time, and we are likely to say "I'm so tired" in a "tired voice" rather than in a "cheerful voice." But what about kinesic behavior, those meaningful movements of the hands and body posture and facial expressions? What of proxemic behavior? Does our physical distance in relation to others and to objects reveal an analogy to our attitudes toward them?

Watzlawick and his colleagues have written that while most speech is digitally expressive, nonverbal behavior is analogical.[9] Nonverbal signs may be far more analogical than speech, but it is quite apparent that nonverbal expressions are not pure analogies for their meanings. If gestures, interpersonal distance, touching behavior were purely analogical we should not find as many misunderstandings as we do. A somewhat more accurate view, for at least some nonverbal expressions, is that they are analogical if you know the basis of the analogy; but with a different logic, quite different analogical expressions can express the same meaning. A few examples should make this clear. In the United States, when a person wants to signal a friend to come, he usually gestures with one hand, fingers more or less together and pointed upwards, with his hand making a roughly clockwise motion. The analogy seems to be something of a pulling motion to draw the friend closer. In many other parts of the world, when someone wants to call a friend, he cups his hand, fingers pointed down, making a roughly counter-clockwise motion. The analogy is about the same, perhaps. However, an American seeing the latter gesture, without knowing its meaning, is likely to guess that the person is waving good-bye, instead of calling him to come. Counting on the fingers is another obvious example. Most Americans count by closing their fist and extending—for each number—one finger, beginning with the forefinger and concluding with the thumb. The analogy is obvious; hold up five fingers and it means **five.** In several other parts of the world, the process is

---

[9] Watzlawick, **Human Communication,** p. 62.

nearly reversed, though the analogical principle is the same. That is, counting begins with an open hand, with one finger drawn into the fist for each number to be counted. What looks like five in one system means 0 in the other, and vice versa. Here is another example: If you come from North America and you want to show how tall your little brother is, you are likely to hold your hand, palm down, parallel to the floor at about the level of the top of your brother's head; in much of Latin America, however, this gesture is fine for showing the height of an animal, but it is not used to show human height. For your little brother, you'd point one finger up in the air, as if testing the wind (or place your hand at the estimated height of your brother). These examples show culturally learned analogies or, if you prefer, digital variations on a basically analogical mode of expression.

Such examples can be added easily: Do you point with your finger, your chin, your lips? In indicating yourself, do you point to your chest, your mouth, your nose? In listening, does looking down show respect, embarrassment, or boredom? Each interpretation can be perfectly analogous to its "meaning," if the principle is known. But the point is that these principles or analogies must be learned, like anything else in a culture.

Saying that the underlying analogy must be learned does not mean that such learning is as difficult as learning a digital system, such as the spoken language of the culture, however. As we have mentioned, at the early stages it is usually much faster to learn analogies than abstracted expressions which give no clue as to their meaning. And despite the impressive potential of nonverbal expressions, the actual number of identifiable problematic nonverbal expressions may be far fewer than the number of words in a basic vocabulary.

One wonders, are some cultures "more analogical" than others? That's an awkwardly put question, but persons who have travelled widely have sometimes indicated that people in some lands were easier to understand in their gestures and movements than were others. The frequency of cultural similarity or dissimilarity must also be taken into account. But just as a good mime or dancer can convey his meanings over a wider range of cultural differences than a public lecturer can, perhaps some cultures are more "dance-like" and analogical while others are more "speech-like" or digital.

Certainly the analogical in a culture is richly woven into the fabric of rituals, and cultures differ markedly in value of ritual. In a religious service or a wedding rite, every movement, every color of clothing, nearly every aspect of behavior may be consciously symbolic of some deeper meaning. But what of day-to-day communication, what Goffman calls "interaction ritual"; might these be similarly expressive of analogies? If so, and if we can discover these, we will have made a great advance in understanding communication, particularly across cultures where we may not be able to easily learn the more complicated digital expressions of speech. We raise this as a possibility but with two warnings. First, the nature of analogy invites specious interpretations, projections of analogies that are consistent in themselves but irrelevant or totally incorrect according to the persons observed. Recall the examples cited at the beginning of this chapter.

A second caution concerns the desire to know the **origin** of a particular nonverbal expression. Perhaps because we expect to find easy analogies in so much nonverbal behavior we more often ask why people do things this way or that way but not so often why they **say** things one way or another. A visitor to the U.S. may ask, "Why, when a couple is walking along the street, does the lady walk on the inside and the man on the street side?" Your friendly American informant may recite a bit of folk-lore picked up from a Sunday magazine and explain something about how in the old days people used to throw garbage out of second story windows and how passing carriages used to splash mud from the street; thus the walking custom developed to protect the good lady from being splattered. Even if true, this story doesn't explain very much. It doesn't say what it means to a lady who finds herself on the inside, a matter more interesting and more relevant than the garbage theory of decorum. Or, if someone asks why "Western peoples" shake hands when greeting, he may be told about the days of swordsmen and how the extended right hand showed the visitor did not have a sword in his hand and was hence friendly. Why do Chinese and Japanese bow their heads before superiors? You may be told that this derives from an ancient courtesy of offering one's head to be chopped off if the superior so wished. These explanations of **why** cultural patterns of nonverbal behavior evolved are far less important, even if true, than the way they function in a society today. Worse, they distract from larger analogical systems of which they are likely to be a part (such as the symbolic expressions of deference toward a woman in some societies and the reverse in others, or whole patterns of vertically expressed humility reflecting hierarchical distinctions of which bowing is but one example). Finally, such questions posed in another culture are often only slightly disguised forms of ethnocentric attitudes, wanting to know why **they** act that way ("funny") instead of the way we act ("natural"). Sometimes persons asked such questions sense this implication and they resent it.

Nonverbal analogies to value orientations

It seems that most studies of nonverbal behavior across cultures have concentrated on the **form** of an expression—smiling, eye contact, distance—as this varies or is consistent in different societies. Perhaps a better approach would be to start with the values of a culture and then relate a variety of nonverbal forms to those values. So far as we know, there has been little systematic study following this approach, although many excellent scholars (including Hall, Birdwhistell, Glenn, Stewart) have occasionally cited specific nonverbal expressions as analogies to broader themes and patterns of organization within a society. There are risks in this approach, certainly, but sometimes this method yields a double advantage. Some understanding of the underlying cultural value orientations should help to make diverse forms of nonverbal behavior immediately more comprehensible, and conversely, sensing patterns of nonverbal expressiveness should give us clues to the underlying value orientations. There is a real danger of being caught up in a circle of reasoning, of course, but that is no more a risk than that of studying language and culture relationships. We will attempt to explain this idea through illustrations based on a few of the value orientations described in the previous chapter.

Activity orientations

Assuming we can at least distinguish cultures which tend to value **doing** from those which value **being** or **being-in-becoming,** can we find nonverbal expressions which mirror these orientations? One likely parallel is in a culture's symbolization of time in the sense that Hall spoke of time: as one of the "silent languages" that has implicit meanings which vary across cultures. As he and many others have observed, what is "on time" in one society may be "early" or "late" in others. An invitation to a Latin American dinner party that reads eight o'clock may mean for the guests to arrive anywhere from 8:30 up to ten or eleven at night—and still be "on time." If the Mexican plumber says he will come **mañana** that may or may not mean tomorrow. It may be that the dominant activity orientation in Latin America as a whole is likely to be one of **being.** The dominant activity orientation in North America is still, apparently, one of **doing,** and for the **do-er** "time is money" or at any rate something that influences doing. Precision, punctuality, scheduling are important. Such attitudes toward time may be reflections of this orientation more than most others, even more than the temporal orientations of valuing the past, present, or future.

The meaning of "silence" is another possible correlate of activity values. It was Clifford Clarke, Foreign Student Advisor at Stanford University, who observed from his many discussions with foreign students at Stanford and Cornell and in intercultural communication workshops that persons from identifiably **doing**-oriented societies tend to regard silence as an absence of words, a waste of time, a period when "nothing is doing."[10] For those who can be characterized as of the being or being-in-becoming mode, silence in conversations has a positive meaning: It is essential to self-fulfillment and to an awareness of the here and now.

What, then, about clothing in cultures characterized by individualism and individuality? The United States, we have said, is generally of the former kind. Certainly in the U.S. there exists a great variety of clothing styles, but these are relatively consistent

[10] Clifford Clarke, personal correspondence.

within groupings by age and by subculture. Fashions vary, of course, and a degree of future orientation makes many alert to the new fashions: one must not look old-fashioned unless the old-fashioned look is again new fashion. In the United States any person is free to buy any kind of clothing, a point that is more surprising than it may seem unless one is familiar with social pressures in other societies which severely limit dress. And yet within that freedom most Americans tend to buy what others are buying. The "hippie style" of the late sixties and seventies broke the pattern by consciously seeking individualistic choices in clothing and hair-styles, but this soon became standard hippie attire, with companies even manufacturing "used clothes." The youth orientation influences dress in the United States, with younger persons' fashions influencing those of adults. Values of sex equality led to "uni-sex" clothing styles.

Individualism, individuality, and group-identification

We cited Japan as a model of a culture based on group-centered identification. Japan is also notorious for its uniformity in clothing: The stereotyped **salariman** (businessman) wears a dark suit, dark tie, shiny black shoes, and company lapel pin. Japanese tourists baffle their foreign hosts with their uniformity in dress, buying habits, and, of course, group spirit, which is always that of doing everything together in the same way.

Clothing is an interesting subject here, for clothing may not only identify some values of a group, it may also help to shape those values. Any person who has had to wear a uniform (in the military, the clergy, scouts, and so on) may recall that the uniform itself helped to influence his behavior at the time. He was identified as one of the group and thus discouraged individualistic behaviors that might be "out of line."

Formalism if not formality, is, of course, a part of this pattern. A Japanese person is more likely to judge another person, foreigner or another Japanese, by his dress than might persons from many other cultures. At a recent meeting of U.S. and Japanese businessmen, where the Americans were attempting to sell real estate to Japanese developers, the overall deportment of the Americans was disconcerting; the back-slapping first-name style of the U.S. team startled the Japanese hosts. But more important, it seemed, was the clothing: bright suits and white buck shoes. "Not one man has dressed here in a manner which inspired confidence," a Japanese electronics executive complained. A similar reaction was reported among some older Japanese people living in Hawaii at the end of the Second World War. In seeing the front-page picture of MacArthur and the Japanese Emperor, some who could not read the English were convinced that Japan had won the war. The reason was that the Emperor appeared in his dignified morning coat, striped trousers and tails, while MacArthur stood, arms akimbo, in the rough military khaki.[11]

Respect

Recognition of valued status differences is expressed nonverbally as often as it is in words of respect. As in other cases, the analogical principle must be understood before making interpretations, but once recognized the nonverbal offers ample evidence of the importance and nature of status differentiation. Where many persons speak, the order of speaking is a frequent indicator: though in some societies the most important person speaks first, in others he speaks last; in some situations the most important may remain silent as an indication of his power, while in others only those of sufficiently high status do the talking. Seating order, too, often marks status: the guest of honor may have a special chair or stool or occupy a recognized position in the room. Height, of course, is another common indicator, one that often appears in verbal metaphors ("your highness," or "the top executive," or the Supreme court). Eye contact is more complicated, though no less analogical; one may look down to show respect—a widespread and clearly analogical gesture, but also a speaker of considerable status may avoid looking at the other to imply, equally analogical, "looking down on him." While hand-shaking may allow some analogical interpretation (firmness of grip, energy and length of the shake, for example), bowing is more visibly analogical. Where bowing—a loose term—is customary, as it is in many parts of the world, usually the lower

---

[11] Mitsuko Saito, personal correspondence.

the bow the greater the respect. Thus at least as much about status relationships between two persons can be conveyed to onlookers as to the parties themselves. Where "equality" is to be symbolized in the bow, the maneuver can be most difficult, each trying to bob up and down at approximately the same time and to the same degree, finishing their performance in unison.

Other probes

Over the years, many writers have suggested some provocative analogies between nonverbal elements of a culture and under-lying values, patterns of social organization and ways of think-ing. Edmund Glenn has offered as indicators of thinking patterns, the organization of trains and subway routes in Paris and U.S. cities.[12] Edward Stewart in a similar vein has compared the placement of signs warning of highway construction in different cultures; whether the sign appears at the point of construction or sufficiently in advance in order to divert traffic reflects, he believes, other patterns of thinking in a culture.[13] Driving cus-toms—including who honks at whom and why, reactions to stop signs, for example—may be appropriate indications of more traditional values and patterns of social relationships. McLuhan, as mentioned previously, sees in the writing system (ideographic or phonetic) **influences**—and not just parallels—in thinking patterns, too. We might go even further to speculate whether cultures with ideographical symbolization retain a greater over-all pattern of analogical symbolization than do societies which use a phonetic alphabet, though there are probably too few ideographic systems available to make much of a comparison.

Housing, in the design and utilization of space, is another sub-ject where the nonverbal and other aspects of culture and commu-nication quite literally come together. Hall has explored this, as have a number of other writers on architecture and design.[14] We will approach the subject in a somewhat different way in the following chapter.

[12] Edmund S. Glenn, "Semantic Difficulties in International Communication" **Etc.** 11 (1954): 163–80.
[13] Stewart, **American Patterns,** p. 17.
[14] Edward T. Hall, **The Hidden Dimension** (New York: Doubleday, 1966).

Where the analogy breaks down

Our distinction between the digital and the analogical marks a difference in the contemporary approaches to nonverbal communication. While we have given more attention to the analogical, the trend in nonverbal studies is in the other direction: studying selected nonverbal behaviors as languages in themselves, systematic, learned and not "natural," and presumably with a kind of vocabulary and grammar. The study of nonverbal behavior, much like its initial perception, can go only so far by following an analogical method. Whether a person engaged in communication in another society must learn new nonverbal behaviors as languages is, of course, another matter.

Hall's widely known work in proxemics is a good example of a mostly digitally based approach. Like other innovators in the field of nonverbal behavior, Hall developed his own methodology, his own terminology, and his own set of symbols for describing proxemic behavior.[15] Although the describing of distances and body orientations of any two people conversing is difficult and time-consuming, it can be done and results can be compared. One wonders, however, if it might be possible to anticipate relations between proxemic behavior and other cultural patterns of communication before completing detailed proxemic descriptions of many different societies. For example, are there likely to be some common value orientations among cultures which are characterized by relatively frequent physical contact (touching, hugging, kissing)? Do relatively noncontact cultures reveal different value orientations? Or is there no more connection between values and such modes of nonverbal expression than there is, for example, between values and the sound system of the language spoken in any given culture? An analogical approach would lead us to seek out such connections, but probably most scholars would ask us to wait until more data has been collected. And that means a long wait. Perhaps the best we can do at this point is to warn of the risks of pushing analogies too far and point out that many codes of nonverbal interaction cannot be treated adequately by analogies to other forms of behavior.

[15] Edward T. Hall, "A System for the Notation of Proxemic Behavior," **American Anthropologist,** 65 (1963): 1003–1026.

Taboos

What is tabooed—or at least just not done—occupies a sub-
stantial portion of the literature on nonverbal behavior and
popular descriptions of cultures. The reasons for this interest
seem obvious enough, but we should not make too much of the
subject. It would be helpful if we could anticipate tabooed behavior from an understanding of broader values and assumptions
about reality, language, and other patterns of nonverbal behavior,
but this appears to be difficult. Why, for example, is belching
after dinner rude in much of the world but regarded as the sin-
cerest compliment to the cook in others (such as in China)? Is
this the sort of thing we must just learn, or can we interpret it
from other information? Why do U.S. kids love to pull the col-
lapsed bubble of their bubble-gum off their faces and stuff it
back into their mouths, while such an action turns the stomach
of a proper Brazilian? Why is showing the sole of the shoe or foot
so offensive in Moslem cultures, when it is not in others—
including those in which the foot is regarded as dirty and the
removal of shoes is required at the door?

The most frequent sources of taboos—bodily functions, sex,
death, and often money—may be anticipated but mostly in terms
too general to be very helpful. Moreover, as we are trying to show
throughout this book, "misbehaving" in another culture is likely
to occur in many ways quite apart from the specifically pro-
scribed behaviors identified as **taboo.** Failing to see a guest to the
door, for example, can weaken a relationship more than can
belching after dinner, even though we do not call the former
indiscretion a **taboo.**

There is much more to intercultural communication than
learning to do all the **do's** while avoiding all the **don'ts.** We remain convinced that culturally influenced patterns of communication are, for the most part, comprehensible, systematic, and,
within limits, adaptable by persons from outside of the culture.

The unadaptable

In some ways much nonverbal behavior seems much easier to
learn than another spoken language. Statistics, which mostly are
based on estimates, about the range of nonverbal behaviors may

impress us ("The human body is capable of over 270,000 discrete gestures, a range of variations which may be greater than the range of possible sounds")[16] but practically speaking, it probably takes more training just to get by in a foreign language than it takes to get by nonverbally. If nothing else we seem to have higher standards for "getting by" in speaking than we do for gesturing. However, as we mentioned earlier, there are some characteristics of nonverbal behavior which can lead to more difficulties in adaptation than we find in speech. The matter of awareness alone is important, and the depth of our nonverbal reactions—perspiration, heart-beat, and so on—is still more important. But even assuming that these can be accommodated, there are some possible problems that seem unavoidable. And there are some aspects of nonverbal communication that seem to defy adaptation.

One is the matter of personal, physical appearance. Of course not everybody in a culture looks alike, though visitors sometimes may say so, but there may be racial or ethnic features which sharply distinguish the native from the outsider. These features are related to physiognomy, not to ways of walking or smiling. They may seem relatively minor to the visitor (he has curly hair while the local people all have straight hair) or they may be more apparent (a white man in a black society or vice versa). In any case, it is obviously more difficult to change physical appearance (skin pigmentation, height, weight, overall build) than it is to change behavior. And often a visitor is made aware of standing out in unsubtle ways, when, for example, people stare or touch (they touch children's hair, especially).

The reason and attitude that prompts the special treatment, no less than the reaction of the stranger observed, makes a difference. A friend from East Africa who has been with his embassy both in England and Japan describes such a difference. "In a London pub, I've had people come up and rub my skin to see if the 'black' came off! They were very direct about it and we joked and I bought them drinks. In Japan nobody has done that, but they stare and that's worse; I can only guess what they are thinking."

If one has ever traveled in a society where he was shorter or

---

[16] Abne Eisenberg and Ralph R. Smith, **Nonverbal Communication** (Indianapolis: Bobbs-Merrill, 1971), pp. 31–37.

taller or fatter than everybody else, he knows the feeling of being different and not being able to do anything about it. Members of "minority groups" in the United States know that feeling, but they may have some advantage—if it can be called that—in sensing how the others feel and think. In a totally different culture, particularly where a visitor is awkward with the language and ill at ease in some other ways, the ambiguity can be oppressive.

There is a fairly extensive vocabulary for describing reactions to perceptions of differentness: prejudice, stereotyped thinking, ethnocentrism, xenophobia, and more. These are all judgmental terms based on a notion of acceptance of others as equals and other characteristic American values which tend to minimize differences. But being perceived as different is neither bad nor good: it is a simple phenomenon that often occurs in intercultural encounters, and one that cannot always be adapted to (without trying to change the whole society).

To what extent perceived or apperceived differences in appearance affect other aspects of a particular discussion between persons from different cultures is difficult to know. Familiar surveys, such as social-distance scales which indicate how people in X group feel about people in Y group, give us some clues but only in general and in the abstract. We know that people can have attitudes about an ethnic group that doesn't even exist. When real people get together the results may be somewhat different from what the social distance scores would predict about the two groups as categories.

More adaptable and yet more subtle are matters of behavior that may seem essential for the person of one culture but are interpretable in other ways by persons in another culture. The U.S. Peace Corps volunteer, for example, is usually provided with a medical kit and reading materials and often with some means of transportation or other equipment with which to do his job. Some have been given portable refrigerators (an early list of perquisites for Tanzanian volunteers, though never followed, included napkin rings!), and many have "practical clothing" of the "drip-dry" variety. At least some of these items can be justified as essential to maintain a sound mind in a sound body of the volunteer. But to the people with whom he or she works, some of these may symbolize something quite different:

wealth, power, outsider status. Indeed, the very presence of the volunteer may be defined differently, with the volunteer seeing this as "service," self-giving if not exactly self-sacrifice, while those in the host nation take more of a bemused attitude about his presence. Of course, the Peace Corps as an organization and, we assume, most volunteers are aware of all of this, but that awareness may not mean that anything can be done about the discrepant perceptions. Volunteer service organizations of other kinds and from other nations, and international exchange programs are not very different in this respect. Missionaries, in recent years, have come to be more aware of the problem, but often missionary work brings even more obvious contradictions. (For one of the strongest criticisms by a most innovative and experienced cross-cultural trainer, read Ivan Illich's "The Seamy Side of Charity"[17] and other essays in **The Celebration of Awareness.** While not all of these reactions are about the nonverbal, many are, such as the reactions to clothes, equipment, housing.

Health precautions are another example of this problem. For many reasons a foreigner may be less capable of coping with illness in the new culture than are the local people. (In many cases, however, the local people suffer as well but may be unable to do anything about their health problems.) A foreign visitor in a locale where there are dangers of dysentery or other such diseases may bring with him many bottles of medicine to stave off or cure such diseases. He may have been warned not to drink unboiled water, or not to eat uncooked vegetables, or not to eat food served on the street, but if he is to participate in the culture he will face a dilemma: Decline the offers of food, and insult the host, or eat what he is served and run the risk of debilitating illness. (Trying to be subtle doesn't always work either; a friend who was a U.S. Peace Corps volunteer in a tropical nation attended a village feast shortly after arriving. He was suspicious about the water served and thus secretly dropped two halazone tablets into his glass. Almost immediately the other guests were astonished to see his glass of water turn bright red. He was embarrassed, the guests were puzzled, and the host quickly threw out that bad water and brought back a fresh glassful.) The very

[17] Ivan Illich, **The Celebration of Awareness** (Garden City, N. J.: Doubleday-Anchor, 1971).

presence of quantities of medicines, much like carrying around foods from home or always avoiding local restaurants and preferring those in the tourist hotels because they seem "safer" are often symptoms of cultural discomfort, a matter which goes far beyond nonverbal behavior. But from the point of view of others looking on, this is nonverbal behavior which communicates quite a bit about this visitor and about his apparent feelings about the land to which he has come. Excuses, apologies, and explanations may not erase the impression.

Looking ahead

In our discussion of some aspects of nonverbal behavior across cultures we have given very little advice about how one might adapt his nonverbal behavior. While noting that some kinds of behavior may be beyond our conscious control, even if within our conscious awareness, we should not conclude with an impression that most nonverbal behavior is unadaptable. However, rather than offer advice at this point, we prefer to wait until the last chapter of this book, after having discussed language and patterns of argumentation and rhetoric. Across cultures, just as within a society, it is important to appreciate the place of nonverbal behavior in the larger context of communication, rather than treating it as a separate, though important and fascinating, mode of communication. To repeat a point made earlier in this chapter, there currently seems to be a temptation to put the burden of communication across cultures on the nonverbal, in part to compensate for having ignored the subject matter for so long and in part, perhaps, because the field is so rich in dramatic illustrations.

When we have a broader view of communication, however, we may be able, also, to locate, more realistically, a place for what we now isolate as nonverbal. We can anticipate that some of the concerns introduced in this chapter may receive a low priority, while others may disappear entirely.

SEVEN

Out of house and home

Although we designate food, clothing, and shelter as life's "necessities," across cultures we find extraordinary variety in each of these categories. So much variety, in fact, that what makes the mouth water in one culture turns the stomach in another; the variation in dress, even within what might be considered a single culture over a relatively short period of time, hardly needs to be mentioned. Housing, too, offers considerable variety even within a single culture, and it may be that people fantasize about their "dream home" even more than they do about food or clothing. The number of popular and folk songs which recall or idealize home is extensive. What should be obvious is that the symbolic values of these three far outweigh their survival functions for most persons. What is less obvious and more intriguing is the extent to which such "necessities" reflect and influence cultural patterns of communication.

In some societies dietary customs have been credited with reflecting and promoting more basic values: spokesmen for vegetarian societies, for example, have often contrasted their values with those of the aggressive, predatory meat-eating peoples.[1] The influence of clothing on lifestyle and outlook is also a frequent source of conscious cultural distinction; Charles Reich's paean to bell-bottom trousers in **The Greening of America** is one of the more recent, as he claims it is impossible to take yourself too seriously while wearing that fashion.[2] (He overlooks the long tradition of bell-bottom trousers in the navy.) In this chapter we will concentrate on the possible influence on patterns of communication of house structure and its use by a family.

"First we shape our buildings and then they shape us," Churchill observed, and it is in this spirit that we approach the subject. Our parents and those who lived before we were born helped shape the home into which we were born, and to some extent that home has influenced us. The same can be said for the language we are "born into" or for any aspect of our culture, of course. But homes are both more personal (each home being notably different, to members of the same culture) and more subtly influential.

Before beginning our brief discussion of house and home styles in several different societies, we must acknowledge the fact that these are described in general terms and without any effort to be comprehensive about any one of them. It is also true that homes in some societies are easier to generalize about than those in others, simply because of greater cultural homogeneity and a relative lack of economic, social, or regional variations. We have tried to limit our observations on house and home styles to a few characteristics that seem to be especially revealing of cultural values and related patterns of communication.

We are indebted to Dr. Ben Goodwin, and Professor Leland Roloff for developing the first of these themes in the American context.[3] Over a period of many years, Goodwin, a psychiatrist in Dallas, Texas, found patterns of behavior in his patients which

[1] A recent expression of this appeared in a letter to **Time** (September 24, 1973), from Shigeo Tahara of Osaka, Japan. He wrote that there was a marked difference between Americans and Japanese in the face of rising meat prices in each country. ". . . Americans are protecting cows and shops with firearms and are experiencing violence and burglary. Here in Japan, prices are skyrocketing faster than in the U.S., but people are still quiet. Meat-eating people seem to get hot more easily than vegetarians. Meat seems to give people an irresistible urge for action."

[2] Charles Reich, **The Greening of America** (New York: Random House, 1970), pp. 235–39.

[3] Leland Roloff, personal correspondence; we express appreciation to Dr. Goodwin for his concept, though interpretations and application here are original.

seemed to be consistent with home styles; the source of such data and the need to generalize into some kind of composite house/home styles should caution us, but the concept of the approach seems valid.

Two styles of homes in the United States

The authority-centered home. In this home there is some "authority" which serves as a standard by which most or many important matters are judged. The authority may be a person, father or grandfather, or it may be a religion or a religious book, such as the Bible. It may be education or some symbol of that, such as a weighty set of **The Great Books.** It might be the family business or the family name. But there is a sense of a fixed authority, a core, around which communication is centered. (Note that this need not be an **authoritarian** home.) While this home is described as one type of American home, arising from Goodwin's observations, it shares much in common with many European homes. Comparisons with a German home will be described later.

In this home there is very often a clear distinction between family areas of the home and guest areas; typically there is a livingroom or parlor where guests are received and entertained, and this room is ordinarily not used by family members. In this room are displayed the treasures of the home: antiques, heirlooms, a portrait, perhaps, and the most sacred and salient symbols of the family.

Ideally in this home the family dines together. Children are expected to be present for dinner, and it is at dinner that the children are socialized into the family and its values. Conversation proceeds typically in a question and answer form, the parents asking the questions, the children supplying the answers: "What did you learn at school today? You came home at 4:30, but school is out at 3:15; where did you go after school! Have you started on your homework yet? Did you do the chores?" The children give the answers. Goodwin notes that among his patients who come from such a background there is often tension associated with eating.[4]

---

[4] Ibid.

There are to be no secrets in this family; anything and every-thing of importance is to be discussed within the home. Mother or father feel free to check on the children's reading materials, and to open and read letters received by the children, and to approve or censor what is found. That which takes place outside of the home, away from the eyes and ears of the parents, is suspect. The house has doors and the doors have locks, but one must not go into a room and lock the door: "What are you doing in there? Why did you close the door? You don't have to close the door; if we're making too much noise for you to study we will be quiet. Open the door."

For these reasons, the bathroom becomes an important room for intrapersonal communication—for being alone and "think-ing" or even talking out loud. The bathroom (and toilet) is the only place where one can be alone without arousing suspicion, and the bathroom provides the added advantage of a mirror for "mirror talk" while shaving or putting on make-up.

The kitchen is often a setting for "negotiation" between chil-dren and their mother, particularly when it is necessary to talk father into something. As many questions and problems and requests by children are likely to be answered by, "ask your father" or "ask your mother," and as mother is more accessible physically and psychologically than father, mother's area in the kitchen is extremely important. (It is interesting that in a study of word values conducted independently, the word "kitchen" was found to rank among the most highly valued words by Americans.)

The parents' bedroom is a setting for **little intimate communi-cation.** Largely off-limits to the children and often symbolically divided between mother's and father's areas (separate closets or wardrobes, often with mother's "little shrine of perfumes," as Roloff describes it, and father's tie rack, comb and brush set) even the sides of the bed (or twin beds) also limit communication between the parents. (In the bathroom, "His" and "Hers" towels may reflect the division.)

Outside of the home, the best place for the children to be—from the parents' point of view—is the school. There the parents assume that control is maintained, and, moreover, competitive values are sharpened. Competition is regarded as essential to the development of character and appears to influence even patterns of speech (such as a reference for ranking evaluations, as we will mention in Chapter Ten).

There is more to be said about this kind of home, but this may be sufficient to contrast this authority-centered home with another style, the social-centered home.

The social-centered home. The social-centered home is embued with an air of social activity, and the entire home is prepared for sociality. In contrast to the authority-centered home, where the parents have clear authority over their children, in the social-centered home the parents often act as assistants to their children's social interests: "Would you like to have a party this week? I will help you plan some games, and Dad can bring the other children here in the car if you like."

There is a great informality about the home, so that there are no clearly marked divisions between "family" and "company" areas. A guest is as likely to be invited to the kitchen as to the livingroom. Movement within the house is free and casual, so that almost no room is likely to be more of a center for communication than any other. In sharp contrast to the authority-centered home, the family is not likely to take meals together: The very social activities may prevent everybody from being home at the same time. The kitchen sometimes resembles a central information exchange, with messages substituting for conversation: **"Johnny—sorry, but I have to go to a meeting—there are leftovers in the refrigerator, fix yourself something for supper. Dad has bowling tonight. Mom." "Mom: Peter came home with me and we made sandwiches. We have play rehearsal tonight. See you about 9:30. Johnny. P.S. Betty called and said she will be home late."**

Along with such activities as scouts, community projects, sports, and music lessons, party-going and dating is urged upon the children at an early age. And one of the significant results of all this socializing is that serious conversations are more likely to take place away from home than within the home. Thus, Goodwin notes, when persons from such home backgrounds marry, they often find it difficult to talk to each other at home! They are so accustomed to going out to parties, dances, and dinners where they are with other people, that the two alone in a home are not prepared for significant conversations. And so they may continue the pattern of socialization very soon after marriage, inviting friends over and going out to parties. A wife may receive some important information second-hand, overhearing her husband saying something to a friend before she herself is told: **"Mat, I heard you telling Mrs. Bensen that you thought we might go to Mexico this summer. You didn't tell me that before." "Didn't I? Oh, I guess I didn't—well, what do you think of the idea?"**

Although both of these **models,** oversimplified and stated very briefly, might characterize American homes, there are clearly different values reflected in each: The authority-centered home seems more traditional and may be associated with older, established families. The social-centered home seems much more typical of the dominant surburban middle class. (Those who have read Reich's **Greening of America** may identify the former with his "Consciousness I," the latter with the values of his "Consciousness II.")[5] The social-centered home is particularly characteristic of those values most associated with American culture: informality, openness, constant busyness, "other-directed," and what some critics might call "superficiality" or fragmentation.

It is no accident that the social-centered home flourishes in a consumer society such as the U.S., with billions of dollars spent on home furnishings and leisure activities (including what is surely the largest producer of 'games' of all kinds). The social-centered home is likely to be in a constant state of rearrangement, and every change becomes the subject of display for visitors. For this reason, too, the kitchen (which is likely to be the most expensive room in the house, with all of the gadgets and luxury utensils) is a more interesting and information-filled room than any other.

Many visitors to the United States are invited to homes as part of any number of "people-to-people" programs, and the kind of homes they are most likely to visit are those of the social-centered type (since inviting foreign visitors is yet one more social activity and an excellent expression of this concept of a home). For many visitors such a home is in startling contrast to their own homes.

[5] Charles Reich, **Greening of America.**

For many of these guests, the visit is likely to be startling, discomfitting. American norms of informality and blurring of host-guest relationships are unique in the world: "Make yourself at home," Americans say, and as this is a most peculiar home, it may be very difficult for a guest to feel at home. To be invited to the kitchen, even to be invited to help prepare a meal or to fix a drink, even to answer the door and invite others inside **("tell whoever it is to come in, and introduce yourself—I'll be out in a few minutes")**.

Similarly, the American abroad is likely to be surprised—sometimes delighted, sometimes disappointed—when he finds that his house and home values and behavior are not appropriate. He may never be invited to a home in the first place, and this he may interpret as unfriendliness. Or if invited, he may be treated so much as a guest that he feels uncomfortable about all of the special attention he is getting. He is afraid that he is causing his hosts too much trouble for he would never go to such trouble for his guests. He is likely to be curious about the house, particularly if he is a first-time visitor in the country, and he may ask if he can see the kitchen and sleeping rooms. But in some countries this is like a visitor arriving at an American home and asking if he could inspect the toilet.

Probably the ideal home for most Americans is one which is occupied by only one nuclear family and one in which each member of the family has his own private room. (Recently there has been a reaction against this norm by some younger members of the society in the so-called "counterculture" who value community living, but even within most of these communes, the members join voluntarily and tend to be of about the same age and with very similar outlooks toward life. Few communes will contain three or even two generations, and in this sense even the counterculture is still an extension of many of the dominant American values.)

In many societies, however, the concept of a family is not restricted to parents and children; grandparents, in-laws, uncles and aunts all may be considered when one thinks of a family. And the home may include many such relations. In Africa it is a common problem for young people who have come from the countryside to find work in the city to soon be visited by other members of their family, who simply move in on them. House complexes, if not a single house, are very likely to accommodate a very large number of family members. And within a home, the divisions and organization of space is likely to be very different.

The Swahili home

A common style of home in the coastal cities of Tanzania is what is sometimes called **the Swahili house.** To the outsider, the house looks like a small single-family dwelling, rectangular in shape with a single door in the middle of the front of the house. When one enters the door, however, he looks down a long hallway often with three doors opening on each side of that corridor. In each of these six rooms, usually, there is a family; as many as six families, often from fifteen to twenty-five people, living in this single house. At the rear of the home is a common area for cooking, and another area for a toilet and possibly a place for bathing as well.

The six families may or may not be related, may or may not even be from the same tribe and thus within the house there may be several different languages spoken. Obviously the values of privacy, community, and many other related values are very different for persons growing up in a Swahili house than for those growing up in a suburban American home. We might assume that this Swahili home is a product of a low standard of living, a point in the socioeconomic process leading to single-family homes. But such an interpretation is clearly biased by values of individuality, privacy, contractual friendships and the like. The Swahili home bears resemblance to many living patterns in the country where all aspects of life are shared among neighbors and members of the extended family.

The socialist program of President Julius Nyerere (**"Ujamaa"** —literally "familyness") is built upon these values which are reflected and reinforced in such living styles. In this case it is possible to extend the influence of home style even to political systems for an entire nation. Nyerere sometimes quotes the Swahili proverb, **Mgeni siku mbili; siku ya tatu mpe jembe,** which means you should treat a guest as a guest for two days, but on the third day, give him a hoe, so he can work like one of the family. Sharing a home, sharing work and problems, and sharing in celebrations and in the simple pleasures of life are all related. Mother rarely prepares her meal alone; she is almost always cooking with the other mothers. The men, who keep away from the women's territory, may sit outside of the home and talk and watch the people pass by the house. Social organizations, community dances, and other such functions are similarly communal and divided among ages and sexes but not usually among individual family units.

Neighboring houses, too, are extensions of the principle. If there is a thief or a fire or a wedding or a baby born, everybody in the neighborhood feels obliged to assist in any way possible. And if a visitor comes, the host is sure to take the visitor around the neighborhood to meet the neighbors just as he would introduce members of his own family. To fail to do so would be impolite. Or worse, if a family remained unto themselves they might not receive the help from the community when problems arose.

Much of this description from East Africa is quite similar to what would be described in traditional communities in most of the world. There are unique patterns to each society, but the spirit of community, of sharing, of a lack of private property and privacy appear throughout the world as the rule rather than as the exception.

The Japanese home

With the exception of some apartments and very small living quarters, most "Western homes" clearly distinguish between a living room, a dining room, and a bedroom. Each is characterized by its own furniture. In the traditional Japanese home, however, a single room can serve all three of these functions, and thus it is sometimes difficult to speak of the bedroom or the dining room, for it may depend more on the hour of the day than the areas themselves. One reason this is possible is that traditionally very little furniture is used in the home; there are no beds as such, for example, but instead **futon** (thick sleeping mats with a comforter-like top) are spread out when it is time to sleep, and folded up and put into special closets when not being used;

cushions rather than chairs are used for sitting, and these, too, are easily moved or removed as required. Where Western homes may have several tables (a coffee table, a dining table, study table) a single low table may serve several of these purposes and may also be put out of the way when it is time for the **futon** to be spread. The lightness and airiness, and the sense of space characteristic of Japanese aesthetics is thus expressed in the practical day-to-day living. Moreover, the doors which separate most rooms are also lightweight sliding doors which thus can be removed entirely when necessary, unlike the fixed, hinged Western doors; and therefore a room may be made to seem larger or smaller as needed by closing or removing these doors.

These sliding doors (both the thicker, elegant **fusuma** and the translucent, thin **shoji**) have no locks. One cannot go into his own room and lock the door. The sliding glass doors and windows which open out onto the garden or street do have locks and there is also an additional set of wooden doors (**amado** or "rain doors"), which completely block out all vision. These, too, are always closed and locked at night.

Although we cannot prove any cause or even significant correlations between home structure and cultural patterns of communication, we would expect less individualism within the Japanese home, and a stronger separation of the home from the outside than would be true in "the West." And, of course, this is exactly what is usually said about Japanese culture.

This aspect of home structure seems very consistent with contrasting values of Japanese and "Western peoples." That is, the family as a whole, rather than the individual, is highly valued in Japan. As the action of any one member of the family reflects on the entire family, individual choices and decisions must be made with great care and after considerable discussion within the family. Moreover, several scholars have noted that there is no word for "privacy" in Japan, at least not in the sense that we can speak of a **private room** or a **private car.** And while Americans are likely to speak of "**my** house," Tanzanians (and many others with similar related values) will always say "**our** house;" in Japanese it is the word for house itself (**"uchi"**) which serves as the pronoun for possession: **uchi no kuruma,** for example, meaning "our car" (or "my car") literally translates as "the house's car."

Although it is impossible to treat all of the characteristics of homes in any culture in so short a discussion as this, it might be worth considering a few other characteristics of the traditional Japanese home style, for in many ways it provides a striking contrast with Western homes.

Bath and toilet. In Japan, the bathing area and the toilet are always in separate rooms (except in some Western-style hotels or apartments); the American euphemism "bathroom," meaning toilet, is thus very confusing to Japanese who take care to distinguish the two as the clean place and the dirty place. In the past, and to a great extent today even in Tokyo there is no large hot-water tank to provide hot running water. Thus in the evening when it is time for a bath, the **ofuro** or Japanese bathtub is filled with cold water, and a small stove is lit which heats the water. Preparing for a bath at home thus requires as much as an hour just heating the water.

Unlike Western bathing, the Japanese style is to do all of the soaping and scrubbing and rinsing outside of the tub; the tub itself is for soaking and relaxing. In this way the same bath water can serve the entire family. (Perhaps the Western counterpart is taking a shower before entering a public swimming pool.) We mention these details not because bathing customs are interesting in themselves, but because even in the bath the individualistic versus family orientation is clearly reflected. An entire family may bathe together, and it is very common for mothers to bathe with their children or for older children to bathe together.

When family members bathe in sequence in Japan, the traditional order of bathing also reflects and reinforces the authority structure of the home. The most important person, father, bathes first. The water is of course hottest and cleanest for the first person who bathes, and thus the order of the bath also reflects cultural values. In Japan the traditional pattern was quite simple: father bathed first because he was the most important person; then the older sons bathed, with the children and wife being the last.

Values are further reinforced by that shared hot water. If one should be the first to bathe and find the water too hot, it is improper to add cold water to lower the temperature, for this makes the water still colder for the next person who may prefer it even hotter. The bathing pattern thus also reinforces in such a subtle way values of group-consciousness, conformity, acceptance of what is provided. No claim is made that cultural values arise from such routines as bathing, but neither are they separable. To some extent for the child growing up, cultural values are introduced in such ways.

While bathing is generally regarded as relaxing and refreshing in the West, there are also those children who avoid taking baths whenever possible ("Do I have to? I took a bath last night."). This attitude is not found in Japan where the bath is consistently associated with relaxation and family ties, rather than the "hurry up I'm waiting to take a bath" attitude sometimes felt in Western families. (The English musical review of several years ago, **At the Drop of a Hat,** by Michael Flanders and Donald Swann, contained a delightful song called "In the Bath." The song extolled the pleasures of bathing and concluded by encouraging all of the political leaders in the world to get together in a bathtub, for this was surely the best of all places to be friendly—and agreeable. Something of that attitude is characteristic of Japan, not so much within a home as at the thousands of bathing spas throughout the country which are favorite meeting places for friends and social groups.) One American girl recently married to a Japanese man confided: "Whenever my husband and I get into a fight, we always find it easiest to make up in the bath. It is impossible to be angry in the bath."

At home and away. It is very unusual to telephone a Japanese home and receive no answer. Somebody is always at home it seems; it is still very rare for a wife to work. **("Okusan,"** the polite word used when referring to any mature woman except one related to the speaker, means literally "deep in the middle of the home," the traditionally valued place for a woman.) And when the wife must go shopping or take a child to school, her mother-in-law, who is likely to live in the home, will answer the telephone. And if there is no mother-in-law in the home, then things may be arranged so that the house is occupied by somebody else.

So near, so far. The Japanese language contains many expressions for organizations of houses. One has obligations toward the neighbors which date back centuries. During the Second World War, this pattern was applied by the military government to make a whole neighborhood of ten houses culpable for the criminal act of any member of any of the homes. The positive virtues of neighborliness remain (except in the tall, grim apartment buildings of large cities) in forms such as offering service on special occasions (such as weddings) or giving gifts to families returning from a vacation. The traditional patterns of obligations extend to neighbors on either side of the house plus the neighbor across the street.

This relationship is similar to the East African pattern in its sense of obligations to neighbors. It differs sharply, however, in the individual's view of his own home, which is far more private in Japan than in any of the other homes described here. For a visitor, even a neighbor, to be invited into a Japanese home brings with it even more obligations: serving tea, food, the obligation of a return visit, and probably gift exchanges as well. Therefore the inside of one's house is regarded as very different from the outside. Again the language reveals the importance of this distinction: **uchi no** (literally means "the house's," but it is used to mean "our") affairs, business, problems, is contrasted with **soto** (literally, "outside," but covering everything else that is not **ours**). Nearly everything in Japan, it seems, from problems to friends, is distinguished in this way.

All of these observations may help to explain the puzzlement felt by foreign visitors in Japan when they find they are treated with generosity and kindness but almost never are allowed to feel "at home." Emotionally and quite literally they must always be **yoso no hito,** "people outside our house."

The Middle Eastern home

The nature of social interaction in the Middle East is reflected in the structure of the average home in the area. In urban or rural settings, a room is usually set aside for receiving and entertaining guests. That room is the pride of the family. Valued heirlooms, pictures of the dear, living or dead, and cherished souvenirs are displayed in the **salon,** an Arabicized word from the French. By the same token, the room's furnishing reflects the family's degree of education, affluence, and modernity. The taste, the quality of furnishings, and the degree of Westernization that the room reflects is a mirror of the family's status and the light in which it likes to be viewed. For example, the family that seats its guests on rugs and hassocks reflects a different structure of internal relationships from the family that seats its guests on sofas and armchairs. The message reflects an advertised measure of identification with the Western, the modern. Although the **"salon"** is a very important room in the home, it is not the most frequently used. It is, paradoxically, both focal and peripheral. It is the center of the family's formal social interactions with visitors, while it is physically located on the periphery of the home.

In the Middle Eastern home, a door usually opens into a family room with a hallway and a number of rooms that are open either on the family room or on the hallway. In the back, close to the kitchen, are the bathroom facilities.

In most homes all rooms look alike. The use and function of every room is decided upon by the family. However, the **salon** is usually the room farthest away from all others and the closest to the door leading to the outside. Actually, in older buildings, the **"majlis"** or the salon or the guest room (which is a literal translation in certain Arabic dialects), a door leading to the outside opens directly into this room on one end and another door opens to the inside of the home. In such a layout the guest knocks at the door and is either led into the **salon** through the home or asked to please wait until the other door leading immediately to the "salon" is opened for him. The behavior reflects two of the primary cultural values of the area. The first is the preoccupation with the concept of face, facades, and appearances. The guest is exposed only to the most shining, formal, and stylized part of the home and gets to meet only the members whom the family intends for him to meet. On the other hand, relationships in the Middle East reflect contextual varieties of guest-host interactions with territorial expectations of welcome and hospitality on the part of the guest and situational obligations of maintaining the traditional image of an open house on the part of the host. Thus, in receiving the guest in the most distinguished part of the home and in having him meet only the members of the family dressed for the occasion, the guest is honored and the family status is reflected.

With close association and the development of friendship, a

guest comes to be accepted by the family and received in the family room or what is commonly referred to in the Middle East as the **sitting room.** However, between the time a guest is received in the salon and the time he is accepted as "one of us," a translation from the Arabic expression, certain social processes take place in terms of the guest's relationship to the family. The pace at which the guest meets the members of the opposite sex in the host family, and the length of the interaction reflect the internal sociocultural norms of the family. For example, it is not unusual in the Middle East for two men to have known each other for a number of years without either of them having met the female members of the other's family, even though they may know a lot about each other's life. This is in contrast to a modern, Westernized family in which a guest may meet most of the members during his first visit.

Until a guest is accepted and received informally in the family room his movement is usually restricted to the salon. Unlike the custom, in the United States, for example, where a guest wanting to use the toilet just gets up and heads toward the bathroom perhaps mumbling an "excuse me" or perhaps not, in the Middle East, the guest asks for permission to go to the bathroom and for guidance to it. The request allows the host to go out first and check to make sure that the way to the bathroom is clear. That is, he makes sure that there are no family members that the host doesn't want to introduce to the guest, that those around are decent, and that the place is tidy and in agreement with the image that the host would like to create. Consequently, because of all these little inconveniences, it is uncommon for a salon-only guest to go to the bathroom in a host's house. The situation is of course different in the case of a guest who is invited to a meal.

In one sense, the most exclusive place in the Middle Eastern home is the kitchen. Its territory is the domain of the household members and mainly the females in the family. To that extent it is the most intimate place in the Middle Eastern home. A guest, whether male or female, has to have achieved the highest degree of familiarity with a family to be admitted into their kitchen.

Depending upon the socioeconomic level of the family, the home may have a sitting room and a family room with one of them the equivalent of a North American den. The use and functions, however, are different. In the Middle East, it is not too frequent that all members of the family gather together in the sitting room. In fact, when the older members are in the sitting room, the young may stay away in the "den" or in their bedrooms out of deference, unless there is something specific that they want to discuss with their parents or aunts or uncles. In behavioral terms, deference is reflected in subduing physical noise or keeping it away from the ears of the elders in the family. Hence the different connotations of silence in certain contexts, for example, for the Middle Easterner and the North American.

In the Middle East, however, the men usually congregate together in the early evening and night hours in indoor or outdoor cafés. Meanwhile, the women visit together, and the young have uninhibited access to all parts of the home, since it is usually the presence of the father or the elder male members in the family that regulates movement and noise in the home. However, with the introduction of television, and the appeal of contemporary programs, family togetherness has begun to center around the television set. Even popular cafés in the Mideast have had to acquire television sets to help maintain their appeal.

The allocation and use of private space in the Middle Eastern home reflect the value system and lines of authority within the family. In some homes, for example, only the elder male members of the family may have access to the whole home. That is, only they are allowed to disturb or invade the privacy of any member of the family who might be alone in his room working, sulking, or visiting with a friend. Also, it is not unusual to find that only the mother has access to the father if he is alone in his room behind a closed door.

The Middle Eastern home, like others, reveals the authority system within the home, the roles and norms of behavior for each sex, and a culture's outlook toward friends and neighbors. The home is a miniature replica of its society and a propagator of many of its values and patterns of communication.

The German home

Doors, hedges, fences: these physical features of a German home reflect an emphasis on privacy which is pervasive throughout German life.[6] Add to privacy formal and regimented behavior, tempered by a love of the out-of-doors, and you have much that is at the heart of the German home and basic to many characteristically German patterns of communication. Two centuries of industrialization, plus the devastation and forced migration wrought by the war have not lessened the ideal of a **Heimat,** a place of one's own, a family home, even if the ideal must sometimes be accommodated to the realities of small apartment living in the larger cities.

In contrast to the kind of neighborhood fostered by the American social-centered home, one which is likely to stress good schools, good companions for the children, and friendly neighbors on the block, in Germany a "good neighbor" is likely to be one who is quiet, knows his place, doesn't object when children make noise, and keeps his own sidewalk clean. Good fences make good neighbors. There is no place here for the welcome wagon, and relatively little "dropping by" for a chat. Even leases are likely to enforce some of these qualities. A lease will often specify who may use the garden or the yard in the back of the house, if there is one, and at which hours. It will probably require the tenant to sweep and wash the stairwell outside of the apartment, and quite possibly the front steps and the sidewalk, too. Time periods for making noise may be prescribed: no running water after 10 P.M.

Even in smaller towns in Germany, formality and social distance are notable in home style and house construction. The door to the average home is made up of two parts, and usually only the top part, about waist height, is opened to receive goods or for conversing with neighbors. When housewives gather for the **Kaffeeklatch,** which is really a gossip session, they usually refer to each other—and to those about whom they are speaking—as Frau or Fraulein so-and-so, not by first names. Thus here, too, the formality of a proper social distance is maintained.

People in small towns and in large cities throughout Germany share a great love for the out-of-doors; the outside is a central part of the concept of an ideal home. However, the outdoors is a private nature and not at all like the expansive front lawns and

---

[6] These observations were provided by Mary Badami and Caroline Yousef.

floor-to-ceiling picture windows glorified in so many American home magazines. Yards are in the back and well shielded from neighbors by shrubbery. Even in city apartments, balconies are very common and well planted. Since city apartments often lack a dining room or a dining-kitchen, the balcony serves to stretch the available space and helps to give the illusion of being in contact with nature. Yards are used for gardening as well as for dining.

Germans eat meals or snacks outdoors at all hours of the day. Garden restaurants, such as the familiar Biergarten, are among the most frequent settings for communication. Indeed, except for family and very close friends, homes are not used for entertaining guests. Restaurants usually have a special table marked by the sign, **"Stammtisch"** (regular's table) for patrons who come every evening to talk, dine, and drink.

For the woman who stays at home, the morning is probably spent in doing housework and shopping and preparing for the mid-day meal, **Mittagessen,** the main hot meal usually served around 1 P.M. As in most countries outside of the United States, both the limitations of space as well as cultural values require shopping daily. When the meal is served, the whole family should be present. School has ended by this time, many shops close, and father has at least an hour free from work. (Increasing problems of traffic threaten this pattern in Germany as elsewhere, however.) Only a serious problem justifies the absence of any member of the family. There is little tolerance for a child's declining to join the family because he says he is not hungry or has promised to eat elsewhere.

After the meal, although school is over, schooling is not. German schools are demanding, and thus mother and child (or children) will spend the afternoon bound together in school work. The parent is a taskmaster (or mistress). Home offers no respite for the child. Headaches, tension, even nervous breakdowns are cause of concern in Germany, but much of the child's day at home is spent under such pressure. And everything may be reviewed again in the evening when father returns. (Except for the hours involved, this description of schooling in the German home is nearly identical to that of contemporary Japan, we might note.)

As we have indicated in our comments on house and home styles in other cultures, the physical plan of the German home also seems to reflect and help maintain many basic cultural values which recur in communication patterns. The ideal German home has foyer or entryway that leads visitors into the house without exposing them to specific rooms and a resultant loss of privacy for the family members. The living room, or **Wohnsimmer,** is the most formal room in the house, and it shares much in common with such rooms in the other homes described (except for the case of the social-centered home in the United States). Whatever the family considers an heirloom is there: a wall scroll showing the family tree, an antique statue, a piano, a Bible, or a wall full of books. Here guests are entertained. If there are children in the family who are old enough to be quiet, they may be expected to appear immediately, greet the guests, and stay quietly for the length of the visit. They speak when spoken to; they are to be seen but not heard. Thus their behavior in the living room is usually quite different from that of many American children who can drop in and say "Hi" and then leave in order to pursue their own interests.

As we have already indicated, a balcony or a back yard may also be a center of social activity, each well hidden from public view and as overflowing with flowers as is possible. Similar guarantees of privacy are provided by heavy drapes on the windows, or with the drapes opened but lighter white sheer curtains drawn. (We recall that Freud's colleague and a noted psychoanalyst himself, Theodore Reich, has also written about the importance of curtains. Reich noted that curtains or drapes were the first things a woman wanted in a house, and he interpreted this in terms of female sexuality and modesty. A better guess might be in terms of German values of privacy.)

The typical bedroom closely resembles that described for the authority-centered home in the United States. The rooms tend to be smaller than those in the American model, but twin beds are far more common than double beds. In fact, double beds are sometimes referred to as **"Franzosische Betten"** (French beds), and many Germans find the idea of such a bed tantalizing if not quite erotic.

Closed doors and massive furniture are themes already explored by Edward Hall in **The Hidden Dimension.**[7] He sees the double doors often used in offices and hotels as evidence of the German search for privacy via soundproofing as well as physical barriers. In this respect the German sense of privacy within a home or office is completely different from that found in Japanese homes, where walls and doors must be among the thinnest in the world. However, in regard to privacy and mutual obligations in regard to neighbors, the German and Japanese patterns show some remarkable similarities. Hall has also observed that the heavy German furniture seems to fill a need for stability and at the same time ensure that social relationships will remain at an acceptable distance.

Finally, we might mention one element of contemporary life we have not considered in the previous descriptions: the use of the telephone. Professor Mary Badami has noted that where homes in Germany have telephones, the use of the phone seems to conform to the general pattern described here.[8] Older Germans are especially prone to follow an elaborate but informal etiquette of phone usage: the morning is a good time to call a private house; calls should not be made around noon (since meals would be interrupted), calls should not be made through the early afternoon (people might be napping); late afternoon is acceptable, but not the evening meal time; a brief after-supper time segment is acceptable, if not too late—calls should not intrude on the bedtime hours.

Concluding comments

Apparent in several of these descriptions of homes is a parallel between a strong central authority in the home and a set of norms which seem to help shape and regulate family life. Formality, a sharp distinction between guest and family member and a related concern for properly impressing the guest; role behavior according to sex and age, and the corresponding use of particular rooms of the home; and throughout a sharply defined hierarchy within the home: These aspects seem so consistent in the previous descriptions of home that it is clearly the Amer-

[7] Hall, **Hidden Dimension,** pp. 123–29.
[8] Personal correspondence.

ican "social-centered home" that stands out in sharp contrast. Such comparisons, for whatever they are worth, should not be twisted into preferential distinctions between "traditional" and "modern," or "stable" and "dissolving" kinds of family structures, however. In any case, our descriptions are intentionally brief and incomplete, for purposes of illustration and comparison.

Perhaps what is of greatest value in this chapter has not been the description of any one composite home or even the more obvious similarities and differences when comparing these; rather it may have been the approach itself—seeing the home as a microcosm of society, the place where each person first learns how to communicate within the norms of his culture. We should each think back to our own homes and recall as best we can where, when, how, and with whom we first learned to communicate. Increasingly now, and not only in the United States, an individual's memories are of more than a single home. And that is significant, too.

EIGHT

Languages and cultures

In the shadow of Babel

It is widely assumed that the major problem in communication across cultures is that of language differences. It is also widely believed that if everybody spoke the same language we would have few, or at least fewer, problems of misunderstanding. There is no question that we might have some different problems, but whether or not we would have fewer is another matter. Within any single community we have disagreements which are not primarily based on language or minor **semantic** misunderstandings, and this alone argues against hoping for a panacea through some common language. Moreover, since a language can be used to express dislike as much as to express attraction and to confuse or conceal as much as to clarify, there is no guarantee that a common language would lead to less acrimony than the poor world suffers now.

Beyond this rather pessimistic view of human relations there are other language-related factors which have to be considered before expressing our total faith in understanding through language. A language is more than a set of arbitrary symbols through which ideas are expressed. Language is a central influence on culture and one of the most highly charged symbols of a culture and a nation. We can laugh at the woman who said that "if King James English was good enough for Jesus it's good enough for me," but it must be difficult for most Americans to imagine any other language but English as the national language of the United States.

In almost every society today there are spokesmen who express concern when their language seems threatened by "corruptions" from foreign languages. Although we do not hear warnings about foreign saboteurs of English today, we can find them if we go back to the time of Shakespeare. Then, Puttingham warned that if English were forever borrowing it would become bankrupt.[1] This cry was sounded, not surprisingly, at a time of great innovation and of intercultural communication, if you will, between England and many parts of Europe. Inevitably along with the sharing of ideas, information, and personnel, comes a sharing of vocabulary. But it seems that far from feeling satisfied that such verbal sharing might in some way make intercultural communication a little easier, the more frequent reaction—apart from that of ignorance and passive acceptance—is one of defensiveness. Today, hundreds of years after English borrowed wholesale the vocabularies for the fine arts, among other areas, the purists in many other nations are reacting against the linguistic onslaughts of American English. So mighty has been the influence of the United States in this century, that American English expressions and words are a part of almost every language. Frenchmen wince at hearing **Franglais,** Mexicans balk at **pochismos,** and the Japanese do their best to keep **Japlish** in its place. Futile as most of these efforts are, they help to reveal the very special symbolic place of language in a culture.

Another indication of the symbolic importance of language in society can be found in language policies of new nations and, occasionally, efforts to modify language policies in long established nations. The rhetoric of such policies is often rooted in

[1] Cited in Karl J. Holzknecht, **The Backgrounds of Shakespeare's Plays** (New York: American Book Co., 1950), p. 187. (Chapter Eight of this book provides an excellent survey of the development of and attitudes toward English in Shakespeare's time.)

selective history, sometimes "destiny," while practical advantages are also cited when convenient. The result is sometimes a greater diversity in official languages than is usually produced by the power politics of conquest or by economic encroachments. Thus Israel at midcentury chose to be the only nation with Hebrew as its national language, even though most of the Israeli immigrants had to learn their Hebrew. Tanzania, for quite different reasons, opted for Swahili—partly to avoid favoring any of the 120 different tribes in the nation, partly to avoid problems of elitism that might result if colonialist English were retained, and partly for a combination of convenience and pride. "Language wars" in India periodically make the headlines, and the 1973 parliamentary elections in Quebec, among the most important in its history, were directly focused on questions of language policy. In the Roman Catholic church the dispute over Latin versus vernacular liturgies bitterly divided many parishes; the dropping of Latin resulted in many advantages, but it also served to diminish the role of the last remaining language that found some expression among all classes in nearly every part of the world. In the United States, for reasons that are practical, psychological, and rooted in concerns for ethnic identity, we have developed an appreciation for "Black English" and have greatly increased the number of classes taught in Spanish. In Mexico, meanwhile, the interest in learning Nahuatl, the language of the Aztecs, grows with each passing year.

If intercultural understanding were a matter of the highest priority and if some common language were the primary means of achieving such a goal, we might find either a diminishing of different languages or at least a more concerted effort at some common second language. Instead, it seems that ethnic or cultural identification is far more important than relating to people who are perceived as different, and the acceptance of an international language has not made such headway.

Language and culture

Roughly a half century ago, the distinguished American linguist Edward Sapir startled some language scholars by upturning the common sense notion that language was no more a kind of neutral medium through which thoughts or ideas were expressed. Though there are disputes about just what he meant, his general position was that language actually shapes the way in which we perceive, think, and therefore act. Such a view had been put forth much earlier, notably through the writings of the German scholar Alexander von Humboldt, who was known even to Thomas Jefferson. Nevertheless, it was not until the writings of Sapir's most famous student, Benjamin Lee Whorf, that the concept began to attract attention. The linguistic relativity hypothesis today is commonly identified with all three men, most frequently labeled "the Whorf hypothesis" or "the Sapir Whorf hypothesis." Since the hypothesis was most congenial with the school of thought of the General Semanticists after Korzybski, it has received an even wider exposure during the past forty years. Today, however, as we shall note later, it is out of fashion among contemporary linguists.

The gist of the hypothesis was stated by Sapir in 1929:

> Language is not merely a more or less systematic inventory of the various items of experience which seem relevant to the individual, as is so often naively assumed, but is also a self-contained, creative, symbolic organization, which not only refers to experience largely acquired without its help but actually defines experience for us by reason of its formal completeness and because of our unconscious projection of its implicit expectations into the field of experience.[2]

In short, a language does not merely record and transmit perceptions and thoughts, it actually helps to shape both. Each language reflects reality as a fun-house mirror, distorted, and the only reality we can know and contemplate is that which we see reflected.

During the past quarter century there have been many academic conferences devoted to exploring and debating the "Sapir-Whorf hypothesis," with several books and many more articles resulting.[3] The hypothesis is also the basis of at least one lecture

---

[2] David G. Mandelbaum, ed., **Selected Writings of Edward Sapir** (Berkeley and Los Angeles: University of California Press, 1949), p. 162; see also Edward Sapir, "Conceptual Categories in Primitive Languages," **Science** 74 (1931): 578.
[3] See, for example, Harry Hoijer, ed., **Language in Culture; Conference on the Inter-relations of Language and Other Aspects of Culture** (Chicago: University of Chicago Press, 1954).

in almost any basic course in the study of language, anthropology, speech, and communication. It enjoys an even more favored position among the General Semantics school. If the hypothesis is "true," the implications are most profound; if "false," then it can be ignored or relegated to an interesting stage in the development of linguistic science. The trouble is, as the conferences, books, and articles so often reveal, it is not the sort of hypothesis that can be proven or disproven. For some, this is sufficient reason to ignore it as an unscientific proposition. And yet, the hypothesis and all it implies will not go away.

Let us ignore what Sapir and Whorf meant, for even this seems to be disputed, and instead restate the general idea for our purposes. And rather than regard the hypothesis as the center of our concerns, let us move one interpretation of it to an extreme position on a continuum. Let us call that position "linguistic determinism," meaning that virtually everything we perceive and think about and hence how we act depends on the language we speak and in which we think. (If necessary, we could selectively quote from Sapir and from Whorf for support of this position.) At the other end of our continuum we should mark a position to represent absolutely no relationship between a person's language and the ways in which he perceives, thinks, and acts. Describing these in terms of an individual may make both positions even more extreme than necessary; however, since individual sophistication toward language and thought can vary considerably, perhaps it would be better to phrase these in terms of percentages of individuals.

Before proceeding further we should also clarify what we mean by "language," although even linguists differ in their definitions. We might want to consider matters of phonology, or sound systems; morphology, or groupings of sounds that make up words (though there are also disputes about how to define a "word"); vocabulary; syntax; and writing systems.

Having mentioned these possibilities, we will immediately abandon the first two. Although attempts have been made to relate phonology and morphology to culture and to patterns of behavior, they are usually outside of the consideration of linguistic relativity. We will thus ignore the many studies which show very similar reactions across cultures to contrastive sounds in "nonsense words" when paired with imaginary objects: the discovery that "gik" is associated with a smaller object, "gok" with a larger object.

Vocabulary, however, seems quite important. Even those persons who deny the importance of the deterministic view readily admit correlations between vocabulary and culture. Similarly, those who have most supported the general Sapir-Whorf position seem to have stressed such correlations for all they are worth. We will appraise their worth shortly.

Syntax was a mainstay of the arguments of Sapir and Whorf and must be considered in any discussion of language influence on thought and action. However, it is far more difficult and, for most students, less interesting to compare syntaxes between languages—unless one is somewhat bilingual—than to compare vocabularies. Perhaps for this reason syntax receives less attention in popular treatments of the subject than does vocabulary.

The last consideration, writing systems, usually is ruled out of bounds by linguists, since a language first of all is a matter of speech, with writing considered only as a substitute for speech. Historically, of course, writing systems appeared late in civilizations and until recently many languages were never written. Nevertheless we want to say something about writing systems and the intriguing possibility that they may influence thinking and perception, even if they are conventionally separated from "language."

Another helpful view of "language" is the three-part division proposed by Charles Morris, called semiotics ("a general theory of signs," including language but also other symbol systems).[4] Morris distinguished: A. **syntactics,** the relationship between signs and other signs, words and other words (grammar, syntax, logic); B. **semantics,** the relationship between signs or symbols and their referents in fact or concept ("book" represents the thing you are looking at); and C. **pragmatics** (the relationship between signs or symbols and human behavior.) In these terms

---

[4] Charles Morris, **Signs, Language and Behavior** (New York: Prentice-Hall, 1946).

we are asking, "Do the syntactic and semantic dimensions of a language in any way influence the pragmatic?" One extreme of the continuum marks an answer of "yes, completely," the other extreme, "no, not at all."

In English we can say, "You should talk to my brothers in the corner." In Japanese we cannot so easily translate that. First we have a problem with "brother," since Japanese has no single word for "brother." There are words for older brother and for younger brother and a generic term roughly comparable to "sibling," though used more frequently, but no exact equivalent for "brother." This may seem strange at first until we realize that "brother" is not fully objective: it is a concept, an expression of a relationship. Many languages do not correspond in their relationship words, some being more general, some more precise than others. "Uncle" in English, for example, is commonly used for at least five kinds of relations which become apparent only when they are made more precise ("my mother's sister's husband"). All this may or may not be very interesting, but the question is: if one's language compels one to indicate older or younger whenever speaking of a brother or a sister, does this influence the way the speaker thinks about his or her brother?

"You" is also a relationship word. We do not need to go so far from English to appreciate that fact. English used to distinguish between two "you" relationships when it offered a choice of "you" or "thou." "Thou" is rarely used nowadays except in some church services, or among some Quakers in conversation together, or by readers of Martin Buber. Most European languages retain a distinction between a "formal you" and a friendly or intimate "you," as students of French, Spanish, and German well know. Does it make a difference if a person's language requires him to choose which "you"? It certainly can be a difficult matter for many students of another language when they are not accustomed to making such a choice, and to not be linguocentric about it, we should appreciate that the single "you" in English can also be discomfitting to one not accustomed to that monolithic relationship.

In Japanese, however, the choices are much greater. Not only must the Japanese speaker consider the intimacy of the "you" he is talking to, he must also consider the relative status of the other person, as superior or subordinate to himself, and the level of formality that is appropriate for the situation. The age and the sex of each party in the conversation also enter into the calculation, with markedly different words for men and for women, and for those of different ages. In all, there are at least ten common alternatives for the equivalent of "you," and a comparable number for "I." (This total does not include regional and occupational alternatives; if these are also considered the number of choices can be multiplied by ten!)

Even "corner" is relatively imprecise. Again, Japanese makes a distinction between what English speakers might call "an inside corner" and an "outside corner." Obviously, English speakers **can** and sometimes do make such a distinction. And that **option** in appraising the linguistic relativity issue is important. However, some languages compel speakers to **always** make that distinction. And that is important, too.

We could continue to point out such differences among languages. The important question is, "Do the differences make any difference?" Certainly if we have always assumed that all languages were more or less alike, apart from their sound systems, then some of these differences are impressive. Surely, we might reason, since we must think as we use language we are going to be directed to think in terms, literally, of our language. On the other hand, if we expect to find great diversity in languages, it is only a matter of time until—as the transformational grammarians seemed to find—we discover how remarkably similar languages are at heart. That is, from the transformationalist point of view, the apparent differences in the ways languages code "reality" are mostly superficial (if not exactly above the surface then at least not below the surface). If we go to a deeper structure on a level that ordinary speakers are not aware of, we can find remarkable consistency across languages.

The so-called "standard theory" of transformational-generative grammar, as developed by Noam Chomsky (**Aspects of the Theory of Syntax** in 1965),[5] has concentrated on "deep structures," but the standard model of grammar did not have much to say about meaning. Two other linguists, Katz and Fodor, pioneered in what

[5] Noam Chomsky, **Aspects of the Theory of Syntax** (Cambridge: MIT Press, 1965).

has been termed "generative semantics," Katz later coming up with a model which allows semantics to be graphed onto the standard model.[6] Thus, using the findings of these three contemporary linguists, we can describe language as having three components: phonological, syntactic, and semantic. And, according to these assumptions, it is the semantic component that interprets the underlying phrase markers in terms of meaning. Thus the role of semantics in this theory is primarily "interpretative."

But not all contemporary linguists are satisfied with such a model. Wallace Chafe, most notably, contends that the generative semanticists are "syntax-biased" and have the cart before the horse. In Chafe's view,[7] which seems more congenial to other communication scholars, "meaning" which is conceptualized comes first. It is this conceptualization which then "generates" sentences which then go through the components of syntax and phonology, a process he has called "literalization."

Despite this divergence in recent American linguistic theory, everyone is still "looking beneath the surface," seeking universals of language. (Thus the "transformations" from language to language are made at this level of deep structure. The same approach, by the way, seems to be that employed—subconsciously—by the translator: He plunges below the surface differences in language to find the underlying meanings, then crosses over to the other language and emerges with a different surface translation.)

The approach described here resembles our approach to cultural values, going deeper to find consistent patterns in many expressions of a culture. It differs in goal, however; the transformationalist seeks a common denominator for different languages; the goal of the values scholar was to find common denominators **within** a culture but not necessarily across cultures.

To do justice to this view of language and thought relationships, then, perhaps requires us to draw a continuum between the opposing campus (linguistic determinism versus language

[6] J. J. Katz, **Introduction to Semantic Theory** (New York: Harper & Row, 1971).
[7] W. L. Chafe, **Meaning and the Structure of Language** (Chicago: University of Chicago Press, 1970).

irrelevancy) on a slant, and not horizontally. At least it seems that the two sides are talking about language in somewhat different ways. Those who deny "the tyrannical hold that linguistic form has upon our orientation in the world," as Sapir put it, base their denial of that view on interpretations made below the surface differences of languages. Those who would agree with Sapir's view—George Orwell's theory of "newspeak" in **1984** is probably the best expression of such a view—martial their evidence at the surface level of speech.

The figure below represents this interpretation. The dotted line, **A** to **B,** represents the conventional continuum from point **A,** marking the extreme Whorfian view or "linguistic determinism," to point **B,** the position that there is no necessary relationship between a language and its impact on perception and speakers' thought patterns. The solid diagonal line, **A** to **C,** serves to illustrate that interpretations at one end are based on structures described below the surface. Continuing with this simple diagram we might say that the transformationalists who reject the Whorfian view do so by assuming that their descriptions of language at the deep level of **C** apply upwards, as it were, to **B:** perception and thought, in other words, are assumed to be mediated at the deep level, emerging in different forms at the surface in only apparently different but unimportant ways. At the other end, **A,** however, the strict Whorfian might argue that any constants or universals that can be described at a deeper level (between **A** and **D**) are irrelevant or, perhaps, that the influence runs downward from **A** to **D.** This diagram is presented only to illustrate one interpretation of different views of the Sapir-Whorf hypothesis which we are considering.

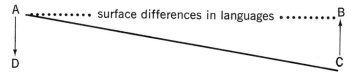

To review briefly, nobody denies that there are many striking differences between languages, in vocabulary, syntax, and of course in phonological and morphological characteristics. As we will note shortly, there is also general agreement that many of these differences correspond to characteristics of the cultures in which the different languages are spoken.

Several considerations arise in this discussion, and each can be interpreted as supporting a view toward linguistic determinism or as irrelevant, if not a refutation of, such a position. For one thing, our very discussion seems to show that one language **can** accommodate expressions in another language, even if the translations are longer ("my mother's sister's husband") or uncommon ("thou"). A basic premise of translation is that anything that can be said in one language can be said in another—but perhaps not so elegantly or simply. Thus those who would support the deterministic position would say that because some approximations of foreign words or expressions take longer or seem unusual, we are not likely to use them or "think that way." There is also sound psychological evidence that it takes longer to conceptualize and takes less time to forget words or expressions that are longer or more complicated than others.

A second consideration goes to the heart of the dispute. Languages conceptualize realities in apparently different ways, and these correspond to distinctions which are important within the culture. Still, if you can say that it is language that is influencing the perceptions and "realities" of a culture, you can just as correctly turn that around and say that the "realities" and demands of the culture are shaping the language.

Students of language who find themselves in opposite camps may agree that there are correlations between vocabulary in a language and aspects of culture, such as between the quantity of words for the same sort of reality, be it snow, camels, or bananas, and the relative importance of that reality in the culture. Where they differ is in how to interpret that correlation: one argues that it is the language one learns that directs his perception of such things (and hence helps to maintain the culture), the other says that it is the culture that directs the language.

Beyond both of these problems of interpretation is an even more practical question. How can we demonstrate that our language makes a difference in our perception, thought, and behavior? Who can say? There are bilingual persons who say they **feel** differently when they speak one language or the other, or that they **prefer** to talk about some subjects in one language rather than another, but this evidence is a long way from proof. Other arguments are advanced supporting the position that there is no necessary connection between language and how one thinks. The fact that languages change with their needs suggests that language must not be all that controlling a factor. This is sometimes countered with the unanswerable speculation, "Perhaps our language accepts only superficial changes—new discoveries or products—while still resisting other ways of conceptualizing and thinking." Transformational grammarians argue that at a deeper level all languages are basically the same, and that they differ only superficially. Just as some differences in languages are striking to one who had always assumed they were similar, the similarities in languages are at least as impressive to anyone who might imagine even more differences. Nevertheless, students of intercultural communication can object to the transformational linguist's implied assumption that perceiving and "thinking" must take place at the level of "deep structure." While "deep structure" might be a useful concept for linguistic analysis, that does not mean it is operative in our thinking.

At the level of theory there is plenty to interest us in this controversy about linguistic influences on thinking and behavior. At the level of practice the questions are even more important for us. If, for example, a language strongly influences the way a person thinks and perceives, then it may be essential to learn another language before being able to see things as a native speaker would. Or, similarly, we might suppose that if one learns a second language, particularly if it is structurally quite different from his own, he will inevitably be compelled to see things differently and think about the world in a manner comparably different from the ways prescribed by his own native language. We will say a little more about these issues in the concluding chapter of the book.

Dorothy Lee, a cultural anthropologist mentioned in our discussion of value theory, offers what we believe to be a more tenable position than that of either extreme.[8] Her dispute with both positions is that we cannot separate language from culture, and indeed we cannot even make the conventional distinction

[8] Lee, **Freedom and Culture,** p. 80.

between "words" and "things." She points out that as soon as you conceptualize "a thing," even if you do not speak the name, you have objectified it, treated it as a substantive or noun, and are thus already using language even if you are only pointing at something. Thus she disputes the assumptions of the basic premise of the General Semantics school, which she ironically calls "the classical view," that "the word is not the thing." By even thinking you are looking at "a thing" (compared to, say, an action or an attribute of some other "thing"), you are already following the dictates of your language. This does not exactly mean that one cannot perceive what a language does not identify or distinguish, however. In Japanese, for example, the word **te** stands for what English speakers call **arm.** It also stands for what English speakers would call **hand. Ashi** means both **leg** and **foot.** But it is ridiculous to assume that Japanese cannot tell the difference between an arm and a hand, or between a leg and a foot. Or that Japanese have trouble counting because their language has no plurals.

Although Lee's position is closer to the deterministic position, it is still some distance from that extreme. It does not claim, for instance, that we cannot see anything we have no words for, or that if our language has only one word for what may take two or three words in another language we cannot even make those distinctions.

To us Lee's position is quite sensible. (A colleague calls it "Dostoevskian.") It hardly resolves the dispute over language and thought, but it provides a rationale for rejecting both extreme positions. To take either extreme means we must employ the very language categories and distinctions that we want to test. Here, then, is a subtle doublebind: if we want to argue that language does or does not determine thought we will have to do so without recourse to language, whether that be a "natural" or ordinary language, or some meta-language devised for the very purpose of denying any necessary relationship between language and thought. If you ask Lee how to get to either extreme you will be told, as they say in the provinces, "You can't get there from here."

Language participates in our perception and in our expression of perception; we cannot divorce language from perception or

thought. It predisposes us to make certain distinctions and minimize others, but allows us more freedom than a strict deterministic view would permit. Language is a tool rather more than a
prison, but we are still limited by our particular tools. And to
extend the analogy just a little further, our tools arise in part
(here thinking of vocabulary more than syntax) from our experiences and needs of a collective culture; some may be
abandoned, some may be refashioned, and others may be added.
In technologies and highly specialized subjects where only a
relatively small number of people use their language in a self-
conscious way, we may feel at ease in changing our tools as
needed. In ordinary language habits, we are far more conservative, clinging even to primative tools. Even the reluctance by
the "pragmatic Americans" to adopt the convenient metric system seems to show that much.

Before leaving this aspect of language and culture, we should
briefly add some remarks about common interpretations of the
linguistic relativity issue. Probably the most often quoted example in this whole area is that of the number of words for "snow"
in the Eskimo language as compared to English. The point made
in this tedious example is that Eskimos need to distinguish carefully about snow since it is such a vital factor in the Eskimo
culture. The example is cited so often and so casually that one
is not really sure how many words for snow the Eskimo language
possesses. In any case, usually overlooked in this example is the
number of words English has for "snow." It is not correct to say
that Eskimo language has ten or twenty words and English has
only one. English has "slush," "fluffy snow," "good for packing"
snow, "wet snow," and many more on a wintery day. Obviously
each of these is not a single word, but that does not mean that
English speakers do not distinguish in language between different kinds of snow. The real issue here is one of equivalences:
There is no reason to expect that a single word in one language
will be equivalent to a single word in another, or that an adjective
in one language will be an adjective in another. We should ask,
rather, if an equivalent concept or "reality" expressed in one
language is conveniently codified in another, even if the form
of expression is different. If it is impossible to express such a
concept or image or if it can be done only through a very cum-

bersome expression, then the linguistic differences may be important. This distinction, we believe, is extremely important and is very often ignored in naive formal comparisons of language.

The different categories of language nearly always reflect the interests, preoccupations, usages, and utilities of a given people. More than a quarter of a century ago in classical Arabic, there were more than 6000 words referring to the **camel**—its color, bodily structure, sex, age, movement, condition, equipment. The natives of the Sahara have 200 words for the **date,** their staff of life, and twenty different ways of describing the shape of sand dunes. In American English the importance of the automobile is reflected in the hundreds of words used to refer to it. Or consider the semantics of what becomes of ground beef or hair styles. How many words do the Eskimos have for pizza?

By the same token, societal conditions and people's interests are reflected in the dropping of words and phrases and the coining and adoption of new ones. Many of the classical Arabic words that refer to the camel have disappeared from contemporary Arabic in recent decades with the disappearance of the conditions they referred to and the related interests involved. Other examples are reflected in the huge array of words relating to electronics, new drugs and biologicals, atomic fission, missiles. In Western countries, especially in the United States, the development of technology has been accompanied by the development of language terms and forms to meet the new needs for new kinds of calculation and organization of techniques and instruments, and the systematization and precise statement of complex ideas, directives, and instructions. And as mentioned at the beginning of this chapter, the developments in one society —if its communications industries, including language, are powerful enough—eventually encroaches on other societies, other languages.

A related issue is that of the absence of certain words or expressions in some languages. We hear that there is no equivalent in most languages for "fair play" in English, or no word for "privacy" in Japanese. The absence of such concepts, if they are truly lacking, may be significant. However, the absence of words for certain artifacts or plants or animals in one language may simply mean that their referents do not exist in the society where that word is spoken. And that is hardly startling. Once such an object, plant, or animal makes its appearance or must be described for one reason or another, the word can be introduced. At what point it becomes a part of that language, however, is another more subtle question. Is **a la mode** English? Or should we say English has no such concept and hence we must speak French when we want ice cream on our apple pie? At some point borrowed words do become a part of a language, even if they seem to retain a foreign accent.

Language and nonverbal behavior

As if there were not enough confusion in the discussion of linguistic relativity, we now have to consider the possibility of nonlinguistic equivalents in one language for linguistic expressions in another. This consideration, too, is often ignored in the heat of the controversy. Just as comparable perceptions of reality may take different linguistic forms in different languages, it is also possible that what is identified through language in some societies is identified nonverbally in others. Take, for example, matters of status differentiation, or formality and informality, discussed earlier in terms of value orientations. In American English, for reasons of values rather than the requirements of the English language, we may minimize status differences between ourselves and those we talk with, and we may usually feel uncomfortable with titles and honorifics. But is it not possible that we substitute comparable nonverbal markers for what we do not express in our speech? Our choice of interpersonal distance (proxemic behavior), eye contact, and direction of gaze, and even autistic behavior reflecting how relatively important or unimportant we feel, may convey the same meaning but in a different form. Of course, there is no reason to suppose that we always compensate nonverbally for what is unexpressed verbally, but at least we must further explore the area of nonverbal equivalence.

Even within the United States the norms governing the use of language in a particular situation may differ considerably across class or subcultural lines. Indeed, there may be greater similarities between some aspects of behavior of some social classes in the United States and comparable norms in other cultures than there are between different classes within the United States. In a fascinating three-and-a-half year field study in a part of Chicago he labeled "Teamsterville," Philipsen sought to discover when and where speech was expected and where a nonverbal expression was more appropriate.[9] His findings show a marked difference between the speech norms of Teamsterville and, presumably, that in the suburbs or within the expensive high-rise buildings along the lakefront. In Teamsterville, to reaffirm and enhance in-group solidarity, as in the neighborhood bar or on the local corner, speaking together was good and important. But to deal with conflicts with outsiders, with people of different ages (such as children), with the opposite sex, or with people from different social groups, a person does not resort to speech. "It just wouldn't be natural" to **talk** back to some little brat—or even to a wife, in some situations. Talking back would not be manly. "The natural thing to do" is to respond nonverbally—here a euphemism for slapping or some other physical attack. (A friend, Karen Carlson, who teaches in an inner city Junior College in Chicago reports a similar reaction in her first "discussion class." Some students had been visibly upset by an obnoxiously over-talkative member of the group, but they assured her after class, "Don't worry about that guy, teacher—we'll take care of him in the alley.") The only point we wish to make with these examples is that we can misinterpret a situation if we look only at language or speech and try to compare across cultures what would be said in certain situations. Usually the Whorf hypothesis looks at alternative forms of speech. We should realize that in many situations, compared in some cultures, nothing would be **said.**

Then there is the matter of cultural expectations about the use of language to apprehend and express **realities** and ideas. It is by no means a universal assumption that **reality** can be apprehended and expressed in **words.** Mystics in all cultures and in all periods of history have reflected the opposite notion, of course, so that William James cited "ineffability" as **the** universal

[9] Gerry F. Philipsen, **Communication in Teamsterville: A Sociolinguistic Study of Speech Behavior in an Urban Neighborhood** (Ph.D. diss., Northwestern University, 1972).

characteristic of the mystical state.[10] In Japan, the tradition of Zen Buddhism, which is not exactly one of mysticism, has stressed a similar opposition toward words, viewing verbalization as the essential barrier to enlightenment. While Zen does not at all hold the position of importance in Japan that some Western readers might suppose, its infuence on the culture and on attitudes toward verbalization and speech is strong; what is unsaid is often regarded as far more important than what is only said. Without becoming involved in the philosophies of knowing, we can at least appreciate how such differing views toward language would complicate the language and culture question as well as posing immediate practical problems for intercultural communication. What one culture may regard as unimportant or even nonexistent because it cannot be expressed in words, another culture, by the same criteria, may regard as supremely important.

Language and values

Value orientations are fundamental to culture and cultural patterns of communication. Apart from those referring to artifacts —plants or animals unique to a particular culture or nation— the words that are likely to pose the greatest difficulty in translating across cultures are those directly related to values. Indeed, explaining or interpreting values is even more difficult than trying to explain or describe some foreign object, since values are abstractions and cannot be clarified with photographs or verbal descriptions. Even with fairly satisfying explanations one is likely to feel that an explanation of a value-related word does not quite express the subject. Hence the apologetic reaction that such a concept cannot be explained in another language.

"Fair play," mentioned previously, is one such example in English that is frequently cited as having no exact equivalent in most other languages.[11] Even better, for American English, is the cluster of words and metaphors related to games. While

[10] William James, **The Varieties of Religious Experience** (New York: Longmans, Green and Co., 1902), p. 380.
[11] See, for example, Stewart, **American Patterns**, pp. 53–55.

particular expressions become first faddish, and then clichés, and might eventually disappear, the game metaphors as a group are remarkably widespread among Americans. Baseball metaphors such as "Out in left field," "He threw me a curve," or "I can't get to first base with her," may seem antiquated in the 1970s, but urgings to "Stop playing games," "It's a whole new ball game," and "The name of the game . . ." are at this writing nearly as fashionable among college students as they are among businessmen or others with whom many of the college students would rather not be associated. During the Watergate hearings the game metaphor may have revealed its supreme value as one humbled witness explained that he did not object to the shady dealings of the Committee to Reelect the President because he wanted to be a good "team player." The underlying values in such metaphors have to do with participating as an equal under certain rules, explicit or assumed, with competition, with action, with detachment of one's "self" or personality from the particular role he has undertaken, and with anticipated outcomes within a specified and limited time period. When one completes a game, he can try again in some other game. Surely part of the appeal of Eric Berne's popular treatment of transactional psychological theory was in its format and title, **Games People Play.** Things are simpler when they are games, everybody who really tries can become a better player, and—win, lose, or draw—it's only a game.

We have in America sensitivity-training games, war games, and there is a huge commercial market for such serious subjects— rendered into games—as race relations, air pollutions, and even the reenacting of the Viet Nam War—in 1973, "The Mi Lai Game" was marketed. The French also use the game metaphor. So did Herman Hesse, in Germany, and so did the Swiss Johan Huizinga in his brilliant book, **Homo Ludens,** man, the player of games. But there the game remained a metaphor, apart from reality. In the United States, the game seems to be something more. The reason seems to lie in cultural values, not in language, per se.

The role of values also is important in interpreting translations. To whatever extent we think in language, we also think in terms of values. The average North American thinks that leaders of autocratic governments are hypocrites when they refer to their countries as "People's Democracies." How can there be a democracy without at least two candidates or two parties for the voters to choose from? The citizen, however, that has grown up in an authoritarian regime may have been trained from childhood to consider democracy as government **for** the people but not necessarily **by** the people. To him a man is no less of a father because he acts in what he honestly believes to be the best interests of his family members even though he does not poll them to find out if they would rather spend a holiday in the mountains or on the beach, if they would rather have a station wagon or a camper. Neither is a woman less of a mother because she does not ask all family members what to cook every day or how or when to do the wash. To the individual that has been raised in an autocratic environment, the idea of polling everybody and following the poll may seem silly and not conducive to the best results. To such individuals, the North American concepts and practices of democracy are hypocritical, since they insist on and represent procedures and values that are considered by such individuals as being basically absurd according to all standards and norms they have grown up with.

Other semantic considerations

It is widely realized that a single word has different meanings (in the sense of evoking different reactions, even "images" among speakers and listeners) within a single culture. Indeed, it is probably safe to say that no word evokes quite the same "meaning" for any two persons, since their backgrounds, experiences, interests, and so on are all a little different. Across cultures, of course, equivalent words for similar realities are likely to evoke even greater differences in reactions. Osgood's semantic differential technique has been used to reveal this, and it has also been used to show rather consistent associations among certain "dimensions of meaning" in many different languages.[12] A simpler and more direct technique for such comparisons is some kind of word association test, starting with the best translations for a word and comparing the associations

[12] Charles E. Osgood, George J. Suci, and Percy H. Tannenbaum, **The Measurement of Meaning** (Urbana: University of Illinois Press, 1957).

these stimulus words evoke. An excellent study among Americans, French, and Japanese conducted by a trilingual scholar revealed quite different reactions to the word "marriage" and its equivalents in French (**mariage**) and in Japanese (**kekkon**).[13] For the Americans marriage was associated with equality and sharing, togetherness, and love. For the French, sexuality and passion were highly salient, confirming some stereotypes, no doubt. For the Japanese, we find family and children at the heart, with a strong pessimistic undertone of obligations and "the end of the line." There was also considerable overlap in the associations in all these languages and cultures, of course, but the differences, particularly in the associations most frequently made, were striking. The same study revealed comparable differences for the concepts of "foreigner," "friendship," and "work." To the question, Are we measuring differences in language or in culture? we might best answer, "Yes." The question, of course, divides what in reality cannot be so neatly distinguished. (One has nearly the same problem in trying to answer if such a test is examining reactions to words or to "concepts.") Getting married in New York, Tokyo, or Paris is, in one sense, not so different. But in the more personal sense of expectations and satisfactions, "marriage" in each part of the world does seem different.

Our point here is simply the familiar semantic one but applied across languages and across cultural lines. What I mean by a word or phrase may not be quite the same as what **you** mean by that; meanings are in **people,** not in language. That seems so obvious that it is hardly worth mentioning. However, in regard to language and culture relationships we are interested more in a sort of "collective meaning" of peoples in one culture as compared to that in another culture. There is no reason to assume that the reactions would be identical. Of course if the reactions are totally different we should suspect that our choice of near equivalents was faulty in the first place.

Further complicating semantics across cultures is the whole range of nonverbal cues and paralinguistic modifications, such

---

[13] Nicole Takahara, "Semantic Concepts of 'Friendship,' 'Marriage,' 'Work,' and 'Foreigner' in the American, Japanese and French Cultures" (Thesis, Tokyo: International Christian University).

as inflection, **tone** of voice, volume. In this respect, dictionaries are not of much help in comparing differences or similarities of any one speaker's meaning at any particular time. Consider, for example, a translation from Arabic of a simple "no" in conversation. To the average North American, "no" is only a negation or refusal or denial. To the native speaker of Arabic, however, if **that** was meant by the term "no" it would be **repeated** several times accompanied by sounds of tongue clucking against the teeth and the head shaking from side to side. In Japan such an emphatic "no" is almost never said; rather there seem to be about twenty different ways of conveying that meaning without ever having to say that nasty word directly.

Language, rhetoric, patterns of thought

If one's language were fully deterministic, there would be no need for an additional category like "patterns of thought" or possibly even "rhetoric." Describe the language and you take care of the rest. But obviously, and fortunately, people speaking the same language do not all think the same way; every language group has its share, disproportionate perhaps, of fools and wisemen. Nevertheless, assuming that language is at least a potentially important factor in influencing "thought," we should say something here about the relationship, although we will develop this further in Chapter Ten.

To start with a relatively safe but little pursued subject, **style** in expression seems very much influenced by language. Long ago Sapir wrote an intriguing essay in which he argued that poetic style was highly determined by language, implying among other things, that it was inevitable that rhyme should enter English poetry late and disappear early, since the English language is not a rhyming language like French or Spanish.[14] One reason, for illustration, is that the rules for noun-adjective agreement inevitably produce rhymes in some languages but not in others: "casa blanca" versus "white house." English poets and songsters may choose to compose rhymes, and we come to expect them in such forms as mnemonic devices ("Thirty days

[14] Edward Sapir, "Language and Literature," in **Culture, Language, and Personality,** ed. D. G. Mandelbaum (Berkeley: University of California Press, 1958).

hath September, April, June, and November") and nursery rhymes. Swahili seems even more euphonic, (**"haraka, haraka, haina baraka"**), including the option to coin words by repeating units (a motorcycle is **"piki-piki,"** garbage is **"taka-taka"**). Japanese poetry, even children's songs and chants have no rhyming at all. On the other hand, onomatopoeia in Japanese is rich in rhyme and rhythm—particularly for the sounds of nature, like the voluminous amount of rain sounds (**"pichi-pichi,"** **"chapu chapu"**). Noticeable here is that these onomatopoeia are used frequently in adult speech. For English speakers, such sound-words are usually limited to audiences of children, or for special effect or irony, like Faulkner's "ding dong of doom" or Brendan Behan's cheerful sneer (in **The Hostage**), that "the bells of hell go 'ding a ling a ling' for you but not for me." Such usages in English are not the stuff of normal adult speech. We cite such examples only to establish a **prima facie** case that the link between language and at least a small part of "rhetoric" cannot be ignored. If rhyming words are associated with children's speech, then the careful writer or speaker should avoid them except for comic or very special effects. We do not take them so seriously: witness Spiro Agnew.

"Rhetoric," of course, is concerned with far more than style, even if some writers would so limit its scope. We can move to the traditional concern of persuasion, and heighten this concern with a view to persuasion for action in issues so fundamental as to alter structures of societies, or even alter the course of history. Of course, most speeches have no such effect, most speakers no such intention. Still, a history of public address will note speeches that were great not necessarily because of their style but because of the way that they came to influence how people later thought. Often such speeches are characterized by the introduction of an especially attractive metaphor, original or not, a symbolic restructuring of realities that altered history and, not incidentally, sometimes added another item to the dictionary. In this century, in English, we could cite "the iron curtain" image of Churchill, or "Black Power" of Stokely Carmichael, and others. The same language-rhetoric principle could be pursued to usages that dull responses, the intentionally soporific rhetoric of bureaucrats and concealers, such as in reports on the Viet

Nam War, where "pacification" had nothing to do with peace. In such issues there appears to be nothing special about **language** that either facilitates or makes difficult such rhetorical coinages. But consider a society where there has been no such thing as democracy, citizenship, voting, and related concepts. The speaker who would introduce such concepts must in some way alter the language even as he works within it. Consider the Christian missionary who preaches about a god image, which to him is unitary and metaphorically male, in a society where the equivalent might be pluralistic or female. The dedicated missionary is likely to try to speak in the language of his would-be converts, but in the process of prosyletizing he might alter at least the semantic reactions to that language. Language and rhetoric cannot be separated.

"Patterns of thinking" seem to lie outside of the narrow view of both language and rhetoric, and yet it is a part or product of such. One of the most intriguing possibilities advanced by Sapir and Whorf is that of the actor-action pattern. The English language, among others, seems to require in its subject-predicate structure a distinction between an actor and the action he (or it) performs. "Rain" sounds like an incomplete statement; "it is raining" sounds complete but the fictitious "it" is not different from the "raining." The language, it seems, requires the addition of the imaginary "it"; not all languages do. The question then is, "does it make any difference in the way we think, or are these only superficial differences in the form of expression?" And that question takes us back to where we were before.

Similar questions, maybe all dead-end questions, can be asked about other requirements of a language, such as how we must mark tenses, plurals, and gender. Such characteristics vary considerably across languages; that is undeniable. Are they simply different ways of "encoding reality," or do they mediate in the perception of that reality so as to influence thought? The answer does not seem as clear cut to us as that which is put forth by the proponents of either end of the linguistic relativity continuum.

At international conferences, the role of a language on the rhetoric of arguments presented is sometimes painfully apparent, particularly to the translator. Later in this book we will deal at some length with the special role of the translator or interpreter, but here we wish to cite one example of the language-rhetoric problem as described by Edmund Glenn, who was formerly the chief of the interpretation branch of the United States Department of State.[15] During a minor procedural matter at the United Nations a dispute arose which had to be handled in the languages of English, French, and Russian. The Soviet representative kept labeling certain Western standards as **nepravilnoe,** "incorrect." He did not mean that they were deliberately false but that they were based on what to him were the wrong premises. When the U.S. delegate referred to his country's economy as an "expanding economy," the Soviet delegate took exception. Expanding, which in English could mean by reasons of outside factors, has to be translated into Russian by a reflexive verb, **self-expanding.** However, by definition a capitalistic economy is a contracting one to the communistic mind, since that is part of the teaching of Marx, Engels, and Lenin. Hence, there was, to the Soviet delegate, an inherent contradiction in the American phrase.

The French verb **deduire,** whose etymological and normal translation into English would be deduce, came out properly as **assume** in the considered context. It was not a scientific deduction but rather an assumption based on the facts presented. The French term **avis,** normally opinion, was in the context presented an assertion or a strong affirmation; the term **prejuger** lent itself to two possible interpretations, prejudice and prejudge. The translator's choice lay between the two which do not at all carry the same meanings and connotations in English.

As we shall discuss shortly, a translator is something of a rhetorician, obliged to try to adapt to the receiver audience. The translator or interpreter is not, however, expected to display his problems of interpretation or to give a lecture on the constraints of language on thought. Thus an audience is likely to receive a speech through translation with certain distortions, which are apparent only to the sensitive interpreter or observed later by some communication analyst. The audience applauds the speech politely or enthusiastically. In any case they are likely to be reacting primarily to what they have heard, not what

[15] Glenn, "Semantic Difficulties," pp. 163–180.

was originally stated. They are also reacting to what their language allows them to hear.

Put it in writing

What Sapir and Whorf did years ago to raise questions about the relationship of a language on the perception and thought of its users, Marshall McLuhan has done for media.[16] Any medium, he has argued, not only structures the reality it would symbolize, it also has an effect on the human nervous system which is unique, different from any other medium. And beyond this, he has argued that the medium is actually more important than the apparent content it would express. Hence his aphorism, "The medium is the message." This is not the book to discuss various media available or even to pursue the assertions of Marshall McLuhan, with one exception: speech systems as compared to writing systems.

As mentioned earlier, "language," to a linguist, is spoken language; writing is usually viewed as a substitute for speech. Communication specialists are well aware of that distinction and of advantages and disadvantages of using each form for a particular purpose. However, we should not treat writing as little more than a technical improvement upon speech. Goody has pointed out that in India the most sacred words continued to be transmitted orally long after literacy was available.[17] Nor in our everyday affairs do letters fully substitute for conversation, or a printed text for a speech. Even more important, perhaps, is the likely impact of writing on rhetoric and persuasion. Goody remarks that it is significant that "the religions of conversion, the excluding religions, are all religions of the book."[18] In our consideration of intercultural communication and the relationship of speech and writing to perception and thought, we would like to call attention only to a few possibilities that should not go unnoticed.

One possibility is the impact of literacy on memory. There is

---

[16] McLuhan, **Understanding Media,** Chapter Nine.
[17] Jack Goody, ed., **Literacy in Traditional Societies** (Cambridge: Cambridge University Press, 1968), p. 12.
[18] Ibid., p. 7.

evidence that people in societies which have no written language have better memories than those who are accustomed to reading and writing.[19] Certainly before literacy was widespread and books were inexpensively available, a person was compelled to draw from memory information that today is found in books. Even in Europe in the Middle Ages, university examinations were all conducted orally. Among other effects, this seems to have required people to rely on mnemonic and other stylistic techniques to recall information as needed or to present a speech; thus we also should pursue relationships between oral and literate societies on rhetoric and argumentation. There is also the suspicion that primarily oral societies have a view of history which is quite different from that of literate societies; the "lineality" of time, best illustrated in those "time-lines" in classrooms, might also be a product of writing.

If we can make a distinction between oral and literate societies, we should also go further to distinguish between at least two different kinds of writing systems. One is that of a phonetic system, such as that of the Roman alphabet or other similar alphabets. Another kind, much older but less widespread today, is that of a pictographic or ideographic kind. Chinese characters (and Japanese, which were borrowed from the Chinese, even though these two spoken languages are totally different) are primarily ideographic. Does it make a difference if the written symbol which represents some referent is based on the sounds of the spoken word which labels that referent, or if it is more a kind of picture of that referent? McLuhan has asserted that it does, going so far as to say that **rationality** is possible only in societies that use a phonetic alphabet.[20] His reasons are more difficult to present than his assertion, unfortunately. These are based on what he regards as different effects of using the ear or the eye, and the view that a reader of a phonetic script is engaged in a more abstract exercise than one who reads ideographic characters, such as Chinese, Egyptian hieroglyphics, or ancient Mayan codices. Probably what McLuhan has pre-

[19] J. C. Carothers, "Culture, Psychiatry and the Written Word," **Psychiatry** 22 1959: 307–20; the point is also made in McLuhan, **Understanding Media,** and in Leonard Doob, **Communication in Africa** (New Haven: Yale University Press, 1961).
[20] McLuhan, **Understanding Media,** Chapter Nine.

sented here resembles the assertions of Sapir and Whorf in another way, it seems impossible to prove or to disprove. Still one can be impressed with novelty of the view and might even suppose that form of writing could make a difference, or even that it **should.** Although we will move on without any further discussion, we should note the parallels between the phonetic-ideographic distinction and that between the digital and analogical distinction which was mentioned in Chapter Six.

Back to Babel: some extra-symbolic considerations

For many years in film, a stock male romantic lead has been an actor with a French accent, a Boyer or Montand; females, **diteaux:** B. Bardot, C. Deneuve. It is not only the voice, but the accent, of course, that is an important part of the romance. Then there is Henry Kissinger. Was it his mind that was so impressive or did the residue of his German youth carry through his voice to help add that extra-symbolic measure of Continental authority? How do North Americans sound to persons with whom they speak in other countries, assuming that the Americans are otherwise doing well at speaking a second language? Since little empirical research has been conducted in this area we can only raise the question as an important extra-symbolic aspect of language in intercultural communication: Do accents matter? A good guess is, yes, they probably do. But if so, in what situations, and with what effect?

At the very least an accent serves to distinguish a speaker from the language-culture group with whom he is speaking. Possibly for certain kinds of emotionally-laden communication, an accent adds mystery, and maybe mystery lends enchantment. Maybe all foreign-sounding lovers sound sexier. For the cognitive we may have different standards or possibly different preferences in accents. We may react differently if a medical doctor sounds like he is from Germany or from Arkansas. Edward Stewart has observed that U.S. Peace Corps volunteers do prefer doctors from their own culture or at least those trained in the United States.[21] On the other hand he finds that the volunteers

---

[21] Edward Stewart, personal correspondence.

much prefer to get information about a culture from a person who seems to be a native of that culture, even if an American lecturer were somewhat better informed. The distinction between "one of us" and "one of them" is operative, and an accent is at the same time one of the most obvious ways of marking such a distinction.

Another extra-symbolic aspect of language, probably even more telling than accent, is that of slang or in-group speech. We not only use a language to reflect our culture, we use language to constantly identify our relationship to that culture. It is far more difficult for a parent to get by through talking like his or her child than for a speaker of one language to "get by" through speaking like a native. To try to identify with something other than what you are often produces the worst possible reaction, resentment, alienation. It is usually good advice to try to understand the in-group idiom, but not necessarily to try to imitate it.

These considerations bring us back to the starting point of our discussion of the role of language and language differences in intercultural communication, the notion that in speaking a language we take the view that language is much more than "the channel" through which ideas are conveyed. Language is also a rallying symbol, a means of identification. It is a tool and, for some, the lens through which "reality" is perceived, or the structure in which life is lived. Metaphors abound. We must not mark off an area in which to confine language within intercultural communication. It responds to and at the same time influences questions of values, nonverbal behavior, and much that might be included in the realm of "thinking patterns."

The philosophers say that it is language that distinguishes man from animals, that sets all of us apart from other creatures on this earth. And that may be true. But even more obviously, languages set us apart from others of our species in the shadow of the tower of Babel.

NINE

The man (or woman) in the middle

A sharp distinction is usually made between interpersonal or face-to-face communication and "mass communication," where words and images are conveyed through some intervening media such as print or electronic impulses. Our interest is clearly with the former, although we should also remember that even the study of mass communication ultimately involves the individual. Nevertheless, when looking at interpersonal communication across cultures, there is very often **another** kind of intervening factor, a **human** factor that is rarely touched upon in discussions of intercultural communication.

Who's that?

They are guides, go-betweens, translators, interpreters (or "interrupters," as a British colleague working in Africa calls them with characteristic disdain). Some are highly paid, traveling as part of an official party wherever they are called; some are recruited on the spot and not so well paid. Most are nameless, though their faces sometimes appear in news photos along with world leaders meeting to discuss trade or peace. They are the

men (or at least as often, women) in the middle of most intercultural communication. But it is odd that we pay more attention
to (and know more about) the electrical circuitry that connects
speaker and listener than we know about the human connection
which makes even the most rudimentary communication possible between persons speaking different languages.

While we are more concerned with speaking than writing, the
case for literary translators is not much different. We say we read
the works of Nobel Prize Winners, but what we often are reading
are the translations of works, just as the Nobel Prize Jury did;
we say we are reading the words of Pasternak, Kawabata,
Jimenez, but we are probably reading the words of . . . who can
name the translators?

Some day the field of translation and interpretation will be
recognized in its own right and paid due—overdue—respect.
When that happens and when the field is studied in detail we
may make a quantum leap in our understanding of many aspects
of intercultural communication. But that day may be several
years away. Right now in the United States, in Europe, and in
Asia, the interpreters are mostly ignored, un-united, underpaid.
If they ever were united and went on strike, communication
across cultures would be paralyzed as fast and as severely as with
a global power failure.

At this writing, there are fewer than a dozen universities teaching interpretation and translation—and this is the figure for
the world, not for any one nation. In both the United States and
in the U.S.S.R., the two universities teaching interpreting
(Georgetown and Moscow University) offer courses only at the
graduate level. In Japan, at International Christian University,
the course is a part of a broader discipline of intercultural communication, but it appears that this is unique.[1] Elsewhere, if
formal training is provided it is treated as a part of language
learning or is further specialized as a discipline in itself. And
this is odd, too, since so much is required of a first-class professional interpreter: the awareness of a range of topics of a

---

[1] At International Christian University there are three courses in interpretation
offered for undergraduate students in the Communication Department; there
is also a two-course sequence in written translation, also at the undergraduate
level.

renaissance man, the sensitivity to nuance and implied messages of a psychotherapist, the caution of a diplomat, and the facility with expression of a professional speaker on the lecture circuit. All this plus a command (and the metaphor is significant) of at least two languages.

The reasons for the lowly position of translators and interpreters are not clear, but they seem to be based on erroneous notions about communication itself. For one thing, there is the old notion that language is a neutral medium—that ideas exist apart from language, that the significant differences between languages are phonological or morphological only, so that translation is simply a matter of matching words. It follows from this assumption that any bilingual is a good interpreter; as we shall note later, this is not such a simple matter. Another assumption seems to be that "information" is totally separable from the manner in which it is conveyed; and thus the words of a German professor emeritus will be unaffected if expressed by a twenty-two-year-old girl from Malaysia. This seems unlikely, but there has been no empirical research to support or refute this. There are other assumptions as well, involving empathy and rapport, status differences, the number of people involved in a transaction, delay of feedback, awareness of potential distortion, and much more that any student of interpersonal communication can easily imagine.

The matter is even more puzzling given the attitude—particularly in the United States—toward foreign language abilities. There are high and low prestige languages and peculiar equations of more and better, but as a rule the polyglot impresses the monolingual, often for the most primitive of reasons ("Does that really mean something?").

Being bilingual is a mixed blessing. As a rule, bilinguals who have learned both languages at an early age score lower on IQ tests conducted in a single language, that is, all IQ tests. This of course, says something about the nature of IQ tests and not about the intelligence quotient of bilinguals. Moreover, linguists divide bilinguals into two camps, the compound and the coordinate. For the compound bilingual, it is as if "reality" is all one that can be symbolized by alternative names in either language. For the coordinate bilingual, "realities" are clearly distinguished by separate language systems. The compound bilinguals usually find it difficult to become good simultaneous interpreters, while coordinate bilinguals can be trained more easily. From that point of view, if a person wants to become a professional simultaneous interpreter it is better to study a foreign language than to grow up in a bilingual world. But there is a catch: For biological reasons, as Lenneberg has demonstrated, learning a second language after puberty is a substantially different matter than learning one earlier—and this becomes more difficult with each passing year.[2] So it seems that the best potential interpreters—at least simultaneous interpreters who can start expressing language A as soon as they hear language B—should learn their second language as a separate language before they go to high school.

Wallace Lambert's studies of Canadian bilinguals have led him to some encouraging conclusions about the outlook and psychic well-being of bilinguals.[3] In contrast to earlier studies of Italian-Americans, who suffered conflicts between identification with their Italian born parents and identification with their American peers, Lambert's French Canadians seemed to avoid that kind of identity crisis and appeared to be far more open-minded and appreciative of other cultures and languages. Whereas Irvin Child in his study of the Italian-American children found many so frustrated by the identity conflict that they simply withdrew into themselves, Lambert's findings show the bilinguals to be positively bicultural, enjoying the best of two worlds instead of acting as victims of the clash of cultures. It is suggested that bilinguals also have the advantage over monolinguals of being able to escape from one real world of problems and annoyances into another language world, but one equally grounded in reality; monolinguals in contrast may find their only escape route into a world of fantasy.

Any person who has spent even a few days in a land where he cannot comprehend the language knows of the relief provided by language ignorance. Neighbors' problems rarely intrude, news-

[2] Eric Lenneberg, **The Biological Foundations of Language** (New York: John Wiley and Sons, 1967), Chapter Four.
[3] Wallace Lambert, **Language, Psychology and Culture** (Stanford: Stanford University Press, 1972).

paper headlines and radio or television reports can be ignored, and unmanageable events of the world are cut down to human size. The bilingual, to some extent, can do the same, not retiring into the bliss of ignorance but traveling linguistically to another less threatening world. This is a new argument in the old theme that foreign language learning is good for you, though it doesn't much bolster the case for learning Latin.

Lambert's subjects were bilinguals who, for the most part, did not employ their dual language skills professionally. We need more studies of the psychological aspects of the men in the middle, for as professional interpreters and translators (in journalism rather than literature) these people cannot escape the problems symbolized in one world—or, if they can, they would seem to do so in a very special way. We have not met any interpreters, simultaneous or otherwise, who can clearly say how they do what they do so well. Most say that they are aware of pressure and the resulting fatigue, but they also say that they do not, cannot, think very much about the content of their interpreting at the time. If they did they would be incapable of performing well. For the same reason, it seems, most cannot remember very well what was said—they were too busy interpreting to be able to recall details. On the other hand, since their abilities are far from being mere mechanical skills (they are not about to be replaced by translating machines), it would seem that their experiences would influence in some way their personality and "cognitive structure." Much more is known about bilingual children, and second language acquisition than about the mental world of the interpreter. Although even professional interpreters themselves cannot explain very clearly how they perform, it would seem to be very important to understand the process. It would be helpful to know, for example, what kinds of unintentional distortions are most common in interpreting, to be able to estimate the percentage of information loss in translation, and to know something of the psychological impact of interpretation on the audience and on the speaker, as well.

Spoken interpretation is usually of two kinds, consecutive and simultaneous. The difference in form is readily apparent. In **consecutive interpretation** a speaker presents part of his speech (or all of it, if it is a relatively brief remark), and the interpreter, who has been taking notes, then expresses the translation. For a long speech this results in the alternative speaking of the original and the interpretation. **Simultaneous interpretation** is usually possible only with the aid of a special microphone and earphones, since the interpretation comes simultaneously with the original; of course this is not completely simultaneous, since the interpreter must hear some of the original before beginning to translate it. Nevertheless, there are almost always two voices, in the two languages, being expressed at the same time, with the good interpreter beginning only a fraction of a second after the speaker begins and concluding a second or two after he is finished. In a multinational conference or world assembly, such as the United Nations General Assembly, the delegates and visitors can adjust their receivers to listen in through any of several languages.

There are other objective differences as well: consecutive interpretation, approximately doubling the length of time needed for a presentation, for example, allows the interpreter to appear before the audience just like any other speaker; a simultaneous interpreter, most often, is hidden away in a booth or at the back of the room and thus unobtrusive if not completely invisible. The subtler differences may be more interesting, however. Newsmen at press conferences often prefer consecutive interpretation to simultaneous interpretation. Many are sufficiently capable in two languages to benefit from (and compare) both presentations, and redundancy has long been known as one of the best checks against distortions. The person giving the press conference himself may prefer the longer, consecutive method, too, for similar reasons and for the added gain in time to consider how to answer a question and sense the mood of the audience. But for a person unaccustomed to speaking through a consecutive interpreter, the experience can be unnerving: Timing and pacing is destroyed and rapport is minimal, the speaker knowing that this audience is listening to him without comprehending, partly curious and polite, partly impatient for the interpretation to begin. The good interpreter will often try to empathize with the speaker in tone of voice, even in gestures and facial expressions where these are comparable. But sometimes a faithful rendering of the original into the second language but without adjustment to culture differences can lead to new misunderstandings. An American woman speaking to women in a culture where the woman's role and communicative style is sharply distinguished from a man's, can sound in "direct translation" bold, masculine, abrasive and probably, as a result, unconvincing.

Keep in mind that translating from one language to another is never a simple process of word-for-word substitution. In some languages a verb may come near the beginning of a sentence, while in others it may always come at the end. This makes it difficult to be fully "simultaneous." What is expressed as a verb in one language may be a noun or a phrase in another. What is an idiom in one language may have to be explained in another. Mechanical problems? Then what of a term that is tabooed or a joke in one language that is the opposite in a second? What happens when word order and jokes are combined in one language and must be rendered without delay into another language: **What is more difficult than getting a pregnant elephant in a Volkswagen? Getting an elephant pregnant in a Volkswagen!** Try that in Swahili or Urdu and start speaking **now!** Difficult? Think of the pressure: Your speaker has said it to relax everybody and show what a sense of humor he has; make sure that mood is conveyed along with the joke. In his culture speeches always start with a joke, but in the receiver language a man in his position should be serious: Convey that to your listeners. It is not surprising that in part of the folklore of interpreters is the story of the interpreter who told his audience: "Our guest has just told a joke. Please be so kind as to laugh."

In fact, good interpreters rarely have such confidence to be so cavalier with their entrusted task. They cope with what they hear, often without being told ahead of time exactly what will be said. They would seem to be servants of two masters, the speaker and the audience, and their service is best when both speaker and audience remain convinced of that fidelity. The Bible tells us that one cannot serve two masters, but one's status as interpreter requires just that. Experience at re-telling something even in the same language indicates that one version will probably be better than the other, but the goal of the best interpreter is to favor neither the original nor the translation. Research into information distortion occurring when the news, good or bad, is sent upward to superiors or downward to subordinates shows what filtering takes place in any serial communication. But the interpreter is supposed to be impervious to that. We might assume that anything related in a second language involves some loss, like photographing a photograph, or Wiener's entropic interpretation: Things fall apart, they cannot get better.[4] The interpreter is to defy the Second Law of Thermodynamics. Of course, if there are sentiments about the sound or feel of a foreign language things may be different—the American poet remarked that in the translator's French version of his poems, something was **gained** in translation, but this is unlikely and even if true it would then not be a good translation. You can't win for losing.

What is needed, perhaps, is not further perfection of the art, but further appreciation for what is inevitably involved in translation and interpretation. With the study of interpersonal communication in general, where the constant theme is not so much "Here is how we can do better" as "it's a wonder we do as well as we do, considering"—and the urging of caution, sympathy, double-checking, and not blaming—we might do better to lower the expectations instead of raising the demands.

Anthropologists in the field who have had to recruit interpreters on the spot without sufficient knowledge or skill to judge the abilities of their assistants have developed some tests for judging their skills. (Even these tests, such as back-translation, are recent and often may not be followed. In published scholarly research the name of the interpreter utilized may be "credited" in a footnote but the accuracy of interpretation may be checked only indirectly through consistency of results with other related research.) Someday scholars may evolve a set of standards for interpretations, much as statistical tests have become standardized, but that day may be a long way off.

By convention, the distinction between the use of "translation" and "interpretation" is mostly one of media, the former used for written works, and the latter with speech. The nuance in English, however, suggests more—that translation is more faithful, interpretation more beautiful (recalling the analogy of

[4] Norbert Wiener, **The Human Use of Human Beings** (Garden City, N. J.: Doubleday-Anchor, 1950), Chapter Two.

a translation and a woman: if she is faithful she is not beautiful, if she is beautiful she is not faithful). In fact, however, media is a better basis of distinction than fidelity, since interpretation obviously involves translation and translation almost always involves an individual's interpretation of what was probably meant and what will probably best serve as an equivalent. Translators and interpreters currently debate the same semantics of identity that rhetoricians have argued for thousands of years: Is interpreting an art, a craft, a science, or, as Plato said of public speaking, just a knack? One senses a universal ambivalence toward communication that is public. That is, we allot the scientist the role of pursuing "objective reality," and grant the artist the right to express his own view of reality; but the interpreter, like the public spokesman, is the man in the middle, neither fully objective nor personal. In defense, the interpreter can justifiably claim he must be both: sufficiently objective to be faithful to the original, and enough of an artist to render the original into an eloquent equivalent, but this still places him in the middle.

Eugene Nida, the foremost teacher of Bible translation (which, theology aside, constitutes one of the most extensive and impressive fields of translation), uses the term "dynamic equivalence" to identify the goal of a good translation.[5] The term appropriately identifies the tension of translation, "dynamic" pulling in the direction of what would be contextually appropriate in the receptor language, and "equivalent" pulling in the direction of fidelity to the original. A translation which is "too dynamic," in this sense, may be criticized as a paraphrase or, worse, as a totally new expression only "inspired" by the original. Fitzgerald's "translation" of the **Rubáiyát of Omar Khayyam** is one of the best known examples of this. A translation which is "too equivalent," in the sense of being rigidly bound to the original, comes off as "too literal," unnatural, self-conscious, or, worse, unintelligible unless one already knows the original! Good translations may be said to reside uneasily between these poles, with the constant danger of having gone too far one way or the other.

As Nida and others have stressed, the translator is attempting

[5] Eugene Nida, **Toward a Science of Translating** (Leiden: Brill, 1964), pp. 120–144.

to convey "meaning"—not words—from one language to another. And so translation begins, as it were, by going backwards —from the words of the original to the inferred meaning that evoked those words. The fields of literary and rhetorical criticism document the problems of that stage even without being concerned with translating that meaning into symbols which are comparably meaningful in another language. But the translator and interpreter must do just that: Having sensed the meaning of the writer or speaker, the goal is to find words in another language which will likely evoke a similar meaning for persons receiving the message in that language.

Thus, the man in the middle stands between a speaker and a listener, a writer and reader. He or she also is in the middle of choices: what was probably "meant" in the original, and what will probably convey that same meaning, more or less, in the second language. We commonly think of an interpreter or translator as only working between **languages,** but this may be the lesser of interlocutor roles. That is, a particular utterance arises **from an individual** and not from a language in general, and it must be re-expressed in a particular choice of words and not just in anything intelligible in that language. Thus there is a double choice that must be made. Often it must be made while simultaneously hearing the original and starting to express the interpretation. And so although the man in the middle is often expected to be neutral, a channel or conduit or, at best, an amplifier of sorts, actually he or she must be extraordinarily sensitive and necessarily subjective. It is hard enough to paraphrase within the same language and within the same value system what a speaker meant; it is obviously far more difficult to act within another language that divides reality differently, is related to a different system of values, and is possibly articulated in a different tone of voice with different expectations.

Malinche's sisterhood

The conquest of the mighty Aztecs by the small band of soldiers led by Cortez continues to intrigue the historian, philosopher, and poet. Some give credit to Aztec prophecy of a white god coinciding with the sudden arrival of Cortez; some stress the practical and psychological power of the Spaniards' horses and weapons; for the Mexican poet Octavio Paz, what occurred was not a defeat but a suicide.[6] Part of all such interpretations is the role played by Malinche, who served as Cortez' guide, interpreter, and mistress. Even today Mexicans speak of the **malinchistas** who open the way for the violation of the culture by serving the invader. The image is at least as sexual as it is linguistic: Intercultural communication in this context seems to be a euphemism for violation.

Adventure stories of the Lone Ranger and his faithful Indian guide, for example, imply a cozy relationship between the two, but most likely the relationship between a guide and his or her people is by no means so close. (The ethnocentrism which produces distrust of such a go-between finds a close parallel today in much of the world's attitudes toward ethnically or racially mixed marriages, where the families of the bride or the groom or both may regard their errant children as outcasts.) Warnings to distrust foreign visitors are legion, with allusions to the Trojan Horse appearing in many forms. Be polite but lock up your treasures and hide your daughters. Less conspicuous but probably no less frequent are warnings about serving as or seeking out a go-between. Beware of people too eager to help you.

A professional interpreter, even less a translator, is not likely to be regarded as a **malinchista,** of course. Like any professional, the interpreter is assumed to have personal feelings, and to be loyal to the task at hand, not to one or the other parties in the engagement.

However, it is not possible in a society where the visitor does not know the language to function effectively by relying on a "neutral" objective interpreter. The reasons should be obvious. It does no good to have questions translated into another language if the questions are inappropriate or meaningless in the first place. Over a period of time, even a short period of time, the interpreter is thus likely to try to teach the visitor something about the culture as well as serving him. More than this, some empathy must exist between the two if they are to get along, and such empathy always involves more than professional serv-

---

[6] Octavio Paz, **The Labyrinth of Solitude** (New York: Grove Press, 1963).

ice. Moreover, where the go-between clearly functions as a guide as well as interpreter, the roles of superior and subordinate will frequently be reversed, with the visitor more often obeying the suggestions of the person in his employ, rather than only giving orders to that person. Some visitors from so-called developed nations working in traditional societies may tend to regard their local assistants much like children who are dutiful but unsophisticated. In fact, however, the visitor is more likely to take the role of the child obeying the guidance of the other: "Now stand up;" "Say 'thank you,'" and so on.

We know of no social study of the man in the middle as a "type" nor historical survey of the famous guides and interlocutors in history, though such studies could be of great value in this important and frequent aspect of intercultural communication. Our image is likely to be shaped by the necessarily distorted images from fiction—Robinson Crusoe's man Friday, for example—than the less romantic facts of history.

Conclusion

The middleman, the go-between, the guide, interpreter, interlocutor, has extraordinary powers to influence the outcomes of intercultural communication. Like executive secretaries within organizations, he has access to considerable information, and may know something of the background and purposes of such information. He is far more than a channel or filter in the process of communication. He exerts and is a recipient of pressure. His role as a vital link in the process of intercultural communication must be given much more attention than it has received in the past. More than this, however, his own life, personality, and mental processes deserve much more study, for these men and women in the middle are interesting in themselves. And also, they may tell us something about the possible character of many others who might be like them in the future—if not our children, then surely many of our grandchildren.

TEN

Thinking about thinking

Paul's case

Paul is Swiss. He is also a Jesuit priest, and for over eight years he helped direct a technical training college in Indonesia. There, as elsewhere in developing nations, discovering sources of fresh water and drilling wells are serious problems. Paul often spoke of the ordeal of drilling and the technical difficulties of installing and maintaining good pumps once the well was drilled. We asked Paul how he knew where to start drilling in the first place. He shrugged the question off as a simple one, explaining: "First you select a young tree, cut a Y-shaped branch, grasp it in both hands, pointing the long branch away from you but parallel to the ground. Then you start walking. When the branch begins to vibrate, you know you are over water. When it really shakes, you know there is a good source of water underground." Having explained this ancient method of "the divining rod," he turned again to the more serious problems of maintenance of pumps, obtaining of spare parts, and so on. He had special praise for a West German pump. "That's a beautifully made pump—almost never breaks down. I visited the German company and told the engineer so, too."

Paul is a serious person, a Swiss Jesuit. He was not joking about the divining rod. But we did not quite understand. "Do you close you eyes when you walk?" He laughed, "Of course not, you might bump into something." That we understood. But how, we wondered, could such a technique work? It did not make sense to us. More than that, how could a technical training director like Paul accept such a method? Paul agreed he used to wonder about its rationality too, but he said that since it almost never failed—unlike other methods—he did not think much about it when there were more important problems at hand. Then he added this note: "When I talked to that German engineer, he also asked me the same question about how we knew where to drill. So I told him what I told you. Then he leaned over his desk and said, 'Don't tell anyone, but that's the same method I use!' "

A Swiss Jesuit and a German engineer agreeing on the efficacy of the divining rod! But assuming that none of us can claim any special expertise in finding water underground, why should that explanation surprise us more than any other? Why are some of us likely to judge that such an explanation is "unreasonable?" If Paul had said that he used electronic soundings to discover water or aerial photography or any of a number of explanations that seem to be in the realm of "science and technology" we might have thought no more about it, even though such explanations alone are no clearer than that of the forked stick.

What is reasonable?

What we are likely to mean by "reasonable" seems to be, in part, what is expected, whether or not we fully understand what is said. Yet this is not enough, for we often hear explanations and arguments that are familiar to us and yet seem weak or fallacious. And, perhaps less common, we do hear novel interpretations or explanations that may impress us at least partly for their very novelty. Still, "familiarity" may comprise a large part of "reasonableness," especially when there are cultural variables.

Let us go further. What is "reasonable" is likely to be that which sounds like what **we** would have said. Or, what is "reasonable" is that which might be said by someone whom we regard as an authority on the subject. In the case of finding water, we may not know what to say but we may have some image of appropriate authorities giving explanations.

So far our description of what makes a statement or explanation seem "reasonable" is not very different from what has been said about rhetoric or persuasion for thousands of years. Specifically, often the most important belief factor is the communicator himself, not just what he says. Also, it has long been said that persuasive arguments reside not just in the speaker or his speech, but to a great extent in the expectations and beliefs of the audience.

It should be clear that these matters are inseparable from cultural assumptions and values. What **we** would say, whom we take as **authorities,** and what sounds "familiar" are all, quite literally, **expressions of our culture.** However, since we know there are plenty of disagreements within any culture, we also may be sure that the matter of seeming reasonable is far more complicated than this. But it does appear clear that a great deal of what is "unreasonable" in expressions from another society can be described by no more than this: I would not have said that, my authorities would not have said that, it does not sound familiar to me.

Let us go further. We might say that what is "reasonable" should be grounded in "reality." When we "reason" we must follow some sort of "logic" or some consistent system which allows us to draw valid conclusions. It is in these two assumptions that we may argue that cultural differences **should be** unimportant. After all, isn't the hallmark of the scientific method that chemists or physicists or biologists from dozens of different cultures can observe the same data, follow the same procedures, and arrive at the same conclusions, even though their native languages, religions, their political philosophies are all different? Yes. And No. Yes, so long as the chemists, physicists, and biologists are investigating the same already identified subject in the same manner. But these subjects are historically intercultural in their development and thus can be regarded as an unusual case. Also, these disciplines may be said to constitute sub-cultures in themselves, characterized by their own languages, their own procedures, even their own heroes and villains. We can go further and say "no" or at least "not necessarily" to our question when the subject is not pure science but the application findings; at this point, cultural differences become extremely important. And it also has been argued by many scientists that "discoveries" and "theories" are strongly influenced by the language, cultural background, and milieu of the scientist. So even "the scientist" in his laboratory is very much a cultural creature.

What of commonsense notions of reality? Won't "reasonable men" from any culture perceive more-or-less the same sun and stars and rivers and mountains? No. **Reality** is, practically, inseparable from our perception of the world around us. And what is perceived is influenced by a complex of factors including what we have been taught to see, what a culture distinguishes as important, what we hope to see, and quite likely the semantic components of our language habits if not the language structure (grammar) itself. Keep in mind that "facts" do not exist in the world; "facts" are verifiable statements. about the world. And people in different societies choose to and need to make different observations.

Edmund Leach, a leading British cultural anthropologist, makes this point nicely:

> Travellers have often remarked of the Australian aborigines that they seem to 'read the desert like a book,' and this is a very literal truth. Such knowledge is not carried in any man's head, it is in the environment. The **environment is not a natural thing; it is a set of interrelated percepts, a product of culture.** It yields food to the aborigine but none to the white traveller because the former perceives food where the latter sees only inedible insects.[1] (Emphasis added.)

"Logic" is very different from perceptions of the environment. Logic, or whatever we call the linkages which show consistencies and relationships, is abstract and deductive. As such it can yield validity, but not "truth." One can be logical about facts; but one can be just as logical about nonsense data or nonsense. Thus any

[1] Edmund Leach, "Culture and Social Cohesion: An Anthropologist's View," in **Science and Culture**, ed. Gerald Holton (Boston: Beacon Press, 1965), p. 25.

logic (Aristotelian logic, symbolic logic, or "non-Western logics") is a learned system and a part of the culture in which it is learned. Mathematics, too, is such a system: $2 + 2 = 4$ is no less a product of culture than is a pair of high-heel shoes. As we mentioned earlier, Whorf and those who have pursued his elusive hypothesis have argued that any spoken language is built upon some implicit "logic" ("subject-predicate," and actor and action in SAE languages) and that these logics, like their more apparent language forms, differ widely. Still, it is not necessary to accept the Whorfian theory in order to recognize our point here: There are many logics, each being a system with its own assumptions and consistent in itself, and different cultures will express different logics.

We can say that what is "reasonable" is not fully separable from cultural assumptions. We need not go so far as to say that it is culture-bound. We cannot escape cultural influences by concentrating on perceptions of reality, nor by relying on logic. If nothing else, this recognition should caution us against criticizing statements from other societies which rely on different authorities, derive from different perceptions of the world, and follow a logic which is different from our own. But this general point is still not sufficient to explain more precisely how such reasoning differs, nor to analyze such arguments on their own grounds, nor to come to learn to adopt or adjust to differences when discussing with a person from another culture. For this kind of understanding we will rely upon two related concepts which are among the oldest concerns of the specialist in speech-communication: **argumentation** and **rhetoric.** Here, **argumentation** will refer to the process of determining and providing "proofs"—going from evidence to conclusions, making inferences and deductions, and in one way or another going from what is known or assumed to an appropriate conclusion. By **rhetoric** we will mean the selection and manner of presentation of proofs in an appropriate form for a given audience to secure belief. Included will be conventional topics of rhetoric: not only proofs through reasoning, but also the means of demonstrating the ethos or credibility of the speaker; emotional appeals; the organization of the presentation; aspects of style; and attention to some nonverbal behavior as well—including clothing, gestures, movement. In our actual behavior, of course, it is difficult to make such neat distinctions.

Structures of arguments

Our simplified layout of argumentation is based on a model pro-posed by Stephen Toulmin; it is a form which already has been revised and developed by scholars in the field of argument.[2] Our scheme uses four key terms: **data,** which yields **evidence,** which leads to a **conclusion,** by way of a **warrant.** Sometimes all four are explicitly stated in an argument, but more often the data and the warrant (and occasionally one of the other two as well) are omitted. We can illustrate these four elements in a simple ex-ample: A telegram arrives at a home early one morning. In the United States, a typical recipient is likely to react (reason) be-fore opening the telegram that "this must be important" or "this must be bad news." In terms of our analysis we can say that out of all of the **data** confronting the householder—the morning air, the color of the uniform of the telegraph agent, and so on—the receipt of the telegram stands out and is transformed into the only important **evidence** for the chain of reasoning which leads to the **conclusion** that "this must be important." The **warrant** is likely to be the implicit experience that only important, and particularly bad, news is sent by telegram. But this warrant is related to other warrants, including the relative cost of sending telegrams, which restricts their use to urgent messages.

If this were Brazil, however, the reaction to receiving such a telegram might be quite different, for there telegrams are rela-tively cheap, often much more reliable than ordinary mail, and therefore sent more often and for all kinds of reasons. Thus al-though the **data** might be more or less the same as in the U.S., it is not likely to be treated as evidence for concluding that it brings bad or even particularly important news. The warrants, as well as the conclusion, of course, must also be different.

It is not too much to say that a complete argument is bound to assumptions based on experience and bound also to values; that the choice of "evidence" is as likely to be derived from

---

[2] See, for example, Russel Windes and Arthur Hastings, **Argumentation and Advocacy** (New York: Random House, 1965); see also, Stephen Toulmin, **The Uses of Argument** (New York: Cambridge University Press, 1958).

expected conclusions as the reverse, and that the warrants that link them are not significantly different from value orientations. Later in this chapter we will introduce some additional variations on this basic structure which will complicate the pattern further in an attempt to account for sensed differences in reasoning, even where these four elements of an argument seem to be the same across cultures.

Evidence appears in several forms. It may be observed sense data, such as seeing clouds (or no clouds) in the sky. It may be hypothetical ("**if** there are no clouds in the sky); or, it may be an assertion of something assumed to be true or known to be valid ("since iron is heavier than feathers" or "since the primary colors are red, yellow, and blue"). Conclusions also take many forms: judgments of better or worse, explanations of causes or predictions of future events, directive statements for policies or actions. Our terms of **evidence** leading to **conclusions** by way of **warrants** can usually be phrased in this form: **Given evidence, therefore conclusions, because of warrant(s).**

If we try to apply this simple model to arguments from different societies, we may run into problems not suggested by the model but anticipated in earlier chapters on value orientations and language. "Evidence" for example, is not "raw data," free of cultural influence. The comment by Leach, cited earlier, makes this point. Another example of language influence is the kind of incident that initially led Benjamin Whorf to probe more deeply into possible relations of language and thought.[3] Whorf, who was an insurance adjuster, discovered that many explosions and fires occurred when people thought of drums that had once contained gasoline as "empty drums." Since the drums were "empty," they assumed the drums posed no hazard to people smoking or using matches. In terms of liquid gasoline, the drums were indeed empty; but the gas fumes remained, which meant that the drums were by no means "empty" and, in fact, much more hazardous than those filled with liquid gasoline. If one draws the conclusion that "it is safe to smoke near these

[3] Benjamin Lee Whorf, "The Relation of Habitual Thought and Behavior to Language," in **Language, Culture and Personality: Essays in Memory of Edward Sapir,** ed. Leslie Spier (Menasha, Wisc.: Sapir Memorial Publication Fund, 1941), pp. 75–93.

drums," using the evidence and warrant that "the drums are empty and no danger can come from empty drums," the language habits have already influenced the interpretation of "the evidence."

Or suppose one reasons that two persons who might be expected to be most alike are "identical twins," since they are born at the same time. This premise is possible only in a language that allows a concept of "identical twins." In some languages such a category is impossible; one child is **always** born first, and therefore is always older than the other. In English-speaking countries there are "identical twins." In Japan, there are not; one child is always older than the other. (This is not simply a matter of language, of course. Values toward age differentiation correspond to these verbal distinctions.)

How one classifies something, what one chooses to notice or ignore, depends a great deal on the language and values of the culture. For this reason, it is helpful to attempt wherever possible to distinguish **data** from **evidence:** at the point we have **evidence** we have already symbolically transformed the data through the language and value system of the society in which it arises.

With conclusions and warrants, structurally tied together, the relationship with language and culture is even closer. A cloudless sky may mean "no rain"; it may also mean God's blessing (or punishment, if rain is needed for the crops), or be a sign to go ahead with a new plan, or much more.

What must be stressed is that the relationship of the evidence, warrant, and conclusion in conventional argumentative analyses is one of consistency. Thus across cultures, the "same evidence" can lead to quite different conclusions which are each logically consistent; this is possible because of different warrants directed toward different goals, and based on different values and assumptions of different cultures. To put it another way, what appears to us to be a **non sequitur** in another society may actually be quite logical (consistent) given the assumptions of that culture. At the beginning of this book we mentioned the ambassador's dandruff, which was sufficient "evidence" to lead to the conclusion that "his wife was not a good wife." The unstated warrant that "a good wife is one who attends to her husband's appearance" makes the conclusion a good argument. For that dandruff to have been significant evidence requires other cultural values to make the dandruff data noticeable in the first place and turn it into evidence.

Qualifiers

The model of arguments thus far implies a certainty of conclusions arising from evidence of one kind or another. But it is in the nature of argumentation and rhetoric that conclusions are not certain: Isocrates long ago said that most things in the world happen neither with absolute certainty nor through whim, and thus it was the function of argument to state what was most likely. Later, Aristotle, too, made this idea central to the concept of rhetoric: People do not argue about what is certain nor about what cannot be known—so rhetoric and argumentation fills that vast middle ground of more or less, the better or worse, and so on.

Toulmin added another term, **qualifier,** to identify the stated cautions in an argument: words and phrases in English such as "unless," "until," "assuming," and the ubiquitous 'if." We will find the use of qualifiers important for identifying these cautions, and also as one means of distinguishing cultural patterns of arguments and patterns of some groups within a culture or across cultures.

Aristotle said that elderly men "are positive about nothing; in all things they err by an extreme moderation. They 'think'—they never 'know'; and in discussing any matter they always subjoin 'perhaps'—'possible.' "[4] This may or may not be true of elderly men in general. But it is a characteristic of speech often identified with other groups, including diplomats and academics. Within the language habits of some cultures, too, one can find variations in the forms and frequency of such qualifiers. In Japanese, for example, words equivalent to "maybe" or "probably" appear in many more sentences than in English. Where an English language speaker might say, "It will rain tomorrow," the Japanese is more likely to say, "It will probably (or maybe) rain tomorrow." To be more definite seems to require the certainty of a tautology.

[4] Lane Cooper, ed. and trans., **The Rhetoric of Aristotle** (New York: Appleton-Century-Crofts, Inc., 1932), p. 134.

(Thus the Japanese speaker on Monday must say "Tomorrow **is** Tuesday" but he cannot say the equivalent of "Tomorrow will be Tuesday," for that "will" implies a prediction rather than a rule.[5] Our point here is that speakers of different languages and from different cultures may use qualifiers with different frequencies and for different reasons. This may seem of minor importance, but when the pattern of qualification is consistently different from what is expected, it can be puzzling, even quite annoying, with some people seeming to be unreasonably cautious, others seeming to be unreasonably sure of themselves.

In addition, we should recall from our discussions of value orientations that some cultures may allow forms of qualifiers which are not generally acceptable in other societies. "God willing," as we noted earlier, may be an assumed qualifier in many Moslem societies but rejected completely or relegated to "mere style" elsewhere. Similarly, personal "luck," "accident," or "chance," which take many forms across cultures, may be implicit qualifiers or may be stated explicitly or may in either case be regarded as "unreasonable" according to the values and assumptions of the societies in which the argument arises.

In short, in the same way that we must recognize the cultural influences in evidence, conclusions, and most obviously warrants, we must also consider the influence of cultural assumptions in the qualifiers that are part of stated arguments.

Reasoning values: some additional categories

The value orientations presented in Chapter Five take on a new role in identifying arguments in different cultures. Assumptions about human nature, the natural world, and the supernatural appear most frequently in arguments. To these we will add a few additional but related categories which should prove helpful in examining the argumentation of other societies. Especially relevant to evidence are culturally related predispositions toward witnesses and toward physical evidence. A colleague in anthropology has described his emotional conflict while observing some

---

[5] The distinction here is between an inference, which is a guess about the unknown, and a tautology, which states a rule that is part of some system; for further clarification of this distinction, see John Condon, **Semantics and Communication**, 2nd ed. (New York: Macmillan, 1974), Chapter Five.

court trials in East Africa, where the prosecutor's treatment of witnesses and physical evidence was totally fallacious, at least according to the standards of the visiting anthropologist. He felt torn between wanting to help defend the accused by criticizing the prosecutor's case and feeling compelled to remain detached for purposes of gathering data. (He decided to say nothing.) In many daily events, of course, as well as court cases, how we evaluate another's testimony or regard physical evidence is extremely important. Pertaining to warrants leading to conclusions we will add three categories that also seem especially helpful in analyses across cultures: the concept of a moral order in society, the influence of 'outsiders' in their thoughts as well as actions, and assumptions about natural laws or basic truths. Finally, two qualifiers are added which seem to play a much greater role in reasoning outside of "Western" patterns of acceptable argument: "chance" and luck.

Pertaining to evidence

WITNESSES

1. Reports of witnesses are crucial; truth emerges through reports of qualified observers and through cross-examination. (Essential in law, social science surveys, etc.)

2. Reports of witnesses are of limited value; we perceive and remember imperfectly; all reports contain some bias. "One person's word against the other's" means a case is inconclusive.

3. Reports of witnesses are unreliable; people lie all the time, especially those who are most guilty or most involved in a dispute.

PHYSICAL EVIDENCE

1. Physical evidence is most important. Clues, hard data, "facts" are of primary importance. Where "facts" conflict with theory, the theory must be altered.

2. Physical evidence is of no value without interpretation. The same "evidence" can mean different things.

3. Physical evidence is of little value, and at best "circumstantial." Ideas, principles, theories, motivation, etc., are more important. (Characteristic of

Pertaining to evidence (continued)

(Basis of scientific method; essential in proving legal disputes.)

some philosophies [e.g., Platonism], religious and political ["closed"] systems.)

Pertaining to warrants leading to conclusions

MORAL ORDER

1. Basis for the guiding and interpretation of human events. (Characteristic of drama and dramatistic interpretation of events; e.g., classical Greek drama, Elizabethan drama, current scandals, etc.)

2. Contemporary Western humanist concern; social justice, corporate guilt, etc. Tends toward metaphorical rather than literal interpretations (e.g., "a sick society").

3. Relevant only if internalized; a sentimental expression of social order. (May be regarded by some as a reactionary interpretation by those in power to discourage change.)

OUTSIDER'S INFLUENCE

1. Other people exert influence on what happens through thoughts as well as deeds. These range from curses, "the evil eye," etc., through rumor mongers, "conspiracies of silence," etc. What others think matters. (Especially characteristic of traditional "closed societies," "shame cultures" vs. "guilt cultures.")

2. Other people exert influence only through acts, not thoughts; self-fulfilling prophecy may account for influence; social constraints and power structure of society influence human events. (Bureaucratic societies, 'Kafkaesque' situations within society.)

3. What other people think and say is of little importance. "Sticks and stones" philosophy. Each individual is ultimately responsible for his fate. To think otherwise is to be morally weak or paranoid. (Especially characteristic of individualistic valuing societies such as the U.S.)

NATURAL LAW, BASIC TRUTHS

1. 'Truth' derives from first principles, immutable, universal laws. "Reasoning requires placing of specific cases within the framework of these laws. (Platonism, traditional Roman Catholic "natural law;" "Realist epistemology;" concern with essences; systemic and deductive reasoning. Also premises of political order sometimes expressed in preambles of constitutions— e.g., "inalienable rights," etc.)

2. "First principles" may be points of departure; abstract codification of society's beliefs and values, but relative to societies. Subject to modification and revision by new information. (The meaning of "law" as in "scientific laws" which are hypotheses to be tested and revised; and in explicit laws of a society which can be modified through lawful procedures.)

3. "Basic truths" are usually fictions, myths, reactionary expressions used to deny facts or sublimate problems and criticism. (Nominalist philosophy; distrustful of higher level abstractions; cautious inductive approach, representative of philosophies from Bacon through the logical positivists, General Semantics, etc.)

Variations

a. Anthropomorphism as basic truth: life/death cycle; sickness/health; applicable to all events, institutions, etc.

b. Scientific propositions: inductively based, product of best thinking, reveals "truth" objectively wherever it may lead; all aspects of subjective or mentalistic interpretation should be ignored (B. F. Skinner may be the most outstanding exponent of this position today.)

Pertaining to qualifiers

ACCIDENT, CHANCE, HAPPENSTANCE

1. Most of what happens in life is the result of chance; thus the "if" or "if only" caution must be a part of every interpretation. (This interpretation ranges from religious and philosophical notions in Buddhism to Heisenberg's uncertainty principle. It is frequently expressed as "coincidence," "irony," "it can't be helped," "bad luck," etc.)

2. When all other explanations fail, "accidence," "coincidence," etc., may be applied. The importance of "accident" or "chance" should be minimized though not denied entirely.

3. Nothing "just happens." At best "coincidence" is an aspect of probability; at worst it is only a poor excuse, a sign of insufficient analysis or a superstition.

PERSONAL LUCK

1. Every person has some degree of luck, good and bad. There are also systems of luck: lucky days, lucky numbers, lucky colors, etc. Individual luck must be taken into account in interpreting social events.

2. "Luck" is only a shorthand way of stating a complex of factors which cannot be directly determined. In some cases it may be equivalent to psychokinesis ("mind over matter"), in others it may be interpreted through variations of the self-fulfilling prophecy where beliefs influence acts which influence outcomes.

3. "Luck" is an immature, superstitious attitude of an individual, and unacceptable as a factor in explanations.

Cultural variations of arguments: an illustration and a "quiz"

Before turning to some more complicated aspects of patterns of reasoning and rhetorical expressions of them, we wish to bring together much of what has been discussed through some examples. We will begin with an argument which we will analyze, and then consider four hypothetical cases with alternative conclusions derived from different cultural warrants.

In 1966, this writer was in Uganda very shortly after a brief but bloody civil war between the forces of the Kabaka, the head of the dominant Baganda tribe, and forces loyal to then President Milton Obote. During the fighting very many people were killed, and the Kabaka (King Frederic Mutesa) fled, finally escaping to England where he died several years later. In visiting with Baganda farmers then, we were frequently told something like this:

> We, the Baganda, are dying because our Kabaka has been separated from us. As long as he remains away from this land, part of us is missing, and so we will continue to become sick and we will die. Help restore our life. Help to return our Kabaka.

The evidence, by the way, was more than the assertions of these farmers who spoke to us. Many people were sick. Many people, apart from those who were caught up in the fighting, had died. This argument, at face value, has at least two parts:

One: the problem, from effect to cause:[6]

Evidence: people sick and dying ——→ Conclusion: the Kabaka's
absence caused this misery

Possible warrants: the Baganda are spiritually
unified; if the head (or heart or soul) is lost,
the body dies.

Two: the solution, from cause to effect: if the Kabaka is re-
turned, people will no longer be sick nor die (apart from
normal illness and mortality)

[6] The use of effect-cause/cause-effect may be relationship imposed by this writer.

If you accept the premise (the warrant) that these Baganda felt a social and spiritual unity that most "moderns" have never known in their nations, then it is not unreasonable to argue that if the head of this body is removed, illness and death will result. Metaphors and analogies of the body are convenient, maybe even essential, for us to express this kind of reasoning.

But there are other interpretations, other conclusions stemming from other warrants rooted in different perceptions of reality. A European medical doctor might argue that following a war, sickness and death is inevitable in any land; the shock itself takes a toll, and the sicknesses spread by death, plus the attendant disruptions of vital services, add to the tragedy. The doctor might sympathize with the feelings of the Baganda but say that their explanation is not as reasonable as his.

A U.S. psychologist might have similar views but reason that it is the power of psychological suggestion that is at work. (If enough people tell a person he looks sick, he will soon come to feel sick.) In the land populated by the Baganda tribe, the suggestion spreads quickly to all, much like a physical contagion. To an Ugandan hostile to the Baganda, this may all be a calculated act to persuade naive foreigners to pressure their governments to help return the Kabaka. And so on.

Moreover, each person with his own assumptions and outlook will probably seek other evidence to try to corroborate his own view of things. We may speak of "an argument," but it is rarely singular; it derives from and feeds many others. Moreover, we may speak of the evidence leading to the conclusion, but our "reasoning" perhaps more frequently proceeds in reverse order. These other arguments actually begin with expected conclusions and then seek "evidence" consistent with these conclusions.

If we did seek additional evidence, what kind would we choose? Witnesses, perhaps. But there are many in Uganda who will tell you this is the worst source of "evidence," since "the mouth was made to deceive." Material evidence may be convincing for some, but dismissed as mere "circumstantial evidence" by others. As for qualifiers, some may say that things will not change unless God wills, a miracle occurs, a sign is given. For others, such qualifiers are unacceptable.

We can describe as a basic warrant in this case the assumption of the organic unity of the tribe, of a moral order which here has been disturbed. But many readers of this book are likely to reject that notion as naive, unsophisticated, or in any case no basis for action. But consider for a moment reactions to "the curse on the house of Atreus" or Hamlet's gnawing sense that something was rotten in the State of Denmark. Great drama, like great myths from which so many dramas are taken, often are posited on assumptions of a moral order not so different from those we might deny for the Baganda in 1966. And yet, in the theatre we suspend disbelief and accept such arguments, partly because the truth of the drama is greater than that literal truth, but at least partly because such arguments are convincing in their context.

To better appreciate cultural assumptions embedded in arguments, consider each of the cases presented below. For each we include four alternatives, much like those given in multiple choice tests. In this quiz, however, there is no single correct or even "best" answer; all are equally "correct," but each is based on different assumptions and values. As in the broad area of reasoning these alternatives sometimes take the form of conclusions, and sometimes the form of appropriate attitudes or actions which derive from the situation. For each, attempt to identify more precisely the nature of the apparent "evidence," and then consider each of the alternative conclusions in light of the warrants that make them seem reasonable. Perhaps the best starting point is to choose which seems most reasonable to you. But do not stop there; all of the alternatives are reasonable, assuming:

1. You are a farmer. Now there has been a long dry spell with no apparent indication of rain in sight. If there is no rain soon, and if you and your neighbors remain on your land, many of you may starve during the next year. What is the best thing for you (and others) to do?
   a. Pray for rain. Only God (or the gods) can deliver us from this dry spell.
   b. Check with scientists or technical people to see if they have methods to create rain, perhaps by dropping some chemical on the clouds.

c. Ask the elders and wise-men of the community; they have lived longest, and they know best what to do.

d. We are probably being punished; the dry-spell is a curse. Discover the source of this curse, remove it, and the rains will come.

2. After U.S. Senator Robert Kennedy was killed (preceded by the deaths of his two older brothers and the mental illness of a sister) you think:

a. The good always die young; I am not surprised very much.

b. His death was coincidental; it was a tragic and improbable death, but such improbabilities often happen; we just pay attention when the person is famous.

c. As a public figure who spoke out and who often faced the public, it is not surprising that somebody was able to kill him. It was very probable.

d. God has his reasons; some people die young, some people live on. There is not much point in trying to discover "reasons."

3. A murder has been committed and one man has been accused of the crime. If you want to know whether he is guilty or innocent, you think:

a. The most important thing is to observe the accused man. Guilty people usually give themselves away in how they talk or act.

b. The most important thing is physical evidence. We must look for some footprint or fingerprint or property, etc., that connects the accused man with the crime.

c. The most important thing is to find witnesses. We should talk with anybody who knows the accused man, anybody at the scene of the crime, etc.

d. The most important thing is to put this accused person to a test and see how he behaves. This might be a psychological test or some physical test which will give us proof.

4. I feel I am a very fortunate person. I am happy, healthy, intelligent. I have a strong and loving family. It seems that almost everything I have set out to do turns out well. And so I think:

a. I am just lucky. Some people are lucky, some people are not. I happen to be lucky.

b. I must be careful—good and bad tend to balance, and one of these days things will begin to go badly for me.
c. Life is what you make it. To be happy you have to 'think happy'—it's all up to the individual's attitude and frame of mind.
d. Somebody or some force is watching over me. Call it "God" or a guardian angel or some other supernatural power— I have such faith.

Epistemic structures

In addition to the influence of cultural values, assumptions, and belief systems, argumentation and rhetoric may also be characterized by what we will call **epistemic structures.** These are the scaffoldings on which arguments are erected; they help to determine the **order** in which an argument is stated and what **must** be stated as well as what is left unstated. While related to all that we have already discussed, these epistemic structures are of a different order, more akin to "logic" than argumentation, and deeply rooted in philosophical traditions of a society. They may be identified with formal schools of philosophy or they may be abstracted from the influence of educational traditions, religion, and the social influence of such "specialists" as scientists, lawyers, or even merchants. (It has been said, for example, that British empiricism owes much to the social history of the "nation of shopkeepers" and traders. As accuracy in counting goods shipped and received was crucial to the merchant and trader, the concern with empirical facts became important in British philosophy. Similarly, U.S. pragmatism is seen as arising from the daily experiences of settlers in a "new world" who were both freed from many formal institutions of the old world and also forced to cope with the unexpected.)

Karl Pribram in his book, **Conflicting Patterns of Thought,** and later Edmund Glenn in articles and speeches have done much in recent years to call our attention to this field. Pribram identified what he felt were four distinctive "patterns of thinking" characteristic of much of the Western World.[7] These he identified

[7] Karl Pribram, **Conflicting Patterns of Thought** (Washington: Public Affairs Press, 1949).

as: (a) universalistic reasoning, in which "reason is credited with the power to know the truth with the aid of given general concepts"; (b) nominalistic or hypothetical reasoning, which is distrustful of "pure reason" and broad categories (the nominalists regarding abstract concepts such as "justice" or "beauty" as only "names," in contrast to the "realists," for whom these are real); here, emphasis is placed on induction and empiricism; (c) intuitional or organismic reasoning, which in giving more attention to intuition than to either inductive or deductive systems "is in a position to ignore some of the basic opposition between nominalism and universalism"; it is "organismic" in stressing the unity or organic relationship of the whole and its parts. Finally, (d) dialectical reasoning which resembles "universalistic reasoning" in that it is systemic and deductive, but its system is located in assumed naturally antagonistic forces found in the world rather than "in the mind" of the one who reasons. These four patterns are readily identified with many cultures today: the universalistic pattern is attributed to French, Mediterranean, and largely "romance language" societies, including most of urban Latin America; the nominalistic or hypothetical pattern is said to be characteristic of Anglo-American thought; intuitional or organismic reasoning is, according to Pribram, "associated with extreme nationalism and is prevalent in Germanic and Slavic Central Europe"; and dialectical reasoning is now most associated with Marxism (through Hegel), but also, in another form, characteristic of Aristotelian reasoning of the kind typified in **The Rhetoric** and recognizable in "the golden mean."

This writer encountered a conflict between two of these patterns while lecturing in Brazil to a class of missionaries and technical assistance volunteers which included French and French-Canadian students, and students from Western Canada and the U.S. In trying to make the point that anything may be classified in many ways, we discussed the many classifications and associated semantic reactions for a banana. The point to be made was that the banana was in one case "dessert," in another situation "merchandise," in another the "subject for a still-life painting," and so on. This simple point was easily accepted by the students from Western Canada and from the U.S.: Some said that they "had never thought of bananas that way," but that point was clear as was its relevance to intercultural communication—the need to see things from other points of view, and the danger of imposing their own classification on a situation. The French and French-Canadians, however, were puzzled. They could understand clearly enough that point, but it seemed trivial; the important thing, they argued, was the **essence** of banana-ness, the basic nature of a banana which transcended all momentary or situational classifications. In Pribram's terms, some of us reflected the empirical, pragmatic view of things (the "nominalistic or hypothetical" pattern), in which you can't talk about the banana without knowing how it is being classified and used at the time. Others reflected a "universalistic" reaction, minimizing the immediately perceivable but incidental treatment of the banana and instead, seeking some universal category (the "essence," the "ideal," the "real").

Keep in mind that there was no serious problem in understanding what everybody meant. And to some extent, at least, most values and assumptions were not so very different among the various students, since they had come to Brazil from similar backgrounds and with similar purposes. But there was a very clear sense of difference in ways of reasoning which included, in this case, a dispute about what questions were the most important. It is extremely difficult in such a discussion to reach agreement or even to tolerate the other's notions as "equally reasonable." Similar conflicts can be imagined, if they have not been experienced, when a pragmatist argues with a Marxist.

The four classifications by Pribram marked a promising beginning in this kind of analysis, though Pribram's book appeared in 1949[9] and surprisingly little has been done to follow his lead.[8] Nevertheless an encouraging sign can be seen in interdisciplinary studies such as ethnophilosophy, ethnorhetoric, sociology of law, as well as in the older field of the sociology of knowledge.

The epistemic structure of an argument, then, is grounded in a culture's epistemology. Is truth found in specific facts or in abstract constructs? Is truth derivable from an essential dialectic of which all things are a part, or is a dialectic, any dialectical system, too rigid and antiquated a mold for the flux of reality?

[8] Pribram's approach has been elaborated by Glenn, "Semantic Difficulties," and by Stewart, **American Patterns**.

The student of intercultural communication is not so concerned with choosing the best epistemology as he is with recognizing that there are these differences, which are expressed in individual arguments as well as in entire "bodies of knowledge." Moreover, it is clear that it is possible to translate reasoning expressed in one structure into reasoning in another structure, though perhaps not without losing something in the translation. Classical Chinese theories of medicine reveal a dialectical structure which appears inconsistent with modern Western medical theory. But at a pragmatic level, the applications of that theory, as in acupuncture or moxa, have commanded the respect of Western doctors who might otherwise have little regard for the niceties of positive and negative forces, the sun and the moon, "and all that."

Another cause for optimism in spanning the distance between different epistemic structures is the fact that everyday we seem to employ several different patterns for different subjects. Stewart draws the analogy between representative "non-Western patterns" of decision making and the procedure of a medical doctor.[9] The doctor observes symptoms and then seeks a more abstract classification of "disease" to which the symptoms correspond. He then prescribes treatment according to the disease. There are clear parallels between this procedure and what was identified as "universalistic or deductive" reasoning which is not typical of U.S. patterns. Nevertheless, in this case of the doctor's diagnosis, the pattern is so "reasonable" (or familiar) to us that we may not notice how different it is from other kinds of reasoning we follow every day.

In the case of deciding whom to marry or what major to choose in college, Americans may adopt a pattern that has more in common with intuitional thinking than empirical analysis or even pragmatic concerns for the effect of that choice. The Japanese, in contrast, often describe themselves as illogical, emotional, intuitive people as opposed to "the rational Westerner." And yet today most marriages in Japan take place only after the most detailed empirical analysis and pragmatic concerns, including detective work into each partner's background and the analysis

[9] Edward Stewart, **American Patterns**, pp. 16–25.

of the family history going back generations that is anything but "intuitive" or "irrational."

In an average day in college, a U.S. student can follow very different patterns of reasoning as he moves from his physics class to his literature class to his political science class—and then gets it all together in a rap session. Depending on your point of view, this flexibility is a credit to the human race or a dismal accounting of what passes for scholarship. In any case, it is not surprising that C. P. Snow described the differences between discussions with persons in the humanities and those in the natural sciences as representing "two cultures," further apart in their thinking, as he said, than that of persons living on opposite sides of the ocean.

We mention this diversity of styles of reasoning within a single culture not to contradict what was said earlier, but to (1) show that flexibility is possible; (2) demonstrate that epistemic structures need not be bound to particular languages; and (3) to direct attention to intracultural differences that may yield insights into intercultural differences in reasoning.

Rhetoric

Theories of rhetoric seem to be nearly as old as the practice itself. Rhetoric has been called an art, a craft, a knack, a science. It has been enthroned as the queen of the arts and scoffed at through comparisons of less noble ladies. As one of the classic seven liberal arts it has a special status, though currently its name is more frequently qualified with adjectives such as "mere," "empty," "hollow," and as the antonym of "action." For Aristotle and many in communication today, rhetoric remains, properly, the study of the available means of persuasion. For some English teachers and some linguists, rhetoric is another name for style—linguists preferring the more scientific sound of "stylistics." Some cross-cultural scholars have treated the term with due respect, as Ethel Albert does in her delightful study of "Rhetoric, Logic and Poetic in Burundi";[10] for others, like Leonard Doob in his encyclopedic **Communication in Africa,**

---

[10] Ethel Albert, " 'Rhetoric,' 'Logic,' and 'poetics.' "

rhetoric refers to "a most miscellaneous category that would include any sort of device likely to lend emphasis to a communication."[11]

Much of what we have referred to as argumentation can be
considered a part of rhetoric. But without denying that relationship, we will treat rhetoric as the speaker's conscious use of
symbols, spoken and unspoken, to elicit from his intended or
assumed audience the response he desires. This is not so different from **persuasion,** but the word persuasion means, for many,
changing attitudes or beliefs, while rhetorically a speaker may
seek only to reaffirm what is already delivered, demonstrate his
legitimacy, or otherwise symbolically express what is expected
of him. (Such goals are, of course, very much a part of the
classical concept of rhetoric.) We will also adhere to the classic
notion of "artistic proofs" developed by the speaker in his use
of symbols only; not included are those methods euphemistically
called "inartistic proofs," such as tortures, forced confessions,
"brainwashing," subliminal persuasion, and so on.

Our emphasis in rhetoric will differ in one important respect
from most treatments of the subject. We will be interested primarily in the culturally influenced forms of rhetorical expression
which may characterize the speaking of large segments of societies, including an entire culture. We do not deny the matter
of the individual's choice in, say, how he begins his speech, the
analogies he chooses, or the broad outline of the speech. But
we are more interested in what his culture denies, permits, and
encourges, what his society says he must never do. If he stands
or sits, if he speaks for twenty minutes or four hours, if he cracks
a joke or apologizes, if he rides in a black limousine or walks in
sandals may all be rhetorical choices, too, but they are not entirely up to the whim of the individual speaker.

Rhetorical relativity

If rhetoric were only the study of "style" we might have little
difficulty in describing its function in communication, particularly its relation to argumentation. We might want to think that

[11] Leonard Doob, **Communication in Africa: A Search for Boundaries** (New Haven
and London: Yale University Press, 1961), p. 212.

rhetoric is the stylish way in which that naked body of argument
is clothed. But there is more to it than that. It is possible to extend the potential influence of rhetorical forms to a degree which
sees them as influencing the very argument itself. We might pose
a hypothesis which parallels the Whorfian hypothesis (or is taken
as a variation of it) that our culturally influenced rhetorical forms
themselves help shape our world view, our thoughts, and our
actions. We might. But we need not go that far to make our more
general point. Consider:

It is characteristic of American speech "style" (but not exclusively American) to follow a pattern of three in describing
things. There are the cliché threesomes of: tall, dark, and handsome; Tom, Dick, and Harry; win, lose, or draw; a hop, skip, and
a jump; and so on. We remember Churchill's having spoken of
"blood, sweat, and tears"—though his speech contained a fourth
term, so perhaps we remember in threes, too. In organization we
expect a beginning, middle, and end; we think of dramas as having three acts (though many do not); we usually award three
prizes—first, second, third—and in college three basic degrees.
Our flag is not the only one in three colors, but baseball is surely
the most American of pastimes, since it is virtually constructed
on threes (strikes, outs, fields, and three times three innings and
players on a side). If at first you don't succeed, try, try again—
and the third time's a charm. Many of our favorite children's
fairy tales involve three characters, with the third being the one
who succeeds in killing the wolf or winning the princess. Most
of our narrative jokes are similarly organized, with the punch-
line coming on the third try ("so the third guy came up and **he**
said . . ."). There are patterns of twos, but they function differently; patterns of four or five are hard to find. So we wonder:
if the "reality" we wish to symbolize corresponds to a pattern
of four, might we drop a term in order to produce the more conventional (elegant?) pattern of three? If we are speaking or writing a sentence and we have only two adjectives, might we struggle
to find a third to give our sentence that rhythm of three? If so
—and perhaps this can be tested empirically in some way—we
may have a bit of evidence that rhetoric, even as "style" is not
mere.

Another example very much in the American idiom is

the superlative ranking, an American characteristic that has not gone unnoticed by foreign observers who have equated this with childishness (S. de Madriaga called Americans, "children in the greatest playpen in the world!").[12] Mohammed Ali (Cassius Clay) and Richard Nixon have at least this much in common: Both were exemplary Americans in speaking of achievements (their own or the nation's) as being **the greatest in the world, the greatest ever since the creation.** This is very typical of a style of American speech. If something can be ranked high, it will be identified by that rank, regardless of its significance. A variation of this is the "one of the-" pattern: "one of the best" usually means only approval, "one of the worst," disapproval. Even if there is no basis for comparison, Americans may still attempt to rank the subject as "one of the. . . ." "The tallest building in the world, the busiest airport in the world, the largest water filtration plant in the world"; take a tour of Chicago with a native and you will hear such things, not because a visitor cares or even because the friendly guide cares, but mainly because the cultural style encourages this. Since we are mostly interested in intercultural communication we must stop and consider the effect of such expressions on visitors from other nations. We are likely to find that the impact is not one of awe in the presence of this greatest show on earth, but at times annoyance, at times a feeling of being looked down upon, and maybe most often dismay at the peculiar excitement of the American host.

The superlative style takes other homelier forms. When entertaining foreign guests, the U.S. hostess might say: "Eat all you can, I've spent **all day** fixing this and there are **tons** more in the kitchen!" Functionally, the Japanese equivalent is this: **nani mo gozaimasen** . . . a polite apology which literally means "there is nothing to eat." Both hostesses want to treat their guests well: The U.S. hostess may do so by exaggerating her efforts, the Japanese hostess my humbling hers.

Dichotomous patterns in U.S. speech have been noted by many persons. The tendency to describe in an either/or pattern has been criticized by the General Semanticists as a "two-valued orientation," which is false to the facts of a multi-valued reality.

[12] Cited in Henry S. Commager, **America in Perspective: The U.S. Through Foreign Eyes** (New York: Random House, 1947), p. 64.

It was identified centuries earlier as a fallacy in logic ("the disjunctive fallacy"). The pattern has been attributed to influences of language by some writers, and to cultural assumptions irrespective of language by others. This dualism is quite different from a dialectical system, in that it demands a choice of the better of the two rather than accepting the two as in necessary opposition which will yield a third (thesis, antithesis, synthesis pattern). So consistent is this that some have remarked that even attempts at neutral, objective descriptions which involve a choice will usually imply that one is better than the other. Thus modern or old-fashioned, slow or fast, hot or cold, are often not real choices: built into the usage of the terms is the expectation of one being better than the other. Structures for some kinds of communication follow this same pattern: debate, for example, or the belief that the two-party system is better than any other possible system. Many persons from the United States find it difficult to believe that a "one-party democracy" is not a contradiction in terms, even though historically that was the U.S. political system for some time after independence.

What shall we make of these patterns of speech? They are not the products of language alone, for not all English speaking nations are so characterized. Nothing in the structure of English requires a "rule of three," exaggeration and ranking, or dichotomous choices. We can make a case for their relation to cultural values, but it is a weak case. The ranking style, for example, may develop only in a culture which values individualism, empiricism, a **doing** activity orientation, change, and so on. Maybe. But what of the pattern of threes? We might think of older, more significant threesomes, such as the Trinity, but that does not prove much. Other nominally Christian societies do not express comparable speech patterns of threes. And anyway, the symbolism of three has been endowed with mystery and metaphysical significance (the cult of Pythagorus, for example) since long before the beginning of Christianity and it exists in many lands untouched by Christian missionaries.

Our answer is that these are part of a cultural rhetoric which must be understood in itself. These are acquired habits, widely shared by speakers within a particular society, influencing both the speaker and his own cultural audience, and extremely difficult to translate satisfactorily into another society—even where the language may be the same—without some loss or awkwardness. They are matters of style, but they are more than that. Cultural influences on rhetoric (**ethno-rhetoric** is a name currently used) is far more complicated than the preceding examples suggest. Let us consider the manner of the speaker, what he is expected to say and do, and what he can get away with.

Rhetoric as art

One of Latin America's most colorful leaders, Getulio Vargas, who was twice elected President of Brazil and then committed suicide rather than resign, exhorted, "My enemies say that I am stealing from you. Well, who would you **rather** have steal from you?" The crowd cheered. Vargas was an unusual man, but to be able to say this and be cheered requires more than charisma. The reasons lie, at least in part, in the traditions and values of Brazil and in Brazilian attitudes about political speaking.

Julius Nyerere, President of Tanzania, is a remarkable speaker, as well as a most unusual political philosopher, who remains always close to his people. Nyerere is, one friend observed, the only person who can hold your attention during a two hour speech —even though you don't understand a word of Swahili. In some of Nyerere's speeches which this writer attended during the politically active period in 1966–67, Nyerere would begin by chuckling; the audience would chuckle back. Soon a laughing relationship would be established, a form of rapport quite unlike anything observed in Western speech making. During the speech, Nyerere had occasion to quote what an English adviser said; Nyerere does so, in a flawless British accent, with appropriate gestures and facial mimicry that convulses the audience. He does voices—farmers, women, whatever; he jokes, he gets angry, he teases, but he maintains his dignity and the line of argument is tight. Nyerere is an unusual man, but he draws upon a rich oral tradition and conventions of speaking which are not found everywhere.

Vargas and Nyerere are politically, philosophically, and culturally very different. But both may be representative models of cultures that value speaking as an art, as a means of communication that is as joyfully self-conscious as the samba.

Just as a man's signature in Latin America—even the most routine bureaucrat's endorsing of a check to be cashed—is executed with a flourish, a speech may also be spirited to a degree that seems exaggerated by the standards of other societies.

No speech act exists in itself, between that speaker and that audience on that occasion, although this is a conventional means of distinguishing the speech act from a written text. Speaker and audience have heard many speeches before. They know what to expect and how to take what they get. The foreign rhetorical analyst is likely to project his own interpretation based on his own culture's traditions and expectations and miss not only the subtle nuance but even the import of the entire speech. At a U.S. football game, we do not take the cheerleader's calls to "rock 'em, sock 'em, dump 'em in the lake" literally; we know what that drama means. But when Russian Premier Khrushchev uttered his famous, "We will bury you" in a spirit perhaps not so different from that of a football cheer, millions of Americans took it literally.

Jokes which arise within a society about speaking and other communicative acts, as well as being a society's means of "controlling speech," may give us a clue about how literally to take what is said. There is a joke in Brazil about a speaker who whipped up the crowd calling for them to march tomorrow for the revolution. "Tomorrow we will march! Tomorrow we will fight! Tomorrow victory will be ours!" he shouted, and the crowd cheered. The mood was broken when one man in the audience called out, "But what if it rains tomorrow?"

Heckling in England or Australia is often an integral part of speech making. It is part of the scene, and the speaker who cannot handle hecklers is not a complete speaker. The heckling can tell us as much about attitudes toward speech at a dramatic performance as do the presence of paid claques shouting "Bravo!" at an Italian opera, or hired mourners who are paid to cry at a Greek funeral.

Anything said publicly is not important

In public speaking, as in many other forms of expression, Japan stands in marked contrast with much of the world. The feudal history of Japan ended officially only about one century ago, and many values of hierarchical relationships, politeness, seriousness, conformity, and formalism characterize Japanese speaking. Added to this has been an emphasis on writing, unusual in the world, and a near absence of speaking apart from ceremonial speeches. For these and other reasons, it is difficult to find "a famous quotation" of a Japanese speaker in Japanese history. Indeed, it is hard to find a famous speaker or even many heroes of the kind other nations commemorate in statues and names of cities or streets. One must work for and through the group. One must not stand out. One must follow form and do the expected. One must avoid embarrassment. These are not the qualities which make for great debates.

Nonverbal patterns are also a part of this. Gestures should be controlled: Waving arms and pointing fingers are signs of immaturity or, in any case, an emotional loss of control. Traditionally and even today in many settings, an audience listens by looking down, not toward the speaker, for looking down is a sign of humility and respect. Speakers often reciprocate by looking down.

So it is that a public rhetoric serves primarily to announce formally what everybody concerned knows has been determined already. Anything said publicly is probably not very important, at least in the sense of its being **news.** Consensus is sought behind closed doors. The press, too, works as part of the national establishment not because of censorship or policies of secretiveness, but because of the very values that have helped to maintain homogeneity in the nation for so many centuries.

Direct conflict, "the clash of ideas," is abhorrent. Even in ordinary speech, "yes or no" is not a viable choice. The equivalent of "yes" may be said, but it often means "no." "No" is rarely said. And these days if a choice comes to "yes or no," the Japanese speakers may state that exotic choice by speaking in English, "yes or no."

Many Japanese have said that it is impossible to debate in Japanese. (There are college debating societies, but these are all done in English, primarily for practice in speaking English.) National diet deliberations, often televised, follow the British model, as does the structure of the diet itself. These are interpolations;

there are announcements, periods of questioning, and replies by the appropriate government spokesmen. The style of these is likely to puzzle foreign observers. The famous Japanese polite-ness and self-control seems, at times, to be replaced by angry shouting matches which in no way resemble the British model. A former prime minister was criticized because his speech was too short. A recent finance minister made the headlines of the papers for a grievous mistake for which he had to make an elaborate public apology. The mistake? The pages of his pre-pared speech were incorrectly arranged, so that he read later portions of his speech before the beginning. What in one society is better suited to laughing about then moving on, in another society is the subject of stern criticism, requiring a national apology.

Intercultural problems also arise when someone wishes to report on the speaking of a figure in one society to readers in another society. Japan again provides our example. A friend who is a Japanese reporter for one of the major U.S. newspapers is always asked by his editor to submit usable quotations of the prime minister or other leading political figures. But, the reporter complains, "If I quote what he actually said, it rambles, it seems vague, it is totally unquotable. Yet if I rewrite all that to indicate what everybody here knows he meant, then I am putting words in his mouth that he never would have said." What is interesting here is not just the particular characteristics of contemporary Japanese political rhetoric, but also the U.S. editor's demand to have "exact quotes." That, too, stems from values and assump-tions of reasoning and is itself a part of a particular rhetorical style very typical of the United tates. (U.S. journalists often supply information by inventing a quote attributed to "a spokes-man," "a reliable source," or "a close friend.")

Other styles, other goals

Between the dramatic and the bland exists a vast area of rhetor-ical modes. Any good book on rhetorical theory, even though most give no attention to cultural variations, will provide the interested reader with many possibilities. Or compare, for example, the rhetorical forms of lawyers arguing cases in a courtroom, a commencement speech, the spiel of a tour guide, and a news report on television. For each ask yourself how much humor is desired, permissible? How much of the speaker's personality and his own opinions should obtrude? How much should be implicit, how much stated in so many words? And so on. Some of the differences are subtle, some may depend to a great extent on **who** the speaker is (who he thinks he is, who his audience thinks he is); but there are also norms for the culture. The same kind of sensitivity is necessary in comparing speeches with the apparently same goal but expressed in different societies. A few relevant examples follow.

Organization

Speech organization is a complicated problem: where to begin, where to stop, how to move from point to point, how many and which points to stress are almost always difficult matters for the speaker to decide. But he does not decide all by himself. The audience and occasion obviously provide constraints. Cultural background does so as well.

Conventional advice of speech teachers, where they exist, may codify some of these assumptions. Advice to "stand up, speak up, and shut up," or the analogy of the length of a speech and a woman's skirt, "long enough to cover the subject but short enough to create interest" are very much in the American mode of getting right down to business with a minimum of "frills." We like to "make a few points," often enumerating these as 1, 2, 3. Speeches in the Anglo-American style, if they are judged "effective speeches" of the informative kind, are likely to follow a pattern of organization for as many "points" or conclusions as there are in the speech:

    I. **First conclusion (or generalization)**
       A. Reason and support or proof (more specific)
       B. Reason and support
       C. Reason and support
   II. **Second conclusion (or generalization)**
       A. Reason and support
       B. Reason and support
       C. Reason and support

In this pattern, the speaker starts with a generalization or conclusion—a theory, an assertion, a problem, and then clarifies or supports that abstract or general statement with details. The "topic sentence" style is the model here. Thus the speaker might say, "Every day the world is shrinking. Jet planes criss-cross the Atlantic in less time than it used to take to go from New York to Boston. It is faster to dial a telephone number in another continent than to walk down the block to meet a friend. . . ." Or, as a variation, the speaker may begin with a series of specifics—examples, news items, and so on—and lead into a more general or abstract statement which brings them together: "All of these events show that the world is shrinking."

A speaker who presents only abstract or general statements is likely to seem **too** general or vague, confusing, boring, and quite possibly unsure himself of what he is talking about. A speaker who presents only details and examples is likely to create a similar impression; we are impatient with him and want him to "come to the point." In courses in speech and written composition, students will be given reasons for needing to maintain a balance between the abstract and the concrete, the general and the specific—reasons we do not need to go into here. But there is another, usually unstated, reason: These are cultural norms. Different cultures have preferences and tolerances for different forms of organization and support.

The organization just described for Anglo-American speaking is not necessarily confusing when presented in some other societies, but it may not be expected and may be identified as foreign. A lecturer in Japan, for example, might follow one of two other patterns of organization:

I. Abstraction or Generalization
II. Abstraction or Generalization
III. Abstraction or Generalization
   or
I. Specific Point
II. Specific Point
III. Specific Point

This distinction has been pointed out by professional interpreters who sometimes find more difficulty in translating patterns of organization than specific words or whole paragraphs.[13] If the speaker is accepted by the audience as an authority, there is no need for him to give specific proofs. And if not everybody understands what he is talking about, maybe so much the better —it makes him even more of an authority. If he moves from specifics to generalizations which relate those points he may be insulting his audience: Their job is to make the connection, just as the reader of a **haiku** poem is to sense a full literary experience from the briefest image in the poem.

An examination of the rhetoric of the women's liberation writers in the United States and in Japan shows some striking differences. The American writers typically stress **action:** what's wrong, what must be done, and how to do it **now.** Their Japanese sisters describe the plight of women in Japan and then, sadly, just stop.

We should note in passing that literacy, as well as devices arising out of radio and television speaking, influence speech organization. In a primarily oral culture, patterns of organization are likely to be different from those in a literate society. The outline form with its numerals and letters ("remember if you have an **A** you must also have a **B**") and sub-sub-points is a product of writing and literacy. Many anthropologists have been struck by the superior skills in memory which are found in still predominantly oral societies, including much of Africa. The capacity for remembering, as well as learned techniques—such as mnemonic devices, influence speech organization. Care for precise temporal sequences in recalling events and analysis and synthesis in a methodical fashion may be possible only with a speech prepared with (not necessarily delivered with) written notes. (McLuhan has commented on this, but for more detailed comments see Ethel Albert's article on Burundi and Walter Ong on rhetoric.[14])

The speaker's goal in relation to his audience also relates to organization. If a goal may be likened to a debater's case, the organization should stress points which clash with those of his

[13] Explained by professional interpreters, Masao Kunihiro, Sen Nishiyama, and Mitsuko Saito.
[14] Both McLuhan and Albert have been cited previously. For Walter Ong, see **In the Presence of the Word: Some Prologomena for Cultural and Religious History** (New Haven: Yale University Press, 1967).

opponent. As in so many U.S. college debates, the organization from beginning to end may be directed to saying: This is what I believe, this is true, my opponent is all wrong, and I am completely right. But if the cultural context is one that seeks consensus, the organization, as well as the strength of conviction, may have to be different: cautious, tentative, complimentary toward the others, incomplete and seeking others to make the position complete. In such a form, one may carefully organize his speech so as **not** to come to a point.

We might suppose that if we could ignore such culturally and personally related factors as persuasive purpose and speaker-audience relationship, comparing, instead, simpler expository styles we would find relatively little differences across cultures. There is evidence, however, from teachers of English (as a second language) that cultural differences are quite apparent in routine theme papers written by students. One writer, Robert Kaplan, has described the problem as emerging at the level of the paragraph; that is, at the unit of a sentence a paper may seem to be "good English," but "the foreign student who has mastered the syntax of English may still write a bad paragraph or a bad paper unless he also masters the logic of English."[15] While noting that not all English writers follow the same "logic" (". . . Ezra Pound writes paragraphs which are circular in their structure, and William Faulkner writes paragraphs which are wildly digressive"), he points out marked differences between native English writers and foreign-student writers by quoting extensively from theme papers. Kaplan summarizes the differences by way of a diagram which appears below.[16]

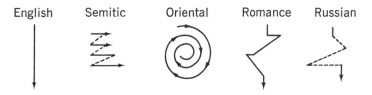

| English | Semitic | Oriental | Romance | Russian |

This exploration seems promising. We might expect that if

---

[15] Robert B. Kaplan, "Cultural Thought Patterns in Inter-Cultural Education," **Language Learning** 16 (1970): nos. 1 and 2, 1–20.
[16] Ibid., p. 15.

diagrams such as these are helpful they reflect not only the "logics" of the areas identified but also something of the languages and cultural values as well.

Rhetorical proofs

The rhetorical components of "proofs" are more complicated than strictly argumentation proofs. With regard to cultural differences, they may be evaluated on at least three levels: (1) their apparent content; (2) their frequency and consistency; (3) their function within the speech and in the entire context of culture. Again we can mention only a few examples to show this.

"Old sayings" and maxims are one form of support which is found throughout the world. Taking one famous example cited in many countries in Africa, a speaker may remind his audience that **"when the elephants fight the grass is trampled."** This has several meanings, including that when two African governments fight, it is the innocent citizens who are harmed; and sometimes that when the Great Powers fight, the weaker African nations suffer. There are, no doubt, comparable expressions in other languages in other cultures which lament the injuries suffered by the innocent during a power struggle, though no equivalent expression in English comes to mind. At any rate, the saying has that meaning at the level of "content." But how often and in what context will such sayings be used? In some societies such folk wisdom is a dominant proof. To be able to recall a fitting saying or, better, to be able to top an opponent's saying with an even better one, is highly valued. One thinks of the wit of Sancho Panza, or of preachers bantering scripture for proofs. In the United States today, at least in major public speeches, this form of proof is seldom heard. Americans may be distrustful of old sayings as being too vague or old-fashioned, or there may be other reasons why we seem to prefer facts, statistics, personal experience, and other forms of support. And so in noting differences in the frequency of usage we can also note that the function is much more than mere style. For an Arabic speaker to recite the proper **hadith** at the proper time shows that he is well schooled, respectful of the traditions, particularly in quoting from the Prophet or Koran. A Chinese businessman may do the same, drawing from a vast resource of ancient wisdom, with much the same effect. A U.S. businessman literally "would not think of doing so."

We could make a similar point with the use of humor generally and with specific forms of humor (irony, sarcasm, exaggeration, self-directed humor, etc.) We can find significant differences in the meaning, frequency of usage, and function of humor within a speech. So many U.S. speakers think they should begin their speech with a joke, though audiences may wish they had saved it for relief much later. The reasons are partly conventional and partly related to other values of informality, wanting to be accepted as a nice guy, and all that. When well used, there may be a belief that some things can be said better through humor than said straight. The potential for misundertsanding humor is obvious enough and causes problems for interpreters as we have indicated. But beyond this is the same question about cultural assumptions in the meaning, frequency, and function of humor as rhetorical support. What is funny (humorous) in one society may be funny (peculiar) in another.

Common ground, too, would seem common enough across cultures. But the role expectations of the speaker, the philosophical and political realities of the society in which he speaks, and the values which lie beneath these all suggest some culturally related differences. A culture may value a leader as one who is above and beyond them, as with the **personalismo** of many a **líder** in Latin America. A culture may demand the leader to speak as one of the people, seeking all possibilities for cultivating that common ground.

In speaking across cultures, many speakers seem to seek common ground with their audience, showing that the two nations are really very much alike. In this writer's opinion, that approach rarely is very effective.

Credibility (ethos)

For centuries it has been said that the most important factor in persuasion is the speaker's **ethos:** those qualities of the speaker's character which make him trustful, sincere, a good man. Aristotle stated this through his observations, and in recent times a very large number of empirical studies seem to consistently confirm this. In the typical experimental study different audiences will be given the same speech or written text but it will be attributed to different speakers or writers for each audience. Words attributed to a person of high credibility consistently are judged "more reasonable and more persuasive" than those attributed to a person of low credibility. There have been similar studies using slang, "substandard speech," and other factors related to credibility, and these have shown similar results. Outside of the laboratory, of course, concerns with the credibility of a political candidate or a brand of merchandise are well known. The "credibility gap," the difference between what is said and what is true, is by now a cliché. In the 1972 presidential campaign the name "Nixon" had a lower credibility than the office he held, hence the title of "the Committee to Re-elect **the President.**" The next year, of course, all that seemed incredible.

As a general principle the ethos of the speaker may universally be the most important factor in persuasiveness. However, what constitutes good **ethos** is not necessarily universal. Again the value orientations will give the best guidance for discovering the ideal ethos of a particular culture. In many societies age will be crucial: The best ethos may accrue to one who is over sixty or under forty. Sex may be crucial: In many societies women are believed to be competent to speak only of women's matters. Family background, achievement, education, relation to the military, religion, and more are likely to be constituents of ethos. As these will differ from culture to culture, their influence in intercultural communication should be obvious.

Something lost in translation

Given the cultural variations in argumentation and rhetoric, it is a wonder that we do as well as we do in public intercultural communication. We need only mention again the difficulties faced by a speaker from one society in addressing an audience from another, particularly when he must speak through an interpreter. This point was developed at some length in Chapter Nine, "The Man in the Middle." Here we note the potential for loss (in rare cases gain) through interpretation.

The warrants which support arguments are, as we have noted,

frequently unstated and exist within the assumptions and experiences of the audience. The speaker who knows this faces a dilemma: If he does not state these he runs the risk of seeming illogical or incomplete at least; if he attempts to make such warrants explicit, he may spoil his natural style and possibly seem to be talking down to his audience.

The rhetorical constraints of occasion, length of speaking time, and many such expectations of an audience may be known to the speaker ahead of time and he can adjust his speaking to some extent. But to the degree that he wishes to represent himself and his society, he may face some difficult choices, even in the matter of what kind of clothing to wear. If at home he relies heavily on humor or allusions to events of his culture, he may have to sacrifice something in speaking with an audience which is not prepared to appreciate his wit and folk wisdom.

As for more obvious matters of style which have special meaning in his language and culture—the rhetorical question, the periodic sentence, anaphora—it is a rare interpreter who can match these with equivalent forms of style in the receiver language. Something will be lost.

But there may be some gain across cultures. The converse of the saying "the prophet in his country is without honor" often holds true: A foreign speaker is often treated with more respect and sympathy than a local equivalent speaker might be. Special problems of misinterpretation, if necessary or expedient, can be blamed on "language problems" or the interpreter himself. At times an audience may read into what is said something that actually favors the speaker (old sayings in a foreign language may seem more profound). The potential for gain is speculative; the inherent dangers of loss are quite apparent.

Why speak?

Many acts of rhetorical analysis and criticism are attempts to discover (1) the speaker's intention, and (2) his success in those terms. In examining the rhetoric of other societies, these questions are at least as important but often much more difficult to answer. For one thing, many speeches that would be subject to analysis by a foreign critic have been directed at several audiences. A government leader's impassioned plea to prepare for war may be intended more to warn a neighbor or ask for help of a third party, and not to actually mount an offensive campaign. Speeches in the United Nations which seem directed from the representative of nation A to the representative of Nation B may actually be ways for the representative to tell the folks back home that he is representing them. And representative B probably knows that.

Why does the United States periodically send some representative, such as the secretary of state, on a speaking tour (good-will tour) of other nations? Some Latin-American editors have said that whenever the United States has no Latin-American policy and doesn't know what to do, they send a secretary down to speak. Cynical or true, that interpretation must be recognized when attempting to evaluate any given speech. The choice of speaker, the choice of nations selected to receive the guest, and the timing are likely to be much more important than anything said.

When President and Mrs. Kennedy visited Mexico on a good-will tour in 1962, they were welcomed in an extraordinarily warm manner that belied the sad history of United States-Mexican relations.[17] Although many of the crowds that lined the streets were required to be there—school children dispatched from classes, labor union members directed to attend, the enthusiasm was sincere. Kennedy's speeches, by most standards, were effective. But it seems that a large part of the success was due to a symbolism not limited to his kind words. They were a handsome couple. Mrs. Kennedy was beautiful and she spoke Spanish. They were Roman Catholic, though not all members of the government fully appreciated that appeal. They were young and, it was hoped, liberally inclined. Oddly enough, the President's father was noted for his criticism of big business (the President had clashed with the steel companies and quoted his father as having told him such businessmen "were all sons of bitches"; some Mexicans took note). Some of these factors lie outside the province of rhetoric as the conscious choice of symbol and symbolic acts; nearly all lie outside of the words of the speeches.

One might wonder why it was necessary for the Kennedys to give any public speeches at all. Not just a U.S. president but

[17] For an analysis of this event, see John Condon, dissertation, cited previously.

perhaps most foreign visitors in any land will probably say more or less what people expect them to say, so why bother to speak in public? The important business will be conducted in private, so again, why bother to speak in public? News reports and cultural products related to the visitor will "communicate" much more to the host nation than any number of polite words from the visitor, so why bother? The answer—or one answer, anyway —is clear: Speech-making remains the fundamental form of public expression. One must say something. And if one is careful, what is said will at least not make matters worse.

Conclusion

Instead of trying to summarize what has been presented in this chapter, we conclude by mentioning a few of many possible items that were not included. We limited our treatment of argumentation and rhetoric to the public speech form, with implications for discussions, debates, question-answer sessions, and so on. There are many other rhetorical forms. Songs, for example, are often rhetorical; President Jomo Kenyatta of Kenya noted that African songs are traditional means of communicating many ideas and that this resource should be exploited anew. Dances in many societies are a part of many rhetorical acts and might be treated as rhetorical forms in themselves. The special characteristics of film, radio, television, the press—all forms of mass media— require special treatment, though it is odd that more research is being conducted in the utilization of mass media across cultures than in the older and still primary form of oral communication. Different effects of messages printed or spoken; nonverbal symbols as rhetorical expressions, clothing, such as the national dress of a newly independent or post-revolutionary nation; massive public displays on national holidays, including the gymnastics of thousands of school children so often characteristic of communist ceremonial rhetoric; the symbolism of faces on banknotes, names of streets and cities; even "the rhetorical calendar," marking the days of displaying the salient symbols of the society and the gaps of time between such holidays: These and many more should keep the student of rhetorical aspects of intercultural communication busy for several more years.

ELEVEN

I'm a stranger here, myself

"Is it more important to speak a foreign language than to be 'fluent' in the corresponding nonverbal expressions?" "Do people in another culture usually admire a visitor who tries to ape their nonverbal expressions, whether or not he also speaks their language?" "Where does so-called 'culture shock' fit into all this?" "Can we really say that all cultural values are equally good?" "Should a person try to adapt to a form of reasoning that seems, to him, 'unreasonable?'" Such questions always arise in a survey of the subjects we have considered in this introduction to intercultural communication. They require somewhat more specific answers and reflect more "practical" concerns of one who wants advice on how to communicate effectively across cultures rather than being content to theorize about the subject. They also serve to bring the human factor back into focus: The cultural is obviously important in intercultural communication, but it is **people,** not cultures, that communicate. In this chapter we will look at several questions frequently asked and venture some cautious answers. But do not expect to receive detailed directions for finding what you might be looking for; the subject is vast and complex and changing all the time. To be honest, any person, no matter how long and varied his experiences in other cultures, must admit: I'm a stranger here myself.

When in Rome

Let us begin with the old advice, "When in Rome do as the Romans do." Superficially this seems to be as modest and practical a suggestion as could be made. Surely it is also safe, or it would not have become such a universal cliché. The trouble is that as advice it is unclear. Setting aside questions about applying the rule equally to weekend tourists in Rome and to immigrants, what does it mean "to do as they do?" Does it mean, at the very least, to speak as the Romans speak? Servants and senators do not speak in quite the same way. Does it also mean to behave nonverbally as the Romans do, in hand gestures, in facial expressions, in dress and interpersonal distance patterns? If these patterns are regarded as analogous to languages, then if we are going to speak like the Romans we had better also gesticulate like them, too. Indeed, to do otherwise is likely to cause confusion where there is a conflict between speech and gesture. But if it means this much, then does it also mean that we should adapt to the value orientations of our Roman hosts? Many of these values are already reflected in the language and in the nonverbal behavior, and besides, most of what the Romans do **as Romans** is influenced by their values. Then why not also try to reason like a reasonable Roman and be persuaded like a persuasable one?

At this point the advice seems to be: **When in Rome be a Roman!** But is that possible? Can any outsider physically, psychologically, and culturally transform himself into someone from another culture? Probably not. Even if some approximation could be made, is that person likely to want to completely transform himself? The usual experience of a person in another society is that he likes some aspects of that culture and dislikes others. (The same can usually be said about his feelings regarding his own culture, too.) We doubt the desirability, let alone the possibility, of following this conventional advice to its conclusion.

So let us consider another approach.

The universal communicator

Not quite so widely shared, perhaps because it lacks a succinct maxim for intercultural ventures, is another kind of advice. This urges one just to "be yourself." Perhaps Polonius' advice to Hamlet as he was sent off to another culture expresses the idea: "This **above all,**" he said, "to thine own self be true," adding that the result would be good for everybody else he encountered, too. In a different and modern context this belief has been called by some scholars, "the myth of the universal communicator." William Howell, in his studies of communication patterns in joint-venture and multi-national corporations throughout the world finds the myth everywhere. This is the belief that there exists in every organization a man (less often a woman) who is going to be liked, respected, understood, and effective in any society he visits. The cultural factors we have been discussing may impede this person, of course, but his own knowledge of the task at hand, his sincerity, and good will carry him through. For the business executive this faith pays an added dividend: language and cultural orientation training programs may be minimized or done away with entirely, saving time and money. To be less hard-nosed about it, we might say that this faith reflects an optimism about good will and the brotherhood of man.

There are drawbacks to trying to follow this advice, however. The first problem is in finding the right person. This is a problem because he does not exist. In reality, "the universal communicator" is likely to be **any** person who is selected to go abroad (or to play host to foreign visitors) and who can successfully disguise the problems he encounters. If he cannot disguise all the conflicts, he is the one who can blame the others with whom he has to deal, whether they be businessmen, teachers, political officials, or even "all those people." If there are other universal communicators who have also had experience with persons in the other culture, they are likely to confirm that **they** are to blame for misunderstandings, delays, or complete failures.

This myth seems to parallel the myth of the great leader. Many studies have been conducted to discover the common traits of those men and women who have been credited with remarkable powers of leadership, but all such studies conclude that there are no common characteristics. "Leadership" is a transactional quality that occurs among men in a particular situation; leadership does not reside exclusively within any one individual. The same must be said of any aspect of communication, including that which transpires between men from differing cultures.

In rejecting this belief in the universal communicator we do not want to take the position that sometimes appears in self-critical books and articles about "the ugly American," the view that Americans are usually most to blame for international misunderstandings. We only want to reject the notion that what in one culture is effective communication, however defined, will also be effective communication in any other culture. We should also leave open the possibility that persons with serious personality problems in their own culture will be less effective elsewhere than people who generally get along well with others at home. But these are other matters which we cannot take up in this book.

The middle ground

Between the two extreme hopes—total adaptation on the one hand and imposing one's will on the other—is a vast middle ground in which some adaptation is possible and some neither possible nor even desirable. It is in this area that we would like to conclude this book by answering several of the most often asked questions about intercultural communication. Although most of the questions relate to several aspects of cultural and interpersonal communication patterns, we will consider these in the order of: language and culture, nonverbal behavior, values, and reasoning and rhetoric. We believe that this order may correspond to the order of difficulty one faces learning about another society and in adapting. Matters of language may be the least of the difficulties and reasoning and rhetoric may be the most difficult. We will explain why we feel this way after trying to answer a dozen frequently asked questions.

1. Are we usually expected to know the language of the host culture?

As a general rule, facility in the language of one's host culture is usually desirable for a number of reasons, only one of which is the instrumental usage of the language. Usually knowledge of the language of the host society also influences how a visitor is perceived and, by implication, how he regards his host society. Someone who "takes the trouble" to learn at least a few phrases of another language may be considered more thoughtful and appreciative than someone who does not. Then there is the matter of time: It takes much longer, obviously, to learn a foreign language than to travel to a foreign country, and even with a lifetime of studying different languages a person cannot expect to learn more than a fraction of all of the languages of countries he might come to visit. Another problem is that usually the best way to learn a foreign language is to live among people who speak that language. Thus to do so a person must go to another society before he is fluent in that language.

Apart from these considerations which are well recognized, there are other complications. The length of time he will be in a place where a language is spoken, plus his role and perceived role certainly make a difference. There are different standards for tourists, students, reporters, and ambassadors. In the United States we are likely to assume that all foreign embassy personnel, foreign students, and maybe even most tourists as well, speak English. We do not impose the same standards on Americans in these roles in other countries, however. We do not even hold such standards when we visit or work in neighboring nations like Mexico or in French-speaking Canada, even though Spanish and French are the languages most often taught in our high schools and colleges.

These considerations still suggest a "yes, ideally" answer to the question. There are other factors that sometimes recommend the opposite answer. There are nations and sub-cultures within nations where an outsider is not expected to speak the language, or at least not to speak it too well. To a great extent Japan is such a nation: a foreigner who learns Japanese "too well," being able to read and write as well as speak, is likely to be regarded ambivalently, with a mixture of curiosity, admiration, and suspicion. Japanese tend to regard their culture as unique, even feeling that only a "pure Japanese" can really understand the culture and its language. Where tribal or sub-cultural languages are spoken in smaller areas within a nation, not only in Africa but in Latin America and Asia as well, an outsider who speaks the language of the people may also be regarded with a mixture of delight and suspicion or even fear. By speaking their language he may implicitly flatter his hosts, but he may also threaten them. As a Tarascan-speaking friend in Mexico said: "The **gringo** who learns Tarascan may take from us all we have left—our secrets."

In a quite different situation, as mentioned in Chapter Nine, an ambassador may choose to speak through an interpreter even if he speaks and understands the language of his host nation quite well; the interpreter protects the official from making any serious mistakes which could lead to political problems, and he also gives the diplomat added time to consider matters before responding to them.

One other consideration should be taken into account before leaving this question. Between the extremes of total ignorance of a foreign language and complete fluency in that language is a wide range of language facility. This point is usually appreciated better by speakers than by listeners, however. That is, if a person appears to be able to speak a second language, his listeners sometimes forget his limitations. Thus should a conversation turn from the usual pleasantries to more subtle or more serious matters, such as politics or religious beliefs, the poor speaker may stammer that he cannot explain his position except in his native language. This bit of awkwardness very often occurs when a person is called upon to explain some controversial aspect of his own society. Some listeners may appreciate that these are language problems, but others may take it as a hollow excuse to avoid a serious discussion.

2. What does "knowing a language" mean?

Often it means whatever you can get away with. When there is no need to demonstrate ability in another language, one can easily claim to **know** that language. There even seems to be an inverse correlation between claiming to know a language and being in a position where one has to speak it. So saying that we know another language or even believing that to be true is not the same as actually knowing a language. Nor does "having had" French, Spanish, Russian, or some other language in high school or college constitute "knowing a language." Praise from native speakers does not prove that one speaks their language, either, for often this is said as small talk or affective communication only. Across cultures, praising the visitor's command of the local language occupies about the same place as talking about the weather. Probably the less a society expects a visitor to speak its language, the more the visitor will be praised. In this, Tokyo and Paris are truly on opposites sides of the world.

In general it is much easier to understand what is being said than to speak about the same subject, and easier to understand a topic we know something about ahead of time than to enter into midst of a conversation or to converse about something totally unfamiliar. For these reasons, too, it is usually easier to read about international news in a newspaper (recognizing the issues and proper names, at least) than to read about local news of which one has little knowledge. All of these observations reflect a point made previously, that "knowing a language" is a matter of degree. And this is partly why a person who feels he has command of a language on Monday may feel he is a complete dolt on Tuesday; the demands of his conversing—not to mention differences in tensions or state of health—change from situation to situation.

The most difficult expressions in a language, to comprehend and to express, are commonly thought to be slang and jokes (and for special reasons, songs). It is not coincidental that both slang and jokes are likely to be the most intimately bound to matters of cultural values and to reasoning and rhetoric. To understand slang and local jokes is an excellent language test, for compressed into a few words are many of the culture's values and ways of thinking that give life to the language. We are saying that it is hard "to know a language" without also knowing a great deal about the culture in which the language is spoken.

3. Can we understand another culture without understanding its language?

This question is often posed by scholars who conduct research in or on another culture. Sometimes the answer depends mostly on whether or not the scholar knows the language of the culture he is investigating. As we have tried to show throughout this book, a language in many ways reflects and directs much of what is at the heart of a culture, culturally distinctive patterns of communication. For one who holds to the Whorf hypothesis (that language influences thought), an understanding of a society's language is crucial; for many linguists today, particularly those transformational grammarians who follow Chomsky, the role of a language per se is minimal.

We would do better to avoid the debate at the level of theory and try to be more precise about what is meant by "understanding a language," the question considered previously. One cannot understand a language without understanding its syntax, but an understanding of syntax may be a long way from understanding most of the characteristics of a culture. A child understands his first language well, a linguist will say, even with a very limited vocabulary; and yet vocabulary may be one of the most important indices of what is important in a culture. When learning another language we are likely to want to say in that language the equivalents of what we would say in our own language; but if knowing a foreign language means only that, then we are not learning anything that is culturally distinctive. In short, depending on what we are capable of and sensitive to, knowing the language of the culture we are studying may or may not be so important.

There are many ways of learning about **some** cultures without speaking their respective languages, but the means and the cultures are limited.[1] Translations of literature of all kinds is important, even if something is lost in translation. However, only a very small percentage of the writings from any one culture are available in translation. (In this regard, information from and about the United States is far more available in other languages than is information about other societies available in the United States.) There are also books, articles, monographs, and other resources of varying quality and reliability about many cultures. Many of these are written by foreigners or for foreigners or for foreign publication and thus in such cases knowing the language of the culture studied may be of no help whatsoever. Today scholars and government officials in many countries are especially sensitive about writings on their cultures which are not available in the language of that culture. Another problem with these writings, as any person who has attempted to study

[1] For an excellent sourcebook on studying cultures from afar, see Margaret Mead and Rhoda Metraux, eds., **The Study of Culture at a Distance** (Chicago: University of Chicago Press, 1953).

cultural patterns of communication in another society quickly finds, is that most of them seem either too general or too specialized or biased or out of date.

Some of these problems can be avoided by attempting to comprehend expressions of a culture directly, as through architecture, fine art, clothing, and even foods. This mode of comprehension, despite problems of interpreting such expressions will no doubt be exploited more fully in the future. Films and videotapes of many kinds, both purely ethnographic, as well as those prepared for popular consumption, offer some obvious advantages but also some subtle traps for misinterpretation. Finally there are the "informants," visitors, students, immigrants, and others, who are so often tapped as cultural resources. If a culture studied is distant and inaccessible for some reason, such means may be the only ones open to us. Ruth Benedict wrote in her classic description of Japanese culture, **The Chrysanthemum and the Sword** without ever visiting Japan and without knowing Japanese.

A person who does not know the language of the culture he wishes to better understand is hindered in two ways. First, he may be missing the source of some very important insights reflected in its language. Second, he is cut off from direct access to much information from and about the culture. There is another limitation, too. Without ability in the language (and participation in the culture), a person can never feel the impact of these cultural patterns on his own behavior, and come to appreciate the complex problems of **inter**cultural communication.

4. Is it more important to speak a language than to be "fluent" in nonverbal expression?

Although "fluency" does not mean quite the same thing in the two modes of expression, we can say this much: Practically anything cognitive and anything at all abstract must be expressed in language, whether spoken or written; for emotional (affective) expressions—anger, frustration, friendship, love—nonverbal expressions may suffice and in some instances be far more effective. So much depends on the purposes and functions of communication.

If a person learns a second language at a young age and in a culture where the language is spoken, he or she inevitably learns the corresponding nonverbal behaviors, too. Indeed, a child is more likely to learn many of the nonverbal expressions first, just as he does in his own culture. If one learns a foreign language as an adult, he is unlikely to learn the appropriate nonverbal behavior, however.

More important than these distinctions, however, are the expectations of the people with whom one is communicating. As mentioned earlier, we much more readily expect, excuse, or correct errors in spoken language than errors in nonverbal behavior, presumably because we do not realize that nonverbal behavior differs from place to place and must be learned much as a spoken language must be learned. The greater the fluency one exhibits in a foreign language, the more the listeners are likely to assume the person knows about all aspects of communication, including nonverbal behavior.

Therefore language fluency carries with it a burden of comparable nonverbal facility; the two modes of expression are complementary, not alternatives.

It is uncommon to find situations where nonverbal behavior leads to expectations about spoken language behavior, with one notable exception. This is where there is a perceived physical similarity between the visitor and those in the host culture. We have seen cases of second or third generation Japanese visiting Japan, black Americans visiting Africa, and Chicanos and persons with a North American Indian ancestry in Mexico who startled their hosts because they could not speak their respective languages. It was as if each "looked" fluent. The problem was compounded because, not knowing the language they were presumed to speak, they could not explain their plight, much to the confusion and sometimes irritation of those they encountered.

5. Do persons in a host culture usually admire a visitor who tries to adapt nonverbally, whether or not he speaks the language of that culture?

Because the range of nonverbal behavior is so great and, for the most part, outside of our conscious awareness, it is difficult to think of adapting to all aspects of nonverbal behavior. Thus in asking this question we are likely to have in mind only certain behaviors which we are aware differ across cultures. Such behaviors are likely to be chiefly of two kinds, those that are most obviously different from our own (such as greetings by shaking hands, embracing, or bowing), and those which have attracted special attention in theory and limited research (such as proxemic behavior). In other words, even when we think we have adapted to other patterns of nonverbal behavior, we have probably only done so to a limited extent.

With caution we might say that it is better to try to follow the nonverbal patterns in the host culture which are most directly related to interpersonal communication patterns and those which are not generally recognized within the host culture as being culture-bound. On the other hand, to try to "go native" in such ways as adopting local dress, particularly if one is ignorant of the subtler aspects of nonverbal behavior or the spoken language, may seem odd if not ludicrous. (This is not to say that any other kind of dress will be acceptable, of course.)

Thus far the advice follows along the lines of the "when in Rome" philosophy, but there is also something to say about the visitor's own personal comfort and ease in communication. Too much of a concern with misbehaving nonverbally is likely to produce an anxiety which itself is communicated. Without going so far as to recommend completely the "be yourself" philosophy, given the choice of a relaxed self and a tense imitator, the former seems preferable.

Overlooked by always putting the burden of adaptation on the visitor is the question of "who adapts to whom?" In terms of spoken language, the answer usually depends on the facility of the two persons who are communicating. If both are mutually bilingual they may even switch back and forth within the conversation. But nonverbal behavior poses other problems and possibilities. Sometimes two patterns of nonverbal behavior may be combined, such as shaking hands and bowing, or shaking hands and embracing. But sometimes this is impossible, as in trying to strike a comfortable interpersonal distance. To attempt to satisfy both parties, when one wants to be relatively close, the other more distant, may produce a bizarre dance of the kind Edward Hall has described in **The Silent Language.**[2] Another example is the confusion when a group of men and women, some

[2] Hall, **Silent Language**, p. 164.

from "ladies-first" cultures, some from "men-first" cultures attempt to make a graceful exit through a door. (Despite the awkwardness, this situation could be taken in good humor and may also show the common awareness of different cultural patterns —so everybody is doubly happy. Obviously not all such confusions are so amusing.)

6. Is learning to avoid taboos the most important aspect of nonverbal behavior in another culture?

"Taboos" are probably much overrated as a problem in intercultural communication. One can frequently learn to avoid the most troublesome or embarrassing expressions without having to encounter them directly. Even if a person should violate a deep-seated cultural taboo, if he is congenial company he is likely to be corrected immediately or taken aside and told. Since many taboos are so obvious and a culture's rules so explicit, the manner of explaining the problem is similar to that of an error in speech. Far more problematic are the subtler errors, such as failing to offer a guest a drink (if this is the custom), failure to see a guest to the door, opening a gift in the presence of the giver or failing to do so, etc., depending on the pattern. Such behaviors may not be dramatic or even apparently severe enough to be designated as "taboos" and then explained to the naive visitor, but they are far more common. In combination or over a period of time such behaviors may be far more damaging to smooth interpersonal relations than a single more blatant indiscretion. They are also likely to be interpreted on a personal, rather than cultural, level. That is, they may be blamed on the visitor's lack of respect or family upbringing and so on, rather than simple ignorance of cultural patterns.

In passing we might also note that while "taboos" are more frequently associated with nonverbal behaviors, comparable problems occur at least as often in speaking. Apart from vulgarisms or impolite speech which is commonly known as a problem area, there are other more frequent indiscretions. Among these are asking questions about topics which people in the society "just don't talk about" (at least not with strangers), such as certain social problems (discrimination against ethnic or caste groups, for example) and topics which seem innocuous in one society but are tabooed elsewhere.

7. Is "culture shock" largely a nonverbal problem?

If one is living in another culture quite different from his own, sooner or later he will experience a period of frustration, anger, alienation, depression, and other such reactions that have come to be labeled "culture shock." (There is another "culture shock" often not noticed: that is the reaction of the people in the host culture to the visitor's behavior!) It seems that no matter how well a person has prepared himself, some degree of "shock" is inevitable and, some would say, necessary for better adjustment. What is important is to recognize these feelings and to know how to respond to them. Withdrawal, excessive sleeping, a consuming desire for news from home, day dreaming about foods, alcoholism, or other escapist behavior are some of the most common symptoms. It is risky to offer general advice on how to deal with these problems, since each case is personal and the problems are more psychological than cultural. If such a problem persists, see a doctor. If it still persists, go home.

One interesting characteristic of "culture shock" is that it often occurs after the person believes he has adapted to a culture and even while he thinks he understands the causes of the problems. Nevertheless, it is as if the body rebels: the person is, quite literally, sick of smiling or hugging his friends or not smiling or being crowded or having to wait or having to hurry or whatever might trigger the reaction at some unexpected moment. Understanding his conflict may help, but he finds it difficult to rationalize such feelings and make them disappear. Thus the familiar fight-flight reaction occurs: striking out, verbally or nonverbally against "these people," or withdrawing to a familiar, safer, fantasy world. While cultural values are invariably bound up in the conflict, it does seem that the catalyst is most often nonverbal, revealing the depth of behaviors established since infancy.

8. How can we learn to recognize the value orientations of a person from another culture?

It is far more difficult to identify value orientations in another culture than to identify patterns of speech and nonverbal behavior, and yet as we have argued in this book, it is extremely important to try to appreciate such values. One reason for the greater difficulty lies in the nature and concept of "values": they are abstractions, even for persons within the culture. Another reason not previously mentioned is that a visitor from another culture may not be representative of the dominant values of his society. Among tourists and even among many foreign students, only the wealthiest and best educated or best "connected" will travel abroad, so that their perception of their culture may differ in some significant ways from those of the majority of the population. This situation is not always so very different when a person visits another society briefly, particularly if his visit is tightly circumscribed: the people he talks with, the places he visits, may all exist for his benefit and for those like him, and thus be unrepresentative.

The best starting point for appreciating differences in cultural values is, of course, some understanding of our own values. At the same time we must acknowledge that often the best means of recognizing values in our own society is to become immersed in another culture—just as we understand characteristics of our own language through studying a foreign language. Hopefully, the loose scheme of value orientations and beliefs sketched out in Chapters Four and Five will be helpful, although these must be modified and specified in any particular situation. Beyond that we should be careful not set up the values of our own culture as standards against which other values seem inferior, a matter we shall say more about later.

If a person is engaged in communication with someone from another culture and has neither the time nor the inclination to undertake a full-scale study of the culture, there are some things he can do to aid communication. If the other person is a visitor, his difficulties in trying to adjust away from home should be appreciated. Clues about strain or confusion should be sensed and might be dealt with openly, much as a counselor might. A sincere concern about another person can help to surmount specific conflicts based on cultural differences. A sympathetic manner toward the visitor's problems which inevitably include adjustments to values and value-related behaviors, is surely more important than trying to objectively study his culture. We would also discourage someone from talking about "value orientations" or any of the categories proposed in this book; probably the other person will have no idea of what you are talking about. This is not so true of direct questions about language or even nonverbal behaviors. Finally, realize that while possibly significant value orientations may characterize the two cultures, the communication is first of all between **people in a particular relationship.** Only some value orientations are likely to come directly into play as a source of conflict. Similar advice may apply when a person finds himself in another society.

9. Isn't it possible to say that some values are preferable to others without going so far as to say that one culture is superior to another?

This is a difficult but important question, and it carries with it still other questions. Can we change only certain values without thereby changing a culture? Can we ever be free of our own value standards, even while trying to be objective? We believe the answer to these two questions is "no."

Each person is likely to have his personal system of values which he believes to be preferable to some others. Those values he prefers are likely to be heavily weighted in favor of those in his own cultural background, whether or not he realizes it. However, so long as a person is content to state preferences in terms of his own values, he remains aware that he is being subjective. The greater difficulty arises when he tries to be objective by thinking he can compare values without recourse to other values, for this appears to be impossible. As best he moves from one set of value standards to another set, or, as some would say, from questions of values to meta-values (values about values). Thus a person who says that "all cultural values are equally good so long as they lead to happiness in life" has not gone from values to objectivity; "happiness," whatever he might mean by that, is still a value even if it is abstract.

We may sometimes think that in programs of technical change (those that Stewart believes Americans are most comfortable with) we are not really changing cultural values, let alone asserting that some values are better than others. But the very choice of encouraging change, the view that techniques are separate from goals and the standard of "happiness," are still culturally based. Since so much of what constitutes intercultural communication is grounded in change, we are never far from at least implicitly viewing some values as better than others. The matter is further complicated by the fact that individually we are mostly unaware of the values we live by and the functioning of those values in a society.

In lieu of objectivity in comparing values we should at least encourage more caution, even humility, in comparing values and in urging changes in other cultures.

10. In communicating with a person from another culture, will some values be more difficult to adapt to than others? Taken as a whole, are some cultures more difficult to adapt to than others?

Our answers to these questions will depend partly on the level of abstraction or generalization on which we approach the questions. At the minimum we should consider three levels. At the most general level, we might compare cultures as a whole; without regard to the individual in a particular situation and ignoring certain value differences between similar cultures we can assume that some cultures have more values in common than others. England and the United States have more in common with each other than either has with Mexico or Japan, for example. Thus at this most general level we might assume that any representative Englishman would find it easier to get along in the United States than he would in Mexico, or in Japan or, indeed, in most of the other cultures in the world. Brazil and Colombia, despite differences in language, have more cultural patterns similar to each other than either has in relation to Macao or Goa, where Portuguese is spoken.

However, we know that communication does not occur at such an abstract level. We must also consider both specific value differences and the particular individuals in any given situation, for differences in these factors may override the broader cultural similarities. While England and the United States are similar in many ways, they differ in some value orientations, such as formality and informality, as discussed previously. Should such differences come into play, particularly if the Englishman and American are expecting no differences, misunderstandings or conflicts might result.

Beyond these aspects of differences in specific values is the **personal** factor. In a particular situation a person from one culture may find more personal satisfaction outside of his society than he enjoys at home. A Japanese college coed, for example, may come to enjoy a kind of freedom (after a period of confusion and uncertainty) in the United States or England greater than she ever knew as a woman in Japan. For this reason, she may find it very difficult to return to Japan and once again act according to her society's norms. Irrespective of specific cultures, one frequently finds he is accorded more respect and deference in a situation outside of his culture (if only because he is a guest) than at home, and therefore this may lead to specific satisfactions.

Personality differences, too, must be considered. A person who longs for the constant stimulation that living in another culture often provides may feel more satisfied abroad than at home. An American male who by temperament likes neither the aggressiveness nor talkativeness that characterizes large portions of U.S. society may find it more comforting in cultures which do not make such demands. Whether the feelings override other conflicts in cultural values is another question that could be answered only in specific cases.

It would be interesting to know if certain values or value-related behaviors are more difficult to change or adapt to apart from the matters discussed above. We suspect that such questions would have to be answered in the case of specific cultures only, and not across all cultures. We assume the answer would depend on the relative importance of specific value orientations within a culture as well as for the particular individual. Although our value orientations scheme makes it appear that all value orientations are equally salient in any society, it seems more likely that some are more at the core of the culture than others.

Keeping these things in mind, can we be more specific about which of the many value orientations are more easily adjusted to than others? Are we more resistant to changing evaluations toward the self than toward nature, for example? These are questions that might be answered with further study of the growing numbers of persons with intercultural experience. Thus far the groups that have been most often studied are foreign students, and perhaps U.S. Peace Corps volunteers, with results usually showing a general trend toward more critical awareness of one's own culture and a more realistic understanding of other cultures, particularly of the host culture. No study that we know of, however, has focused on the kinds of categories provided in this book.

11. Is it possible to "reason" or argue in the patterns expressed in another culture without also utilizing the language and values of that culture?

As in the case of language translations, we assume that anything argued in one language can be said in another language but
not, perhaps, without some loss and distortion. The real problem
here, however, is not in the mental exercise of mechanically
expressing an argument that seems "unreasonable" to the
speaker, but in having the speaker respond sympathetically—at
least to the extent of appreciating why it seems reasonable to
others. Perhaps there is some analogy here to that of a college
debater who, compelled to debate both sides of a proposition,
may feel one side is the stronger while still reserving an appreciation for the weaker case which resulted from having had to
defend it. That kind of appreciation for culturally varied arguments and rhetorical style would seem to us to require an understanding of the values and realities of the culture in which it
exists. As we have already indicated, this is likely to involve even
factors of perception of reality, often literally "seeing it from the
others' point of view."

The role of language in argumentation and rhetoric continues
to be a moot question, not very changed after years of attacking
and defending the Whorfian hypothesis. Obviously if a language
lacks a particular category that is crucial in an argument, it will
be difficult to phrase that argument without also supplementing
the language with the needed term. This, of course, is what we
constantly find in translations of, say, a particular German philosopher whose English translations contain a residue of German
words for which there are no English equivalents. Since language, argument, and persuasion are linked, it is likely that a
style muddied by borrowed words will be less persuasive; the
opposite is also possible, of course, with people persuaded precisely because they are impressed by the unusual style. Although
this example is based on the lack of vocabulary, the same consideration could be made of arguments which retain a vocabulary deemed irrelevant (as in the old concept of "ether" in
physics, or "God's will" in the social sciences), and presumably
to matters of grammar as well.

So long as one conceives of language only as a system apart
from human uses and responses to it, the role of language in
reasoning and argumentation will be discounted. The network
of human reactions to language, in the spirit if not the usual

treatment of the General Semantics school of Korzybski, must be a crucial factor in what is considered reasonable and rhetorically effective. Nevertheless, of the two influences, language and values (extending to beliefs), language seems to be less of an influence, assuming for the moment that we can make a neat distinction between language and values.

12. What if a particular way of reasoning or a particular argument in another culture seems "unreasonable"? Should one try to adapt to that, too?

This question, if not its answer, helps to show why we have ranked problems of reasoning and rhetoric as more difficult than any of the other topics we have considered. There is little moral or intellectual hesitance about trying to alter language or nonverbal behavior to aid communication across cultures. Problems of values are more difficult, but still we may try to keep an open mind. Now, however, we have to consider the possibility of violating standards which we had supposed were culture free.

Let us explore the question through a hypothetical situation in Mexico. In Mexico, reflexive verbs are often used in a way to avoid designating the responsibility for some action. The verbs do not have to be interpreted that way, but the cultural values of many Mexicans seem to exploit that possibility. If, for example, a dish breaks in the kitchen, and one in another room asks "What happened?" the answer is frequently **"se rompió,"** literally meaning "it broke itself." Linguistically, "it broke itself" is good English, but it may not "make sense" in terms of an English speaker's assumptions about causality. At the very least we might demand clarification: "**How** did it break itself?" In many situations in Mexico, however, that question in Spanish will only evoke the same answer: **"se rompió,"** it broke itself. If some people in Mexico are content with that answer, should we be too? Or should we retain standards of cause and effect by always demanding to identify the cause and place of responsibility?

We can easily think of at least five reactions based on different standards of what we accept as "reasonable":

1. Do not accept such an argument when it is presented, since it is obviously just an excuse; and certainly do not "adapt" to the point of using such arguments yourself.

2. Do not accept such an argument **literally;** instead simply translate it into something like "for some reason it broke." And if using **"se rompió"** yourself to explain some action, do so with the intention of your translation, not the literal meaning. Better still, avoid using such a vague or incomplete expression.

3. Come to accept such arguments on whatever terms they seem to be presented, but as in the previous alternatives do not use such arguments yourself.

4. Come to accept such arguments, and even express them yourself. However, always retain the understanding that dishes don't just break themselves.

5. Go even further by trying to convince yourself that in at least some situations in Mexico dishes actually do break themselves.

We suspect that in incidents of this kind, the tendency is to start with reactions like the first one, and then later come to think and talk in ways similar to positions two or three or maybe four. The last choice, however, is likely to seem extreme. We may fear that to try to actually think that way risks the deadening, if not the loss, of all that our education has taught us. Despite this understandable reluctance to try to think that way, we wonder if it is not necessary, at least in many cases, in order to better comprehend the other's point of view. That is, after all, what communication is mostly about. Perhaps without making that effort, many other patterns of interaction and communication can never be understood.

The levels of difficulty

Language, nonverbal behavior, values, and reasoning and rhetoric: These topics embrace the most important cultural considerations in interpersonal communication. For many reasons this stated order of the topics may be the order of increasing difficulty for both understanding and adaptation. We know more about languages and the theory of language than about the subject of nonverbal behavior which only recently has begun to be studied systematically. But nonverbal behavior as well as language can be studied overtly; their expressions can be recorded and patterns discovered. We even can anticipate that "foreign" nonverbal behavior can also be taught, much as foreign languages are taught.

Values are a more complicated matter. They are abstractions, they take many forms, and researchers disagree about how they might be described and interpreted. More than this, however, we are likely to be far more resistant in altering our values to accommodate those of persons from another culture than we are with either language or nonverbal behavior. That last category, reasoning and rhetoric or argumentation, at present appears to be the most difficult to describe and maybe the most threatening and difficult to adapt to. We say threatening because we are likely to regard as unscrupulous a person who seems able to argue with conviction any position on any subject.

There is a word for the kind of person who is willing to claim anything and persuade anybody of anything: We call him a **sophist.** The original sophists, as students of speech and communication well know, were not so criticized. They were the first lawyers, the people who would try to see things from another person's point of view and argue in their terms on their behalf. They provided a beginning for this oldest of academic studies which has now come to be called **communication.**

Many persons who come to learn about the study of intercultural communication express a real fear of a modern day **sophistry.** Many are afraid that cultures will be subverted and destroyed through techniques of manipulation learned in such a study. There may be such a danger, though our problems today seem to be more based on ignorance and selfishness rather than conscious subversion. And, anyway, the tenacity of culture in our communication—the same factors that make communication sometimes so difficult—also act as a check against truly effective manipulation by advertisers or political propagandists. The risks in intercultural communication come not nearly so much from the international sophists as they do from some well-meaning people who are little more sensitive to their own behavior than they are to those of the people they encounter in other societies.

Nothing so sensitizes us to our own culture as living outside it and then trying to return. One can't go **home** again. To try reveals a new home, and a new self seeing it for the first time.

For the person sensitive to interpersonal communication, a trip away, physically or vicariously, is a round trip ticket through the looking glass. **Bon Voyage.** And many happy returns.

Bibliography

Albert, Ethel M. " 'Rhetoric,' 'Logic,' and 'Poetics' in Burundi: Culture Patterning of Speech Behavior." **American Anthropologist (The Ethnography of Communication:** Special Publication) vol. 66 (1964): no. 6, pt. 2, 35–54.

——. "Value Systems." In **International Encyclopedia of the Social Sciences,** pp. 287–91. New York: Macmillan, 1968.

——, and Kluckhohn, Clyde. **A Selected Bibliography on Values, Ethics and Esthetics in the Behavioral Sciences and Philosophy, 1920–1958.** Glencoe, Ill.: The Free Press, 1959.

Almond, Gabriel A., and Coleman, James S. **The Politics of the Developing Areas.** Princeton, N. J.: Princeton University Press, 1960.

Appelbaum, Stephen A. "The World in Need of a 'Leader': An Application of Group Psychology to International Relations." **British Journal of Medical Psychology** 40 (1967): 381–92.

Apter, David E., ed. **Ideology and Discontent.** London: Free Press of Glencoe, 1964.

Ardener, Edwin. **Social Anthropology and Language.** London: Tavistock Publications, 1971, distributed by Barnes and Noble, Inc.

271

Arensberg, Conrad M., and Niehoff, Arthur H. **Technical Cooperation and Cultural Reality.** Chicago: Aldine Publishing Company, 1964.

Argyle, Michael. **Social Interaction.** New York: Atherton Press,
1969.

Aristotle. **The Rhetoric.** Edited and translated by Lane Cooper.
New York: Appleton-Century-Crofts, 1932, 1960.

Arnheim, Rudolf. **Art and Visual Perception: A Psychology of the
Creative Eye.** Berkeley, Calif.: University of California Press,
1957.

Asch, S. E. "On the Use of Metaphor in the Description of Persons." In **On Expressive Language,** edited by H. Werner, pp.
29–39. Worcester, Mass.: Clark University Press, 1955.

Ashford, Douglas E. "Patterns of Consensus in Developing Countries." **American Behavioral Scientist,** 4 (April, 1961): 7–10.

Bach, E., and Harms, R. T., eds. **Universals in Linguistic Theory.**
New York: Holt, Rinehart and Winston, Inc., 1968.

Back, G. W., Mahl, G. F., Risberg, D. F., and Solomon, S. S. "Some
Linguistic Indices of Anxiety." Unpublished manuscript,
Yale University, 1955.

Bagby, James W. "Dominance in Binocular Rivalry in Mexico and
the United States." In **Cross Cultural Studies of Behavior,**
edited by Ihsan Al-Issa and Wayne Dennis, pp. 49–56. New
York: Holt, Rinehart and Winston, Inc., 1970. Originally in
Journal of Abnormal and Social Psychology 54 (1957): 331–
34.

Baier, Kurt, and Rescher, Nicholas. **Values and the Future.** New
York: The Free Press, 1969.

Bales, R. F. **Interaction Process Analysis.** Cambridge, Mass.:
Addison-Wesley, 1950.

Barber, Bernard, and Lobel, Lyle. " 'Fashion' in Women's Clothes
and the American Social System." **Social Forces** (December,
1952) 124–31.

Bar-Hillel, Yehoshua. "Can Translation be Mechanized?" **Journal
of Symbolic Logic** 20 (1955): 192–94.

Barker, G. "Social Functions of Language in a Mexican-American
Community." **ACTA Americana** 5 (1947): 185–202.

Barker, Larry L., and Collins, Nancy D. "Nonverbal and Kinesic
Research." In **Methods of Research in Communication,**

edited by P. Emmert and W. D. Brooks, pp. 343–72. Boston: Houghton Mifflin, 1970.

Barnlund, Dean. "Toward a Meaning-Centered Theory of Communication." **Journal of Communication** 20 (December, 1962): 197–211.

——, ed. **Interpersonal Communication: Survey and Studies.** Boston: Houghton Mifflin, 1968.

Barry, H., and Paxson, Leonora M. "Infancy and Early Childhood: Cross-cultural Codes." **Ethnology,** 10 (October, 1971): 465–508.

Basu, A. K., and Ames, R. G. "Cross-cultural Contact and Attitude Formation." **Sociology and Social Research** 55 (October, 1970): 5–16.

Beals, Ralph L. "Native Terms and Anthropological Methods." **American Anthropologist** 59 (1957): 716–17.

Bedau, H. A. "Review of Whorf." **Philosophy of Science** 24 (1957): 289–93.

Bell, Daniel. "The Disjunction of Culture and Social Structures: Some Notes on the Meaning of Social Reality." **Daedalus** 94 (Winter, 1965): 208–22.

Bender, I. E., and Hastorf, A. H. "On Measuring Generalized Empathic Ability (Social Sensitivity)." **Journal of Abnormal and Social Psychology** 48 (1953): 503–06.

Benedict, R. **Patterns of Culture.** Boston and New York: Houghton Mifflin, 1934.

Berlinsky, S. L. "Loudness of Speaking: The Effect of Heard Stimuli on Spoken Responses." **Journal of Experimental Psychology** 39 (1949): 311–15.

Berlo, D. K. **The Process of Communication.** New York: Holt, Rinehart and Winston, Inc., 1960.

Berreman, Gerald D. "Behind Many Masks: Ethnography and Impression Management in a Himalayan Village." **The Society for Applied Anthropology,** monograph, no. 4, 1962, pp. 4–24.

Bernstein, B. "Elaborated and Restricted Codes: Their Social Origins and Some Consequences." **American Anthropologist (The Ethnography of Communication,** special publication) vol. 66 (1964): no. 6, pt. 2, 55–69.

Bettinghaus, E. P. **Message Preparation: The Nature of Proof.** Indianapolis: Bobbs-Merrill, 1966.

Binder, Leonard. "National Integration and Political Development." **American Political Science Review** 57 (1964): pt. 3, 622–31.

Birdwhistell, Ray L. **Introduction to Kinesics.** Photo-offset, Foreign Service Institute. Louisville: University of Louisville Press, 1952. Now available in microfilm only, University Microfilms Inc., 313 North First St., Ann Arbor, Mich.

——. "Field Methods and Techniques: Body Motion Research and Interviewing." **Human Organization** 11 (1952): pt. 1, 37–38.

——. "Paralanguage 25 Years After Sapir." In **Lectures in Experimental Psychiatry,** edited by H. Brosin, pp. 43–63. Pittsburgh: University of Pittsburgh Press, 1961.

——. "The Kinesics Level in the Investigation of the Emotions." In **Expression of the Emotions in Man,** edited by P. H. Knapp. New York: International Universities Press, 1963.

——. "Some Relationships between American Kinesics and Spoken American English." In **Communication and Culture,** edited by A. G. Smith, pp. 182–89. New York: Holt, Rinehart and Winston, Inc., 1966.

——. "Communication." **International Encyclopedia of the Social Sciences,** vol. 3. New York: Macmillan, 1968, pp. 24–29.

——. "Kinesics." **International Encyclopedia of the Social Sciences** 8 (1968): 379–85.

——. **Kinesics and Context.** Philadelphia: University of Pennsylvania Press, 1970.

Black, J. W., and Moore, W. E. **Speech: Code, Meaning, and Communication.** New York: McGraw-Hill, 1955.

Black, Max. **Language and Philosophy: Studies in Method.** Ithaca: Cornell University Press, 1949.

——. "Linguistic Relativity: The Views of Benjamin Lee Whorf." **Philosophical Review** 68 (1959): 228–38.

——. **Models and Metaphors: Studies in Language and Philosophy.** Ithaca: Cornell University Press, 1962.

Boas, Franz. **The Mind of Primitive Man.** New York: Macmillan, 1938.

Boddle, D. "On Translating Chinese Philosophical Terms." **Far Eastern Quarterly** 14 (1955): 231–34.

Bohannan, Paul. "On Anthropologists' Use of Language." **American Anthropologist** 60 (1958): 161–62.

Bolinger, D. L. "Visual Morphemes." **Language** 22 (1946): 333–40.

Bostian, L. R. "The Two-Step Flow Theory: Cross-Cultural Implications." **Journalism Quarterly** 47 (1970): 109–17.

Boulding, Kenneth E. **The Image.** Ann Arbor, Mich.: Ann Arbor Paperbacks, 1961.

Bowie, Theodore R. **East-West in Art: Patterns of Cultural and Aesthetic Relationships.** Bloomington, Ind.: Indiana University Press, 1966.

Bradnock, Wilfred J. "Religious Translation into Non-Western Languages within the Protestant Tradition." **Babel** 9 (1963): 22–35.

Braibanti, Ralph, and Spengler, Joseph J., eds. **Traditions, Values, and Socio-Economic Development.** Durham, N.C.: Duke University Press, 1961.

Brewer, W. D. "Patterns of Gesture Among the Levantine Arabs." **American Anthropologist** 53 (1951): 232–37.

Bridgman, P. W. **The Logic of Modern Physics.** New York: Macmillan, 1927.

Broadbent, D. E. "Effects of Noise on Behavior." In **Handbook of Noise Control,** edited by Cyril M. Harris. New York: McGraw-Hill, 1957.

———. **Perception and Communication.** New York: Pergamon Press, 1958.

Brown, Roger W., and Lennenberg, Eric H. "A Study in Language and Cognition." **Journal of Abnormal and Social Psychology** 49 (1954): 454–62.

———, Black, Abraham H., and Horowitz, Arnold. "Phonetic Symbolism in Four Languages." **Journal of Abnormal and Social Psychology** 50 (1955): 288–93. (Also in **Cross-Cultural Studies of Behavior,** edited by Al-Issa and Dennis.)

———, and Lenneberg, Eric H. "Language and Categories." In **A Study of Thinking,** edited by Jerome S. Bruner, Jacqueline J. Goodnow, and George A. Austin, pp. 247–312. New York: Wiley, 1956.

——, and ——. "Studies in Linguistic Relativity." In **Readings in Social Psychology,** 3rd edition, edited by D. Maccoby, T. Newcomb, and E. Hartley. New York: Holt, Rinehart and Winston, Inc., 1958.

——. **Words and Things.** Glencoe, Ill.: Free Press, 1959, 1966.

——, Ford, Marguerite, and Gilman, A. "The Pronouns of Power and Solidarity." In **Style in Language,** edited by T. Sebeok, pp. 253–76. New York: Wiley, 1960.

——. **Social Psychology.** New York: Free Press, 1965.

Bruner, Jerome S., and Goodman, C. C. "Value and Need as Organizing Factors in Perception." **Journal of Abnormal and Social Psychology** 42 (1947): 33–44.

——, Goodnow, J. J., and Austin, G. A. **A Study of Thinking.** New York: Wiley, 1956.

——, and Taguire, Renato. "The Perception of People." In **Handbook of Social Psychology,** vol. 2, edited by G. Lindsay and E. Aronson, pp. 634–54. Reading Mass.: Addison-Wesley, 1968.

Bryson, Lyman, ed. **The Communication of Ideas.** New York: Institute for Religious and Social Studies, 1947.

Bryson, Lyman. **Symbols and Values.** New York: Harper, 1954.

Buchanan, William, and Cantril, Hadley. **How Nations See Each Other: A Study in Public Opinion.** Urbana: University of Illinois Press, 1963.

Burke, Kenneth. **A Grammar of Motives.** New York: Prentice-Hall, 1945.

——. **A Rhetoric of Motives.** Berkeley, Calif.: University of California Press, 1969. (Originally published by Prentice-Hall in 1950.)

——. "What are the Signs of What? A Theory of 'Entitlement.'" **Anthropological Linguistics** 4 (1962): 1–23.

Burling, Robbins. "Linguistics and Ethnographic Description." **American Anthropologist** 71 (1969): 817–27.

——. **Man's Many Voices: Language in its Cultural Context.** New York: Holt, Rinehart and Winston, Inc., 1970.

Butler, Jack H. "Russian Rhetoric: A Discipline Manipulated by Communism." **Quarterly Journal of Speech** 50 (1964): 229–39.

Byrnes, Frances C. "Americans in Technical Assistance: A Study of Man's Perceptions of Their Cross-Cultural Experience." Ph.D. diss., Michigan State University, 1963.

Campa, A. L. "Language Barriers in Intercultural Communication." **Journal of Communication** 1 (1951): pt. 2, 41–45.

Campbell, Donald T. "The Mutual Methodological Relevance of Anthropology and Psychology." In **Psychological Anthropology Approaches to Culture and Personality,** edited by F.L.K. Hsu, pp. 333–52. Homewood, Ill.: Dorsey Press, 1961.

——. "Systematic Error on the Part of Human Links in Communication Systems." **Information and Control** 1 (1959): 334–69.

——, and Le Vine, Robert A. "A Proposal for Cooperative Cross-Cultural Research on Ethnocentrism." **The Journal of Conflict Resolution** (March, 1961): 82–108.

Cantril, Hadley. **Tensions that Cause War.** Urbana: University of Illinois Press, 1950.

Capell, Arthur. **Studies in Socio-Linguistics.** The Hague: Mouton, 1966.

Carlson, Karen A. "The Kenya Wildlife Conservation Campaign: A Descriptive and Critical Study of Inter-cultural Persuasion." Ph.D. diss., Northwestern University, 1969.

Carothers, J. C. "Culture, Psychiatry and the Written Word." **Psychiatry** 22 (1959): 307–20.

Carpenter, Edmund, and McLuhan, Marshall, eds. **Explorations in Communication.** Boston: Beacon Press, 1960.

Carroll, J. G. **Language, Thought and Reality: Selected Writings of Benjamin Lee Whorf.** New York: Wiley, 1956.

——, and Cassagrande, J. G. "The Function of Language Classifications in Behavior." In **Readings in Social Psychology,** 3rd edition, edited by E. Maccoby, T. N. Newcomb, and E. L. Hartley. New York: Holt, Rinehart and Winston, Inc., 1958.

Cassagrande, Joseph B. "The Ends of Translation." **International Journal of American Linguistics** 20 (1954): 335–40.

Cassirer, Ernst. "The Influence of Language upon the Development of Scientific Thought." **Journal of Philosophy** 39 (1947): 309–27. (Also published as: "L' influence du language sur le developpement de la pensee dans les sciences de la nature." **Journal de Psychologie** (1946): no. 2, 129–53.)

——. **An Essay on Man: An Introduction to a Philosophy of Human Culture.** New Haven: Yale University Press, 1944.

——. **Language and Myth.** New York: Harper and Row, 1946.

——. **The Philosophy of Symbolic Forms,** vol. 1. New Haven: Yale University Press, 1953. (Translated by Manheim from **Philosophie der symbolischen Formen,** Die Sprache. 1923.)

Caudill, W., and Plath, D. W. "Who Sleeps by Whom? Parent-Child Involvement in Urban Japanese Families." **Psychiatry** 29 (1966): 344–66.

——, and Weinstein, H. "Maternal Care and Infant Behavior in Japan and America." **Psychiatry** 32 (1969): 12–43.

Chafe, Wallace, ed. **Aspects of Language and Culture: Proceedings of the American Ethnological Society, Washington, D. C., 1962.** Seattle: University of Washington Press, 1963.

Chas, Yuen Ren. **Language and Symbolic Systems.** Cambridge, Mass.: Cambridge University Press, 1968.

Cherry, E. Colin. **On Human Communication; A Review, A Survey, and a Criticism.** Cambridge, Mass.: Technology Press of Massachusetts Institute of Technology, 1957, 1966.

Ching, James C. "Public Address in the Formation of the Congo." **Quarterly Journal of Speech** 51 (1965): 225–33.

Chomsky, N. "The Logical Basis of Linguistic Theory." In **Proceedings of the Ninth International Congress of Linguists, Cambridge, Mass.,** edited by H. G. Lunt. The Hague: Mouton, 1964.

Chu, Goodwin C. "Sex Differences in Persuasibility Factors among Chinese." **International Journal of Psychology** 2 (1967): 283–88.

Clark, Herbert H. "Linguistic Processes in Deductive Reasoning." **Psychological Review** 76 (1969): no. 4, 387–404.

Cleary, Norman B. "Cross-Cultural Communication, Powerlessness, Salience, and Obeisance of Professional Change Agents." Ph.D. diss., Michigan State University, 1966.

Cleveland, Harlan, Mangone, Gerard J., and Adams, John C. **The Overseas American.** New York: McGraw-Hill, 1960.

Cohen, R. A. "Language of the Hard-Core Poor: Implications for Cultural Conflict." **Social Quarterly** 9 (1968): 19–28.

——. "Conceptual Styles, Culture and Non-Verbal Tests of Intelligence." **American Anthropologist** 71 (October, 1969): 828–56.

Colby, Benjamin N. "Behavioral Redundancy." **Behavioral Science** 3 (1958): 317–22.

——. "Ethnographic Semantics: A Preliminary Survey." **Current Anthropology** 7 (1966): pt. 1, 3–32.

——. "The Analysis of Culture Content and the Patterning of Narrative Concern in Texts." **American Anthropologist** 68 (1966): pt. 1, 374–88.

Collison, Robert. "The Continuing Barrier: Translations as a Factor of East-West Communication." **UNESCO Bulletin for Libraries** 16 (1962): 296–300.

Condon, John C. "Value Analysis of Cross-Cultural Communication: A Methodology and Application for Selected United States-Mexican Communications, 1962–1963." Ph.D. diss., Northwestern University, 1964.

——. **Semantics and Communication,** 2nd ed. New York: Macmillan, 1974.

——. "Communication and the National Community, II: The Arusha Declaration—Spreading the Word." **Mbioni** III (March, 1967): no. 10, 28–41.

——. "Nation Building and Image Building in the Tanzanian Press." **The Journal of Modern African Studies** V (November, 1967): no. 3, 335–54.

——. "Language in Reasoning and Rhetoric." In **Studies in Descriptive and Applied Linguistics,** edited by S. Sakurai, pp. 62–75. Tokyo: International Christian University, 1972.

——, and Mitsuko Saito, eds. **Intercultural Encounters with Japan: The Proceedings of the 1972 Conference on Intercultural Communication.** Tokyo: Simul Press, 1974.

——. "Intercultural Communication from the Perspective of a Speech Communication Scholar." In **International and Cross-Cultural Communication,** edited by Fred Casmir, in press.

Condon, William S., and Ogston, W. D. "A Segmentation of Behavior." **Journal of Psychiatric Research** 5 (1967): 221–35.

Conklin, Harold C. "Linguistic Play in its Cultural Setting." **Language** 35 (1959): no. 4, 631–36.

Crawford, R. W. "Culture Change and Communication in Morocco." **Human Organization** 24 (Spring, 1965): 73–77.

Crowell, Laure Irene. "Speech in the Building of a Modern State." **Quarterly Journal of Speech** 41 (1955): 118–26.

Damle, Y. B. "Communication of Modern Ideas and Knowledge in Indian Villages." **Public Opinion Quarterly** 20 (Spring, 1956): 257–70.

Dance, Frank E. X. "Speech Communication in the Soviet Union: The Psychogenesis of Speech According to Frederich Engels." **Speech Teacher** 13 (1964): 115–18.

Darwin, Charles R. **Expression of the Emotions in Man and Animals.** New York: D. Appleton and Co., 1959.

Davis, Martha. **Understanding Body Movement: An Annotated Bibliography.** New York: Arno Press, 1972.

Davitz, J. R., ed. **The Communication of Emotional Meaning.** New York: McGraw-Hill, 1964.

Dean, Vera Micheles. **The Nature of the Non-Western World.** New York: New American Library, 1957.

DeCharms, R., and Moeller, G. "Values Expressed in American Children's Readers: 1800–1950." **Journal of Abnormal and Social Psychology** 64 (1962): 136–42.

Dettering, Richard. "The Prospects for Semiotic Unity." **Etc.** 21 (1964): no. 1, 39–71.

Deutsch, Karl., ed. **Nation Building.** New York: Atherton Press, 1963.

——. **The Nerves of Government: Models of Political Communication and Control.** London: Free Press of Glencoe, 1963.

Deutschman, Paul. "The Sign Situation Classification of Human Communication." **Journal of Communication** 7 (1957): pt. 2, 63–73.

DeVito, Joseph A. "Levels of Abstraction in Spoken and Written Language." **Journal of Communication** 17 (1967): 354–61.

Diaz-Guerrero, Rogelio. "Mexican Assumptions about Interpersonal Relations." **Etc.,** (Winter, 1961): 185–88.

Dollard, J., and Mowrer, O. H. "A Method for Measuring Tension in Written Documents." **Journal of Abnormal and Social Psychology** 42 (1947): 3–32.

——, and Miller, Neal E. **Personality and Psychotherapy: An Analysis in Terms of Learning, Thinking, and Culture.** New York: McGraw-Hill, 1950.

Domnitz, Meyer. "Educational Techniques for Combating Prejudice and Discrimination and for Promoting better Intergroup Understanding." A report of **UNESCO,** 1965.

Doob, Leonard. **Becoming More Civilized, A Psychological Exploration.** New Haven: Yale University Press, 1960.

——. **Communication in Africa: A Search for Boundaries.** New Haven and London: Yale University Press, 1961.

Dumont, Rene. **False Start in Africa.** New York: Praeger, 1966.

Duncan, Hugh Dalziel. **Communication and Social Order.** New York: Bedminster Press, 1962.

DuToit, Brian M. "Pictorial Depth Perception and Linguistic Relativity." **Psychologia African** 11 (1966): pt. 2, 51–63. (Abstracted in **Psychological Abstracts** 40: no. 11, 1164.)

Easterbrook, W. T. "Problems in the Relationship of Communication and Economic History," **Journal of Economic History** 20 (December, 1960): 559–65.

Edwards, Harold T. "Power Structure and its Communication Behavior in San Jose, Costa Rica." **Journal of Inter-American Studies** 9 (April, 1967): 236–47.

Efron, David. **Gesture, Race and Culture.** The Hague: Mouton, 1972. (Originally published as **Gesture and Environment.** New York: King's Crown, 1941.)

Eisenberg, Abne M., and Smith, Ralph R. **Nonverbal Communication.** Indianapolis: Bobbs-Merrill, 1971.

Eisenstadt, S. N. "The Perception of Space and Time in a Situation of Culture-Contact." **Journal of the Royal Anthropology Institute** 79 (1949): 63–68.

——. "Communicative Systems and Social Structure: An Exploratory Comparative Study." **Public Opinion Quarterly** 19 (Summer, 1955): 153–67.

Ekman, Paul. "A Methodological Discussion of Nonverbal Behavior." **Journal of Psychology** 43 (1957): 141–49.

——. "Body Position, Facial Expression and Verbal Behavior during Interviews." **Journal of Abnormal and Social Psychology** 68 (1964): pt. 3, 295–301.

——. "Communication through Nonverbal Behavior: A Source of Information about an Interpersonal Relationship." In **Affect, Cognition, and Personality,** edited by Silvan S. Tompkins and Carroll E. Izard, pp. 390–442. New York: Springer Press, 1965.

——, and Friesen. "The Repertoire of Nonverbal Behavior: Categories, Origins, Usages, and Coding." **Semiotica** 1 (1969): 49–98.

——, Friesen, Wallace V., and Ellsworth, Phoebe. **Emotion in the Human Face: Guidelines for Research and Integration of Findings.** New York: Pergamon, 1972.

Ekroth, Laurea Elton. "The Study of Face-to-Face Communications between Cultures: Present Status and Directions." Ph.D. diss., 1967.

Ellingsworth, Huber W. "Anthropology and Rhetoric: Toward a Culture-Related Methodology of Speech Criticism." **Southern Speech Journal** 28 (1963): 307–12.

Erikson, Erik H. **Childhood and Society:** Revised edition. New York: W. W. Norton, 1963.

Ervin-Tripp, Susan. "An Analysis of the Interaction of Language, Topic, and Listener." In **American Anthropology (The Ethnography of Communication:** Special Publication) 66 (1964): pt. 2, 86–102.

Estes, S. G. "Judging Personality from Expressive Behavior." **Journal of Abnormal and Social Psychology** 3 (1938): 217–36.

Fang, A. "Some Reflections on the Difficulty of Translation." In **Studies in Chinese Thought,** edited by A. F. Wright. Chicago: University of Chicago Press, 1953.

Fanon, Franz. **The Wretched of the Earth.** New York: Grove Press, 1968.

Ferguson, C. A. "Language Factor in National Development." **Anthropological Linguistics** 4 (1962): 23–27.

Festinger, L. **A Theory of Cognitive Dissonance.** Evanston, Ill.: Row, Peterson, 1957.

Firth, Raymond. "The Study of Values by Social Anthropologists." **Man** 53 (1953): 146–53.

Fischer, J. L. "Art Styles as Cultural Cognitive Maps." **American Anthropologist** 63 (1961): no. 1, 79–93.

——. "Words for Self and Others in Some Japanese Families." **American Anthropologist (The Ethnography of Communication:** Special Publication) 66 (1964): no. 6, pt. 2, 115–26.

Fishman, Joshua A. "A Systematization of the Whorfian Hypothesis." **Behavioral Science** 5 (1960): 323–39. (Also in **Communication and Culture,** edited by A. Smith, pp. 505–16. New York: Holt, Rinehart and Winston, Inc., 1966.

——. "Varieties of Ethnicity and Varieties of Language Consciousness." In **Georgetown University Monograph No. 18: Language and Linguistics.** Washington, D. C.: Georgetown University Press, 1965, pp. 69–79.

——. **Language Loyalty in the United States; The Maintenance and Perpetuation of non-English Mother Tongues by American Ethnic and Religious Groups.** The Hague: Mouton, 1966.

Fishman, Joshua A., and Ferguson, Charles, and das Gupta, Jyotirindra, eds. **Language Problems of Developing Nations.** New York: Wiley, 1968.

——, ed. **Readings in the Sociology of Language.** The Hague: Mouton, 1968.

Flack, M. J. "Communicable and Uncommunicable Aspects in Personal International Relationships." **Journal of Communication** 16 (1966): no. 4, 283–90.

Flugel, J. **The Psychology of Clothes.** London: Hogarth, 1950.

Foley, J. P. "The Expression of Certainty." **American Journal of Psychiatry** 72 (1959): 614–15.

Fonseca, Luiz, and Kearl, Bryant. "Comprehension of Pictorial Symbols: An Experiment in Rural Brazil." **Bulletin of the Wisconsin Department of Agriculture Journal,** no. 30, 1960.

Foster, George M. **Traditional Cultures and the Impact of Technological Change.** New York: Harper and Brothers, 1962.

Foster, Thomas, Katz, William K., and Otto, Henry J. **Value Orientations in Four Elementary Schools.** Austin: University of Texas Press, 1966.

Frank, Laurence K. "Tactile Communication." **Genetic Psychology Monographs,** 56 (1957): 209–55.

Frank, William W. "An Exploratory Study of Selected Attitudes and Perceptions toward Change among AID Technical Assistance Program Participants." Ph.D. diss., Michigan State University, 1965.

Frenkel-Brunswick, Else. "Intolerance of Ambiguity as an Emotional and Perceptual Personality Variable." **Journal of Personality** 18 (September, 1949): 108–43.

Fried, Charles. **An Anatomy of Values; Problems of Personal and Social Choice.** Cambridge, Mass.: Harvard University Press, 1970.

Galjart, Benno. **Itaguai: Old Habits and New Practices in a Brazilian Land Settlement.** Wageningen: Centre for Agricultural Publishing and Documentation, 1968.

Garfinkel, Harold. **Studies in Ethnomethodology.** Englewood Cliffs, N. J.: Prentice-Hall, 1967.

Gecas, V. "Perceived Parents-Child Interaction and Boys' Self-Esteem in Two Cultural Contexts." **International Journal of Comparative Sociology** 11 (December, 1970): 317–24.

Gerster, Georg. **Sahara: Desert Destiny.** New York: Coward-McCann Publishing Co., 1960.

Gibb, Jack R. "Defensive Communication." **Journal of Communication** 11 (1961): 141–48.

Gibson, James J. "Pictures, Perspective, and Perception." In **The Visual Arts Today,** edited by G. Kepes. Middletown, Conn.: Wesleyan University Press, 1960.

——, and Pick, Ann D. "Perception of Another Person's Looking Behavior." **American Journal of Psychology** 76 (1963): 386–94.

Giedt, F. H. "Cues Associated with Accurate and Inaccurate Interview Impressions." **Psychiatry** 21 (1958): pt. 4, 405–09.

Gillin, John. "Some Signposts for Policy." In **Social Change in Latin America Today: Its Implication for United States Policy,** edited by Lyman Bryson, pp. 14–62. New York: Vintage Books, 1960.

Gladstone, W. H. "A Multidimensional Study of Facial Expression of Emotion." **Australian Journal of Psychology** 14 (1962): pt. 2, 95–100.

Gladwin, T., and Sturtevant, W. C., eds. **Anthropology and Human Behavior.** Washington: Anthropological Society of Washington, 1962.

Glazer, N., and Moynihan, D. P. **Beyond the Melting Pot: The Negroes, Puerto Ricans, Jews, Italians and the Irish.** New York and Cambridge, Mass.: MIT Press, 1963.

Gleeson, Patrick, and Wakefield, Nancy, eds. **Language and Culture.** Columbus, Ohio: C. E. Merrill, 1968.

Glenn, Edmund S. "Semantic Difficulties in International Communication." **Etc.** 11 (1954): 163–80.

——. **Language and Patterns of Thought.** Mimeographed. Washington: Georgetown University Press, 1955.

——. "Introduction to the Special Issue: Interpretation and Intercultural Communication." **Etc.** 15 (1957–58): 87–95.

——. "Meaning and Behavior: Communication and Culture." **Journal of Communication** 16 (1966): no. 4, 248–72.

Goffman, Erving. **The Presentation of Self in Everyday Life.** New York: Doubleday, 1959.

——. **Encounters.** Indianapolis: Bobbs-Merrill, 1961.

——. "The Neglected Situation." **American Anthropologist (The Ethnography of Communication,** special publication) 66 (1964): no. 6, pt. 2, 133–36.

——. **Behavior in Public Places.** Glencoe, Ill.: Free Press, 1965, and New York: Free Press, 1963.

Golden, H. H. "Literacy and Social Change in Underdeveloped Countries." **Rural Society** 20 (1955): 1–7.

Goldschmidt, Walter K. "Values and the Field of Comparative Sociology." **American Sociological Review** 18 (1953): 287–93.

——, ed. **Exploring the Ways of Mankind.** New York: Holt, Rinehart and Winston, Inc., 1960.

Gombrich, E. H. "The Visual Image." **Scientific American** 227 (1972): no. 3, 82–96.

Goodstein, R. L. "Language and Experience." In **Philosophy of Science,** edited by Arthur Danto and Sidney Morgenbesser, pp. 82–100. Cleveland: Meridian Books, 1960.

Goody, Jack, and Watt, Ian. "The Consequences of Literacy." **Comparative Studies in Society and History** 5 (1963): 304–45.

——, ed. **Literacy in Traditional Societies.** Cambridge: Cambridge University Press, 1968.

Gorer, Geoffrey. **The American People: A Study in National Character.** New York: W. W. Norton and Co., 1948.

Green, R. T., and Courtis, M. C. "Information Theory and Figure Perception: The Metaphor that Failed." **Acta Psychologica** 25 (1966): 12–36.

Greenberg, Joseph H. "Concerning Inferences from Linguistic to Non-Linguistic Data." In **Language in Culture,** edited by Harry Hoijer, pp. 3–19. Chicago: University of Chicago Press, 1954.

——, and Jenkins, J. J. "Studies in the Psychological Correlates of the Sound System of American English." **Word** 20 (1964): 157–77.

———. **Language, Culture and Communication.** Stanford, Calif.: Stanford University Press, 1971.

Grinder, R. E., and McMichael, R. E. "Cultural Influence on Conscience Development: Resistance to Temptation and Guilt among Samoans." **American Journal of Sociology** 65 (1959): 59–67.

Gumperz, John J. "Speech Variation and the Study of Indian Civilization." **American Anthropologist** 63 (1961): 976–88.

———, and Hymes, Dell H., eds. **American Anthropologist (The Ethnography of Communication,** special publication) 66 (1964): no. 6, pt. 2, 1–186.

Haas, Mary R. "Interlingual Word Taboo." **American Anthropologist** 53 (1951): 338–44.

Hachiya, Noriko. "A Comparative Study of the Value Differences of Japanese Students and American Studies in Relation to Communication Patterns." Thesis, Tokyo: International Christian University, 1972.

Haiman, Franklyn S. "An Experimental Study of the Effects of Ethos in Public Speaking." **Speech Monographs** 16 (1949): 190–202.

Haley, J. "Cross-Cultural Experimentation: An Initial Attempt." **Human Organization** 26 (Fall, 1967): 110–17.

Hall, E. T., and Trager, G. L. **The Analysis of Culture.** Washington, D.C.: American Council of Learned Societies, 1953.

———. **The Silent Language.** New York: Doubleday, 1959.

———, and Whyte, W. F. "Intercultural Communication." **Human Organization** 19 (1960): 5–12.

———. "A System for the Notation of Proxemic Behavior." **American Anthropologist** 65 (1963): no. 5, 1003–26.

———. "Adumbration as a Feature of Intercultural Communication." In **American Anthropologist (The Ethnography of Communication,** special publication) 66 (1964): no. 6, pt. 2, 154–63.

———. **The Hidden Dimension.** New York: Doubleday, 1966.

Hallowell, A. I. "Cultural Factors in the Structuralization of Perception." In **Psychology at the Crossroads,** edited by J. H. Rohrer and M. Sherif, pp. 164–95. New York: Harper, 1951.

———. "Culture, Personality and Society." In **Anthropology Today,** edited by A. L. Kroeber, pp. 597–620. Chicago: University of Chicago Press, 1953.

Hamada, Ibrahim. "An English Translation of Abu Bishr's Arabic Version of Aristotle's **Poetics** (Tenth Century)." Master's thesis, Indiana University, 1965.

Hamalian, Leo. "Communication by Gesture in the Middle East." **Etc.** 22 (1965): pt. 1, 43–49.

Harding, John, et al. "Prejudice and Ethnic Relations." In **Handbook of Social Psychology II,** edited by Gardner Lindzey. Cambridge, Mass.: Addison-Wesley, 1964.

Harms, L. S. **Intercultural Communication.** New York: Harper, 1973.

Harrison, Randall. "Nonverbal Communication: Explorations into Time, Space, Action and Object." In **Dimensions of Communication,** edited by J. Campbell and H. Helper. Menlo Park: Wadsworth, 1965.

——, and Knapp, Mark L. "Toward an Understanding of Nonverbal Communication Systems." **Journal of Communication** 22 (December, 1972): 339–52.

Harrison, Roger and Hopkins, Richard L. "The Design of Cross-cultural Training: An Alternative to the University Model." **Journal of Applied Behavioral Science** 3 (1967): no. 4, 431–60.

Hastorf, Albert H., Schneider, David J., and Polefka, Judith. **Person Perception.** Reading, Mass.: Addison-Wesley, 1970.

Haugen, Einar. "Dialect, Language, Nation." **American Anthropologist** 68 (1966): no. 4, 922–35.

Hauser, Phillip M. "Cultural and Personal Obstacles to Economic Development in the Less Developed Areas." **Human Organization** 18 (Summer, 1959): 78.

Henle, Paul. **Language, Thought and Culture.** Ann Arbor, Mich.: University of Michigan Press, 1958, 1965.

Henry, Jules. "Rorschach Technique in Primitive Cultures." **American Journal of Orthopsychiatry** 2 (1941): 230–34.

Herdan, G. **Language, Choice, and Chance.** Groningen: P. Noordhoff, 1956.

Herder, J. G. **Social and Political Culture.** London: Cambridge University Press, 1969.

Herskovits, Melville J. "Cultural Relativism and Cultural Values." In **Cultural Anthropology,** edited by Melville J. Herskovits, pp. 348–66. New York: Knopf, 1955.

————. **The Human Factor in Changing Africa,** 1st edition. New York: Knopf, 1962.

Hewes, G. T. "The Anthropology of Posture." **Scientific American** 196 (February, 1957): 123–32.

Hinde, Robert A., ed. **Nonverbal Communication.** Cambridge, Mass.: Cambridge University Press, 1972.

Hintikka, K., and Jaakko, J. "Aristotle and the Ambiguity of Ambiguity." **Inquiry** 2 (1959): 137–51.

Hockett, Charles F. "Chinese versus English: An Exploration of the Whorfian Thesis." In **Language in Culture,** edited by H. Hoijer, pp. 106–23. Chicago: University of Chicago Press, 1954.

Hoijer, Harry. "The Relation of Language to Culture." In **Anthropology Today,** edited by A. L. Kroeber et al. Chicago: University of Chicago Press, 1953.

————, ed. **Language in Culture.** Chicago: University of Chicago Press, 1954.

Holton, Gerald, ed. **Science and Culture.** Boston: Beacon Press, 1967.

Hoopes, David, ed. **Readings in Intercultural Communication,** vols. 1, 2, and 3. Pittsburgh, Pennsylvania: Regional Council for International Education, University of Pittsburgh, 1971, 1972, 1973.

Horton, Robin. "African Traditional Thought and Western Science." **Africa** 37 (January, 1967): 50–71.

Hsu, Francis L. K. **Americans and Chinese: Two Ways of Life.** New York: Henry Schuman, 1953. (Revision: **Americans and Chinese: Purpose and Fulfillment in Great Civilizations.** New York: Natural History Press, 1970.)

————. **Clan, Caste and Club.** Princeton, N.J.: Van Nostrand, 1963.

Hymes, Dell H. "Discussion of the Symposium on Translation between Language and Culture." **Anthropological Linguistics** 2 (1960): 81–85.

————. "Linguistic Aspects of Cross-cultural Personality Study." In **Studying Personality Cross-culturally,** edited by B. Kaplan. Evanston, Ill.: Row, Peterson, 1961.

————. **Language in Culture and Society: A Reader in Linguistics and Anthropology.** New York: Harper and Row, 1964.

————. "The Anthropology of Communication." In **Human Com-**

munication Theory, edited by Frank E. X. Dance. New York: Holt, Rinehart and Winston, Inc., 1967.

Illich, Ivan D. **Celebration of Awareness.** Garden City: Doubleday-Anchor, 1971.

Inkles, Alex, and Levinson, Daniel J. "National Character: The Study of Modal Personality and Sociocultural Systems." In **Handbook of Social Psychology II,** edited by Gardner Lindzey, pp. 997–1020. Cambridge, Mass.: Addison-Wesley Publishing Co., 1954.

Ishikawa, K. I. "Difficulties in Translating Japanese into English and Vice Versa." **Pacific Spectator** 9 (1955): 95–99.

Jacobs, M., et al. "Study of Key Communicators in Urban Thailand." **Social Forces** 45 (December, 1966): 192–99.

Jones, W. R. "A Critical Study of Bilingualism and Nonverbal Intelligence." **British Journal of Educational Psychology** 30 (1960): 71–77.

Joos, Martin. **The Five Clocks.** New York: Harcourt, Brace and World, 1967.

Kaplan, Robert B. "Cultural Thought Patterns in Inter-cultural Education." **Language Learning** 16: nos. 1 and 2, 1–20.

Kecskemeti, P. **Meaning, Communication and Value.** Chicago: University of Chicago Press, 1952.

Keene, Donald. "On Appearing in Japanese Translation." **Twentieth Century** 154 (1953): 225–28.

Keller, Paul W. "The Study of Face-to-Face International Decision-Making." **Journal of Communication** 13 (1963): 67–76.

Kelly, C. **The Psychology of Personal Constructs.** New York: W. W. Norton, 1955.

Kepes, Gyorgy. **Language of Vision.** Chicago: Paul Theobald, 1944.

Khan, M. M. R. "Silence as Communication." **Bulletin of the Menninger Clinic,** 27 (1963): 300–313.

Klineberg, Otto. **The Human Dimension in International Relations.** New York: Holt, Rinehart and Winston, Inc., 1964.

——. **Tensions Affecting International Understanding: A Survey of Research.** New York: Social Science Research Council, Bulletin 62, 1960.

Kling, Merle. **A Mexican Interest Group in Action.** Englewood Cliffs, N. J.: Prentice-Hall, 1961.

Kluckhohn, C., and Kluckhohn, F. "American Culture: Generalized and Class Patterns." In **Conflicts of Power in Modern Culture: Seventh Symposium on Science, Philosophy and Religion,** edited by Lyman Bryson, pp. 106–28. New York: Cooper Square.

——, and Murray, Henry A., eds. **Personality in Nature, Society and Culture.** New York: Knopf, 1948.

——. **Mirror for Man.** New York: Whittlesby House, McGraw-Hill, 1949.

——. "Values and Value-Orientations in the Theory of Action: An Exploration in Definition and Classification." In **Toward a General Theory of Action,** edited by Talcott Parsons and Edward Shils. Cambridge: Harvard University Press, 1951.

——. "Toward a Comparison of Value-Emphases in Different Cultures." In **The State of the Social Sciences**, edited by Leonard White, pp. 116–32. Chicago: University of Chicago Press.

——. "Notes on some Anthropological Aspects of Communication." **American Anthropologist** 63 (1961): 895–910.

Kluckhohn, F., and Strodtbeck, Fred L. **Variations in Value Orientations.** Evanston, Ill.: Row, Peterson, 1961.

Knapp, Mark L. **Nonverbal Communication in Human Interaction.** New York: Holt, Rinehart and Winston, Inc., 1972.

Knapp, Peter H., ed. **Expression of the Emotions in Man.** New York: International Universities Press, 1963.

Korb, George M. "Communicating with the Chilean Peon." **American Journal of Economics and Sociology** 25 (1966): 281–96.

Kouwenhoven, John. **The Beer Can by the Highway; Essays on What's American about America.** Garden City: New York: Doubleday, 1961.

Krampen, M. "Classification of Graphic Symbols and the Scientific Method." Prepared for the Fund for the Advancement of Education. Privately distributed, 1959.

Kroeber, A. L., and Kluckhohn, C. "Culture: A Critical Review of Concepts and Definitions." **Papers of the Peabody Museum of American Archaeology and Ethnology.** Cambridge, Mass.: Harvard University 47 (1952): no. 1, 1–223.

La Barre, W. "The Cultural Basis of Emotions and Gestures." **Journal of Personality** 16 (1947): 49–68.

——. **The Human Animal.** Chicago: University of Chicago Press, 1954.

Lambert, Wallace E. **Language, Psychology and Culture.** Stanford, Calif.: Stanford University Press, 1972.

Langer, Susanne K. **Philosophy in a New Key.** Cambridge, Mass.: Harvard University Press, 1942.

Lasswell, H. D., Lerner, D., and Pool, I de Sola. "The Comparative Study of Symbols." **Hoover Institute of Studies, Sec. C., Symbols, no. 1.** Stanford, Calif.: Stanford University Press, 1952.

Leach, Edmund. "Anthropological Aspects of Language: Animal Categories and Verbal Abuse." In **New Directions in the Study of Language,** edited by Eric H. Lenneberg, pp. 23–63. Cambridge, Mass.: MIT Press, 1964.

——. "Culture and Social Cohesion: An Anthropologist's View. In **Science and Culture,** edited by Gerald Holton, pp. 24–38. Boston: Beacon Press, 1967.

Lee, D. D. "Lineal and Nonlineal Codifications of Reality." **Psychosomatic Medicine** 12 (1950): 89–97.

——. **Freedom and Culture.** Englewood Cliffs, N. J.: Prentice-Hall, 1959.

Leites, N. "Psycho-cultural Hypotheses about Political Acts." **World Politics** 1 (1948): no. 1, 102–19.

Lenneberg, Eric H., ed. **New Directions in the Study of Language.** Cambridge, Mass.: MIT Press, 1964.

——. **Biological Foundations of Language.** New York: John Wiley and Sons, 1967.

Lermas, Jordi. "Gaps in World Translations." **UNESCO Features** (1958): no. 283, 10–11.

Lerner, D., and Schramm, W. **Communication and Change in Developing Countries.** Honolulu: East-West Center Press, 1957, 1967.

Lerner, David. **The Passing of Traditional Society: Modernizing the Middle East.** Glencoe, Ill.: Free Press, 1958.

Levi-Strauss, Claude. "Language and the Analysis of Social Laws." **American Anthropologist** 53 (1951): 155–63.

——. "The Structural Study of Myth." **Journal of American Folklore** 68 (1955): 428–44.

Lieberson, Stanley, ed. **Explorations in Socio-Linguistics.** Bloomington, Ind.: Indiana University Press, 1967.

——. **Language and Ethnic Relations in Canada.** New York: Wiley, 1970.

Lin, Nan. **The Study of Human Communication.** Indianapolis: Bobbs-Merrill, 1973.

Lipset, Seymour. "Some Social Requisites of Democracy: Economic Development and Political Legitimacy." **American Political Science Review** 52 (March, 1959): 69–105.

Lorenz, Konrad. **On Aggression.** New York: Harcourt, Brace and World, 1966.

Lounsbury, Floyd G. "Similarity and Contiguity Relations in Language and Culture. **Georgetown University Monographs on Language and Linguistics.** Washington: Georgetown University Press (1960): no. 12, 123–128.

McGinnies, Elliot. "Some Reactions of Japanese University Students to Persuasive Communication." **Journal of Conflict Resolution** 9 (1965): 482–490.

McLuhan, Marshall. **Understanding Media: The Extensions of Man.** New York: McGraw-Hill, 1964.

McQuown, N. A. "Analysis of the Cultural Content of Language Materials." In **Language in Culture,** edited by H. Hoijer, pp. 20–31. Chicago: University of Chicago Press, 1954.

Maclay, Howard, and Ware, E. E. "Cross-Cultural Use of the Semantic Differential." **Behavioral Science** 6 (1961): 185–90.

Mandelbaum, David G., ed. **Selected Writings of Edward Sapir in Language, Culture and Personality.** Berkeley and Los Angeles: University of California Press, 1949.

Mathieu, George J. "Words before Peace; Translators and Interpreters." **UN World** 3 (1949): 58–59.

Mazrui, Ali. "On Heroes and Uhuru and Uhuru-Worship." **Transition** III (November, 1963): 23–28.

Mead, George H. **Mind, Self and Society.** Chicago: University of Chicago Press, 1967.

Mead, Margaret. **And Keep Your Powder Dry.** New York: Morrow, 1942.

——. "The Application of Anthropological Techniques to Cross-National Communication." **Transactions of the New York Academy of Science** 9 (1947): no. 4, 133–52.

———. "A Case History in Cross-National Communications." In **The Communication of Ideas,** edited by Lyman Bryson, pp. 209–29. New York: Harper and Row.

———, and Metraux, Rhoda, eds. **The Study of Culture at a Distance.** Chicago: University of Chicago Press, 1953.

———, ed. **Cultural Patterns and Technical Change.** Paris: UNESCO, 1953.

———. "National Character and The Science of Anthropology." In **Culture and Social Character: The Work of David Riesman Revisited,** edited by Seymour Lipset and Leo Lowenthal, pp. 15–26. New York: The Free Press of Glencoe, 1961.

Meerloo, J. A. M. **Conversation and Communications: A Psychological Inquiry into Language and Human Relations.** New York: International Universities Press, 1952.

Mehrabian, Albert, and Williams, Martin. "Nonverbal Commitments of Perceived and Intended Persuasiveness." **Journal of Personality and Social Psychology** 13 (1969): 37–58.

Miller, G. A. **Language and Communication.** New York: McGraw-Hill, 1951. (Paperback: 1963).

———, Galanter, Eugene, and Pribram, Karl H. **Plans and the Structure of Behavior.** New York: Holt, Rinehart and Winston, Inc., 1960.

Minami, Hiroshi. **Psychology of the Japanese People.** Honolulu: East-West Center, 1970.

Miner, Horace. "Body Ritual: Among the Nacirema." **American Anthropologist** 58 (1956): 503–07.

Mises, Richard von. **Positivism: A Study in Human Understanding.** Cambridge, Mass.: Harvard University Press, 1951.

Morgan, J. J. B., and Morton, J. T. "The Distortion of Syllogistic Reasoning Produced by Personal Convictions." **Journal of Social Psychology** 20 (1944): 39–59.

Morris, C. W. **Signs, Language and Behavior.** New York: Prentice-Hall, 1946. New York: Braziller, 1955.

———. **Varieties of Human Value.** Chicago: University of Chicago Press, 1956.

Morris, Desmond. **The Naked Ape: A Zoologist's Study of the Human Animal.** New York: McGraw-Hill, 1967.

———. **Intimate Behaviour.** London: Cape, 1971.

Nakamura, Hajime. **The Ways of Thinking of Eastern Peoples.**

Tokyo: Japanese National Commission for UNESCO, 1960.

Nakane, Chie. **Japanese Society.** London: Weidenfeld and Nicholson, 1970, and Berkeley: University of California Press, 1970.

Neher, William, and Condon, John. "Communication and National Integration." In **National Integration in Africa,** edited by Kwamena Bentsi-Enchill and David R. Smock. London: Oxford University Press, in press.

Newcomb, T. M. "An Approach to the Study of Communicative Acts." **Psychological Review** 60 (1953): 393–404.

Nida, Eugene A. **Learning a Foreign Language.** New York: Friendship Press, 1950.

——. **Customs and Cultures.** New York: Harper & Row, 1954.

——. **Toward a Science of Translating.** Leiden: Brill, 1964.

Northrop, F. S. C. **The Meeting of East and West.** New York: Macmillan, 1946.

——. **Ideological Differences and World Order.** New Haven: Yale University Press, 1949.

——, and Livingston, Helen H., eds. **Cross-cultural Understanding; Epistemology in Anthropology.** New York: Harper and Row, 1964.

Notre Dame University. **Values in America,** edited by Donald N. Barnett. Notre Dame, Ind.: University of Notre Dame Press, 1961.

Ogden, C. K., and Richards, I. A. **The Meaning of Meaning: A Study of the Influence of Language upon Thought and of the Science of Symbolism,** 10th edition. New York: Harcourt, Brace, 1952.

Oliver, Egbert S. "Public Discussion in India." **Today's Speech,** 5 (September, 1957): 9–10.

Oliver, Robert T. "The Rhetorical Implications of Taoism." **Quarterly Journal of Speech** 47 (1961): 27–35.

——. **Culture and Communication: The Problem of Penetrating National and Cultural Boundaries.** Springfield: Charles C. Thomas, Publishers, 1962.

Ong, Walter J. **In the Human Grain; Further Explorations of Contemporary Culture.** New York: Macmillan, 1967.

——. **The Presence of the Word; Some Prolegomena for Cultural and Religious History.** New Haven: Yale University Press, 1967.

Osgood, Charles E., Suci, George J., and Tannenbaum, Percy. **The Measurement of Meaning.** Urbana: University of Illinois Press, 1957.

———. "The Cross-Cultural Generality of Visual-verbal Synesthetic Tendencies." **Behavioral Science** 5 (1960): no. 2, 146–69.

———. "Semantic Differential Technique in the Comparative Study of Cultures." **American Anthropologist (Transcultural Studies in Cognition,** special publication) vol. 66 (1964): no. 3, pt. 2, 171–200.

Osser, Harry, and Peng, Frederick. "A Cross-cultural Study of Speech Rate." **Language and Speech** 7 (1964): 120–25.

Patterns of Communication In and Out of Japan (Abstracts of twenty studies) (Tokyo: ICU Communication Dept., 1974).

Paz, Octavio. **The Labyrinth of Solitude.** New York: Grove Press, 1963.

Pickthall, Marmaduke. "Arabs and Non-Arabs and the Question of Translating the Qur'an." **Islamic Culture** 5 (1931): 422–33.

Pittenger, Robert E., Hockett, C. F., and Danehy, J. J. **The First Five Minutes: A Sample of Microscopic Interview Analysis.** Ithaca, New York: Paul Martineau, 1960.

Politzer, R. L. "A Brief Classification of the Limits of Translatability." **Modern Language Journal** 40 (1956): 319–22.

Pool, Ithiel de Sola, ed. **Trends in Content Analysis.** Urbana: University of Illinois Press, 1959.

Pribram, Karl H. **Conflicting Patterns of Thought.** Washington: Public Affairs Press, 1949.

Prosser, Michael H., ed. **Intercommunication among Nations and Peoples.** New York: Harper and Row, 1973.

Pye, Lucien W. "Communication Patterns and the Problems of Representative Government in Non-Western Societies." **Public Opinion Quarterly,** 20 (Spring, 1956): 249–56.

———. "Administrators, Agitators and Brokers." **Public Opinion Quarterly** 22: no. 3, 342–48.

———. **Politics, Personality and Nation Building: Burma's Search for Identity.** New Haven: Yale University Press, 1962.

———. **Communications and Political Development.** Princeton, N. J.: Princeton University Press, 1963.

Queen, Stuart Alfred, and Adams, John B. **The Family in Various Cultures.** Philadelphia: J. B. Lippincott, 1952, 1961, 1967.

Radin, Paul. **Primitive Man as Philosopher.** New York: Appleton, 1927.

Rao, Y. V. Lakshmana. **Communication and Development: A Study of Two Indian Villages.** Minneapolis: University of Minnesota Press, 1966.

Rapoport, Anatol. **Fights, Games and Debates.** Ann Arbor: University of Michigan Press, 1960.

Reichard, Gladys A. "Language and Cultural Pattern." **American Anthropologist** 52 (1950): 194–204.

Reichenbach, H. **The Rise of Scientific Philosophy.** Berkeley: University of California Press, 1951.

Richman, R. J. "Ambiguity and Intuition." **Mind** 68 (1959): 87–92.

Riesman, David, et al. **The Lonely Crowd.** New Haven: Yale University Press, 1951.

Riesman, D. "The Oral and Written Traditions." In **Explorations in Communication,** edited by E. Carpenter and M. McLuhan. Boston: Beacon Press, 1960.

Rogers, Carl R. **On Becoming a Person.** Boston: Houghton Mifflin, 1961.

Rogers, E. M. **Diffusion on Innovations.** New York: The Free Press, 1962.

——, and Bhowmik, D. K. "Homophily-Heterophily: Relational Concepts for Communication Research," **Public Opinion Quarterly** 34 (1970): 523–38.

——, and Shoemaker, F. **Communication of Innovations.** New York: The Free Press, 1971.

Rosenzweig, M. R. "Comparisons among Word-Association Responses in English, French, German and Italian." **American Journal of Psychology** 74 (1961): 347–60.

Ruesch, Jurgen, and Bateson, Gregory. **Communication: The Social Matrix of Psychiatry.** New York: Norton, 1951.

——, and Kees, Weldon. **Nonverbal Communication: Notes on Visual Perception of Human Relations.** Berkeley: University of California Press, 1956, 1970.

——. **Disturbed Communication.** New York: W. W. Norton, 1957.

Samovar, Larry A., and Porter, Richard E., eds. **Intercultural Communication: A Reader.** Belmont, Calif.: Wadsworth Publishing Co., Inc., 1972.

Sapir, Edward. "Communication." **Encyclopedia of the Social Sciences.** New York: Macmillan 4 (1931): 78–81.

——. **Culture, Language, and Personality.** Berkeley: University of California Press, 1958, 1964.

Saporta, Sol., ed. **Psycholinguistics: A Book of Readings.** New York: Holt, Rinehart and Winston, Inc., 1961.

Saul, Ezra V., ed. **A Review of the Literature Pertinent to the Design and Use of Effective Graphic Training Aids:** Technical Report SDC 494–08–1. Port Washington, New York: U. S. Naval Training Devices Center, 1954.

Scheflen, A. E. "Quasi-Courtship Behavior in Psychotherapy." **Psychiatry** 28 (1965): 245–57.

Schelling, Thomas C. **The Strategy of Conflict.** Cambridge, Mass.: Harvard University Press, 1960.

Schramm, Wilbur, ed. **The Science of Human Communication: New Directions and New Findings in Communication Research.** New York: Basic Books, 1963.

Schwartz, Benjamin. "Some Polarities in Confucian Thought." In **Confucianism and Chinese Civilization,** edited by Arthur L. Wright, pp. 3–49. New York: Atheneum, 1964.

Schwartz, Theodore, and Mead, Margaret. "Micro- and Macro-Cultural Models for Cultural Evolution." **Anthropological Linguistics** 13 (1961): 1–7.

Sebeok, Thomas A., ed. **Style in Language.** Cambridge, Mass.: Technology Press, MIT; New York: Wiley, 1960.

Segall, Marshall H., Campbell, Donald, and Herskovits, Melville J. **The Influence of Culture on Visual Perception.** Indianapolis: Bobbs-Merrill, 1966.

Shannon, Claude E., and Weaver, Warren. **The Mathematical Theory of Communication.** Urbana: University of Illinois Press, 1949.

Shigeta, Midori. "An Experimental Study of Ambiguity in Japanese and American Speaking Behavior." Thesis, Tokyo: International Christian University, 1972.

Shils, Edward. "The Concentration and Dispersion of Charisma." **World Politics** 11 (October, 1958): 1–19.

Shouby, E. "The Influence of the Arabic Language on the Psychology of the Arabs." **Middle East Journal** 5 (1951): 284–302.

Silvert, Kalman H. **Reaction and Revolution in Latin America: The Conflict Society.** New Orleans: Hauser Press, 1961.

——, ed. **Expectant Peoples: Nationalism and Development.** New York: Random House, 1963.

Singh, P. H., and Huang, S. C. "Some Socio-Cultural and Psychological Determinants of Advertising in India: A Comparative Study." **Journal of Social Psychology** 57 (1962): 113–21.

Siu, R. G. H. **The Tao of Science: An Essay on Western Knowledge and Eastern Wisdom.** Cambridge: The Technology Press, M.I.T., and New York: Wiley, 1968.

Smith, Alfred G., ed. **Communication and Culture: Readings in the Codes of Human Interaction.** New York: Holt, Rinehart and Winston, Inc., 1966.

Smith, Henry Lee, Jr. "An Outline of Metalinguistic Analysis." In **Report of the 3rd Annual Round Table Meeting on Linguistics and Language Teaching,** pp. 59–66. Washington: Georgetown University Press, 1952.

——. **The Communication Situation.** Washington, D. C.: U. S. Department of State, Foreign Service Institute, 1953.

Sommer, Robert. "The Distance for Comfortable Conversation: A Further Study." **Sociometry** 25 (1962): 111–25.

——. **Personal Space.** Englewood Cliffs: Prentice-Hall, 1969.

Spier, Leslie, Hallowell, A. I., and Newman, Stanley S., eds. **Language, Culture and Personality: Essays in Memory of Edward Sapir.** Menasha, Wisc.: Sapir Memorial Publication Fund, 1941.

Spiro, Melford E. "Human Nature in Psychological Dimensions." **American Anthropologist** 56 (1954): 19–30.

Stephenson, William. **The Family in Cross-Cultural Perspective.** New York: Holt, Rinehart and Winston, Inc., 1963.

Stewart, Edward C. **American Cultural Patterns: A Cross-Cultural Perspective.** Pittsburgh: Regional Council for International Education, 1971.

——. "The Simulation of Cultural Differences." **Journal of Communication** 15 (December, 1966): 291–304.

——, Danielian, Jack, and Foster, Robert J. **Simulating Intercultural Communication Through Role Playing.** Alexandria, Va.: Human Resources Research Office, George Washington University, 1969.

"Symposium: Value Theory and Rhetoric." **Western Speech** (Spring, 1962): 70–91; (Summer, 1962): 133–45.

Takahara, Nicole. "Semantic Concepts of 'Friendship,' 'Marriage,' 'Work,' and 'Foreigner' in the American, Japanese, and French Cultures." Thesis, Tokyo: International Christian University, 1972.

Tanaka, Yasumasa, and Osgood, Charles E. "Cross-Culture, Cross-Concept and Cross-Subject Generality of Affective Meaning Systems." **Journal of Personality and Social Psychology** 2 (1965): no. 2, 143–53.

Toffler, Alvin. **Future Shock.** New York: Random House, 1970.

Trager, G. L., and Hall, E. T. "Culture and Communication: A Model and an Analysis." **Explorations** 3 (1954): 137–49.

——. "Paralinguistics: A First Approximation." **Studies in Linguistics** 13 (1958): 1–12.

Triandis, H. C. **The Analysis of Subjective Culture.** New York: John Wiley, 1972.

Van Nieuwenhuijze, C. A. O. **Cross-Cultural Studies.** The Hague: Mouton, 1963.

Von Bertalanffy, L. "An Essay on the Relativity of Categories," **Philosophy of Science** 22 (October, 1955): no. 4, 243–63.

Wallace, Anthony F. C., and Atkins, John. "The Psychic Unity of Human Groups." In **Studying Personality Cross-Culturally,** edited by Burt Kaplan, pp. 29–164. Evanston, Ill.: Row, Peterson, 1961.

Watson, O. Michael. **Proxemic Behavior: A Cross-Cultural Study.** The Hague: Mouton, 1970.

Watts, Alan. **The Wisdom of Insecurity.** New York: Pantheon, 1951.

Watzlawick, Paul, Beavin, Janet H., and Jackson, Donald D. **Pragmatics of Human Communication.** New York: W. W. Norton, 1967.

Wedge, Bryant. "Nationality and Social Perception." **Journal of Communication** 16 (December, 1966): 273–82.

Weinreich, Uriel. **Languages in Contact.** New York: Linguistic Circle of New York, 1953.

White, Leslie A. "The Symbol: The Origin and Basis of Human Behavior." **Philosophy of Science** 7 (1940): 451–63. (Also in

Etc. 1 (1944): 229–37; and in **The Science of Culture,** L. A. White, pp. 22–39. New York: Farrar, Straus, 1949.)

———. **The Science of Culture.** New York: Farrar, Straus, 1949.

White, Morton. "The Analytic and the Synthetic: An Untenable Dualism." In **John Dewey: Philosopher of Science and Freedom,** edited by Sidney Hook, pp. 316–30. New York: Dial, 1950.

Whorf, Benjamin L. **Four Articles on Metalinguistics.** Washington, D.C.: Foreign Service Institute, Department of State, 1939, 1940, 1941, 1949.

———. "An American Indian Model of the Universe." **International Journal of American Linguistics** 16 (1950): 67–72.

———. **Language, Thought and Reality: Selected Writings of Benjamin Lee Whorf.** J. Carroll, ed. Cambridge, Mass.: Technology Press, MIT and New York: Wiley, 1956.

Wiener, Norbert. **The Human Use of Human Beings: Cybernetics and Society.** Garden City: Anchor Books, 1950.

Williamson, Rene de Visme. **Culture and Policy: The United States and the Hispanic World.** Knoxville: University of Tennessee Press, 1949.

Windes, Russel, and Hastings, Arthur. **Argumentation and Advocacy.** New York: Random House, 1965.

Winter, Werner. "Impossibilities of Translation." In **The Craft and Context of Translation,** edited by William Arrowsmith and Roger Shattuck, pp. 68–82. Austin: University of Texas Press, 1961.

Wright, Arthur F. **Studies in Chinese Thought.** Chicago: University of Chicago Press, 1953.

Yamada, Yoko. "The Rhetoric of the Readers' Column." Thesis, Tokyo: International Christian University, 1971.

Yousef, Fathi S. "Cross-Cultural Testing: An Aspect of the Resistance Reaction." **Language Learning** 18 (1968): nos. 3–4, 227–34.

———. **Cross-Cultural Social Communication Behavior: Egyptians in the U. S.** Ann Arbor, Michigan: University Microfilms, 1972.

———. "Cross-Cultural Communication Aspects of Contrastive Behavior Patterns between North Americans and Middle-Easterners." **Human Organization,** Summer, 1974.

Index

301